HARD HITTING SONGS for HARD-HIT PEOPLE

COMPILED BY
ALAN LOMAX

NOTES ON THE SONGS BY
WOODY GUTHRIE

MUSIC TRANSCRIBED
AND EDITED AND WITH
AN AFTERWORD BY
PETE SEEGER

FOREWORD BY JOHN STEINBECK
PUBLISHER'S FOREWORD BY IRWIN SILBER
INTRODUCTORY NOTE BY NORA GUTHRIE

UNIVERSITY OF NEBRASKA PRESS • LINCOLN AND LONDON

INTRODUCTORY NOTE

Nora Guthrie

A few years ago, I began working on a new project. I wanted to tell the story of Woody's life in New York City. It's not a story that's been deeply covered to date, considering he lived in New York City for almost twenty-seven years, from February 1941 until his death in October 1967. The more I investigated, the more interesting and extraordinary the story became. And reconfirming the old saying, "It's all in the details," the details suddenly took on a new glow. From his acquaintances with artists such as Rockwell Kent, writer Daschiell Hammett, poets Walter Lowenfels and Langston Hughes, modern dance choreographer Martha Graham, composer Marc Blitzstein, and Broadway lyricist Yip Harburg to his evolving education with blues musicians W. C. Handy, Lead Belly, Sonny Terry, and Brownie McGhee and his friendship and collaborations with Nicholas Ray (director of *Rebel Without a Cause*) and Alan Lomax, the cast of characters found in his mid-1940s personal address book is mind-boggling and stunning. After learning about all these connections, I had to ultimately laugh and shrug as it dawned on me, "Well, of course. Isn't that why everybody comes to New York?"

One of the stories that really caught me took place at an artist's loft. In 1940 artist, sculptor, and ceramic tile designer and part-time musician Harold Ambellan was living in a loft on Twenty-First Street with his wife, artist and writer Elisabeth Higgens. Woody returned to New York in late April 1940 following a brief visit to the Library of Congress in Washington DC, where he had recorded his life story and songs with Alan Lomax. Trailing him back to the city was a young banjo player whom he had befriended in Washington, Pete Seeger. Simply put, Seeger stated, "I found we could play together well." Woody was twenty-seven years old, and Seeger was twenty-one. With no permanent home, Woody shacked up with Ambellan and Higgens. The loft was mostly filled with Ambellan's sculptures, which were abstract and very large. However, the couple managed to throw a cot up in the back of the loft for Woody to crash on. In a 1980 interview with author Joe Klein, Ambellan recounted hearing Woody straggle in late nights, greeting each of the sculptures with "Hello, Madame" or "Good evening, Sir."

Evenings at the loft often included impromptu hootenannies, where Woody and Pete's musician friends would gather to raise some money to help pay the Ambellans' rent. Musician Bess Hawes described these hootenannies in another interview with Joe Klein: "We did a lot of singing with the audience. Mostly union people. Most of New York was union! There were lots of garment workers and lots of city workers, lots of taxi drivers and people like that. And some, I suppose, intellectuals. We didn't know. And that was appropriate for New York at that time." By all accounts, it was a time of youthful enthusiasm, exploration, and ambition. Their blood was flowing. Their juices were creating. Only two months earlier, in February, while briefly staying at a boarding house in midtown Manhattan, Woody had penned a few other lyrics that included "Jesus Christ" and a new song that recounted his cross-country journey from Los Angeles to New York, "This Land Is Your Land." A few weeks later came "The Ballad of Tom Joad"; "Vigilante Man" and "Hard Travelin'," both written while living at the Ambellans', followed.

Alan Lomax's father, John Lomax, had collected a group of songs that dealt with migrant workers', share crop farmers', and industrial workers' issues, many of the lyrics protesting workers' conditions and advocating for their rights. At the time, the material was considered "too hot to handle" by government employees, so Alan handed it over to Pete and Woody to browse through. They loved the material, and together with Alan, they decided to create a new songbook that they would embellish with their own writings and commentary, as well as some additional original songs. Working fourteen hours a day, they completed the songbook in about five months. Woody, now in the writer's flow and prodded by Lomax, also began writing down more stories about his early life in Oklahoma. These stories would two years later become the basis for Woody's autobiography, *Bound for Glory*. When the book was published in 1943, Woody sent one of the first copies to the Ambellans, annotated with a short note thanking them and stating that it was at their loft that he began writing the tale that was to become his signature story.

During his time at the Ambellans', Woody was able to land a couple of spots on various NYC radio programs and so was working as a popular performer during the days. "The Ballad of Wild Bill Hickok," written at the Ambellans', was one of the many songs Woody composed especially for his radio broadcasts, which were often scripted by Alan Lomax and Nicholas Ray. Elisabeth Higgens was the scriptwriter for "Cavalcade of America," the multiartist performances held at Town Hall that Woody often participated in. Additional "Cavalcade of America" artists often included W. C. Handy, Lead Belly, Josh White, Earl Robinson, Pete (Bowers) Seeger, and Burl Ives, among others.

When Seeger moved up to New York, he shared an apartment with Lee Hayes and Millard Lampell on East Twelfth Street, where they started up a new folk group they called The Almanac Singers. Woody, however, continued to live with the Ambellans for most of the year, until he was financially well off enough to be able to bring his wife, Mary, and their three children from Texas in November 1940. They set up house in an uptown apartment on 101st Street off Central Park West. Woody's life became a hectic one. With the sudden success from his radio shows, the arrival of his family, in addition to making his first record, *Dust Bowl Ballads*, that same year, his time and energy became absorbed with pressing issues other than the songbook. The manuscript, which they had titled *Hard Hitting Songs for Hard-Hit People*, was left behind at the loft, literally saved by Elisabeth Higgens until its existence became known in the 1960s, when it was first published in 1967.

As you read through these early writings and look through the songs that inspired them, you can clearly see the beginnings of what we now collectively identify with both Woody Guthrie and Pete Seeger. The labor history, the language, the humor, the personal connections to the issues of the day—which both of these icons now historically represent around the world——are all here in this early manuscript, to be discovered in their raw infancy. As it turns out, it wasn't a phase, it wasn't a folly, it wasn't a flirtation. It was the beginning of these two extraordinary people's creative legacies, which have lasted now for over half a century and have inspired countless others around the world to follow.

The songs here first inspired Woody Guthrie and Pete Seeger to think about, to begin writing about, to decide to sing about, and to forge their own destinies from the working class. They are the gold nuggets that true democracies are created from and strive to eternally connect to. They are the thoughts, plans, and progress of the working class, then and now. It was, and is, an extraordinary and pivotal time. Or as Woody concluded, "A folk song is what's wrong and how to fix it." Here they are.

CONTENTS

ILLUSTRATIONS

FOREWORD   by John Steinbeck

The songs of the working people have always been their sharpest statement and the one statement which cannot be destroyed. You can burn
books, buy newspapers, you can guard against handbills and pamphlets,
but you cannot prevent singing.

For some reason it has always been lightly thought that singing people
are happy people. Nothing could be more untrue. The greatest and most
enduring folk songs are wrung from unhappy people - the spirituals of
the slaves which say in effect "It is hopeless here, maybe in heaven it
will be nicer." We have the grunting songs of the weight lifting steve-
dores which tell of a little pleasure on Saturday night. The cowboy songs
are wails of loneliness.

Working people sing of their hopes and of their troubles, but the rhythms
have the beat of work - the long and short bawls of the sea shantys
with tempos of capstan or sheets, the lifting rhythms, the swinging
rhythms and the slow, rolling songs of the southwest built on the hoof
beats of a walking horse. The work is the song and the song is the people.

There is great relief in saying a thing that hurts - I remember a very
little boy who was going to the barber for his first time. He was terrified
and his eyes were filled with tears. He stood very stiffly on the curb
and sang -

"They think I will be scared,
"They all think I will be scared,
"But I will not,
"But I will not cry,
"Oh! No! I will not cry."

Songs are the statements of a people. You can learn more about people
by listening to their songs than in any other way, for into the songs go
all the hopes and hurts, the angers, fears, the wants and aspirations.

A few years ago when I sat in the camps of the people from the dustbowl when hunger was everywhere, I heard the singing and I knew that
this was a great race, for, while there was loneliness and trouble in
their singing, there was also fierceness and the will to fight. A man

might sing - "Goin' down this road a feelin' bad -" but his next line was - "Cause I aint gonna be treated that-a-way."

In a cotton strike a woman spoke and her voice chanted a song -

"My man is in jail for striking -
"It aint agin' th' law,
"My boy is in jail for striking -
"It aint agin' th' law.
"I say- Plead Not Guilty!
"An' rot they dam jails down!"

And that for a statement of survival has not often been equaled.

It would be a good idea to listen very closely to these songs, to listen for the rhythms of work, and over them, the words of anger and survival.

Woody is just Woody. Thousands of people do not know he has any other name. He is just a voice and a guitar. He sings the songs of a people and I suspect that he is, in a way, that people. Harsh voiced and nasal, his guitar hanging like a tire iron on a rusty rim, there is nothing sweet about Woody, and there is nothing sweet about the songs he sings. But there is something more important for those who will listen. There is the will of a people to endure and fight against oppression. I think we call this the American Spirit.

PUBLISHER'S FOREWORD

by Irwin Silber

There is the grime of coal and the smell of manure and even the taste of blood on these pages. And the story of how this collection came to be a book is important to tell, because it, too, has a place in the history of our times.

The starting point, of course, is with the songs and the men and women who fashioned them out of the urgent necessity of their lives. It is probably next to impossible for any person who did not live through it to truly understand the nature of the Depression that wracked the United States in the decade of the 1930's. America had never known such widespread economic dislocation. The central fact was mass unemployment. Everything else -- the soup kitchens, the home relief lines, the unmitigated misery of the old, the sick, the feeble who had no resources and no place to turn -- all these stemmed from the fact that in some basic, incomprehensible way, the system had fallen apart at the seams. Factories, mills, and mines closed down and people were thrown out of work. This began a cycle of business failures, wage-cutting, lockouts, land evictions which shortly began to back up on itself and produced, within a short time, the most massive economic collapse this country has ever known.

It was a time of trial, a time of despair and hunger and insecurity. The "one-third of a nation ill-housed, ill-clothed, ill-fed" was more than a symbol or a political slogan. It was 50 million people living in slums, in shacks, scrambling for pennies and dimes, families moving in together and being evicted together, and always and always, looking for work, looking for a job at honest pay.

> I don't want your millions, mister,
> I don't want your diamond ring.
> All I want's just live and let live,
> Give me back my job again.

It was a time of struggle. After the initial shock, after the emergency soup kitchens and the apple-sellers, came organization. In New York, the unemployed organized and marched on City Hall. In Washington, D. C., the World War I veterans organized and marched on the capitol, where Douglas MacArthur and the U.S. Army used force and violence to break up their demonstration. In San Francisco, they organized a general strike, and on the plantations of the south, even the share-croppers organized into alliances and unions that fought for the land. The greatest symbol of this struggle was the Union. For it was in this period that the CIO was born, bringing to birth the old Wobbly dream of industrial unionism that would give workers the power to bring the system to its knees.

> Come all of you good workers,
> Good news to you I'll tell.
> Of how the good old union
> Has come in here to dwell.

It was a time of dreams. For the first time, the poor and the dispossessed of America could imagine a new kind of world, a life based on brotherhood and mutuality. The political parties of the left grew in size and militancy. The economic reforms of the New Deal -- unemployment insurance, social security, the wage-and-hour law, low-rent housing -- could not keep up with the hopes and demands of the people for government that would be responsible to and for the people. The symbol was Roosevelt -- and the TVA!

> The Government employs us,
> Short and certain pay;
> Oh, things are up and comin',
> God bless the TVA.

That is what this book is all about -- the despair, the struggle, and the dreams of the working people of the United States in the Depression Years as expressed through the songs the people themselves made up and sang.

There aren't many professional song-writers represented in these pages. Mostly, the writers and composers, where we know their names, are people like Aunt Molly Jackson, Jim Garland, Ella Mae Wiggins, Sara Ogan, John Handcox. Or blues singers like Blind Lemon Jefferson, Big Bill Broonzy, Tampa Red. For these and all the anonymous picket-line poets of the time, there was no intellectual problem of "commitment" or whether or not "protest" was "art." When you sing because your life depends upon it, when you sing out of the very bowels of your being with a scream of anguish or when you sing out with a yell that demands and proclaims and asserts your rights as a man or a woman and as a human being --when you sing this way, where the song is an extension of your own life as it is inter-connected with the lives of others, there is no need to weigh the advisability or artistic worth of songs of protest.

Toward the end of the 1930's, Alan Lomax, who was then working in the Folksong Archives of the Library of Congress, began to realize that a great body of song literature had come to birth in the United States during these years. And so he began to accumulate what eventually became this collection. Many songs came naturally into the Archive, where they might very well have been buried if someone less perceptive than Lomax were there. Other songs came from commercial recordings issued by the major record companies, RCA, Columbia, Decca. Each song, taken by itself, made a small statement, but put together in an overall context they became part of the pattern. This, too, was a huge undertaking for Lomax, because it involved going through the files of these companies, listening, culling, copying, from out-of-print highly breakable, 78 rpm discs.

Other songs came from Lomax field trips. One whole spring with Aunt Molly Jackson, a trip to the Kentucky coal fields with Elizabeth Barnicle, and others. Many songs came from picket-line word-sheets or mimeographed migrant newspapers.

Lomax next got together with Woody Guthrie, then only a few years out of the Oklahoma Dust Bowl, to construct the book. They organized it into subjects and chapters. If some subject needed a song that wasn't there, Woody wrote one. Or Woody might write one anyway just being inspired by some particular phrase or idea he got from working on the manuscript. But, most of all, Woody wrote introductions and comments for every song in the book. Somewhere along the way, Pete Seeger came into the project, his work consisting mostly of transcribing tunes from records, from Woody, from other singers.

Finally the book was finished. John Steinbeck, who had met Woody in the "Grapes of Wrath" days, was asked to write a foreword, which he did. Woody wrote an introduction of his own, and then decided to add an auto-biography which ran almost as long.

Then began the job of trying to get a publisher. Lomax says that "every publisher in town" turned it down. Mostly they thought it was "too hot," or too illiterate, or lacking in commercial appeal, or any one of a hundred objections that publishers have when something so startlingly new comes along that there is no precedent by which to judge it.

And then came Pearl Harbor and World War II and the whole project was shelved. The various people concerned went off to war, copies of the manuscript were disbursed, other battles were fought and other songs were sung.

After the war when People's Songs was organized, the original copy of the manuscript (including the only set of musical transcriptions) was deposited in the People's Songs Library, intact as a manuscript. There it sat for more than seven years, accumulating dust, occasionally referred to in search of a song or a story, but slowly being forgotten.

People's Songs folded, Sing Out! magazine was started, and the manuscript of the book went along with the mimeograph machine, the electric typewriter, two battered old desks and half a dozen filing cabinets from one cold loft to another as part of the arsenal of that handful of fanatics who believed that the songs of the people were a mighty weapon of attack and counter-attack in the fight for life.

With the passage of time, various chapters became separated, one from the other. Individual songs were pulled out and misfiled again. Someone was in too big a hurry to get the words to a particular song, so he didn't bother to copy from the manuscript (no, we did not have a copying machine) and simply walked off with the original copy. Eventually, the manuscript was completely broken down and re-filed by subjects along with other songs in the library.

Sometime during this period, John Greenway set out to write the book which eventually was published as "American Folksongs of Protest.' A major portion of the contents of this book was taken from the manuscrpt of "Hard-Hitting Songs" from the files of the People's Songs Library.

Nothing more happened until 1961. At that time, while compiling material for various projects, I came across pages of the old manu-script scattered through our files. The pity of this great book never being published was made clear once again as I read through the handful of pages I could find. And then I realized that it could be published.

I discussed the idea with Moses Asch (we had just organized OAK Publications)showed him some samples of the songs and comments, and told him about the history of the project. He became as enthusiastic as I was. We had never before published anything that ambitious or complicated, but we agreed that it was a book that had to be done. Now all we had to do was reconstitute the manuscript.

I spent several weeks culling through all of the material in the old People's Songs (now Sing Out!) library. I trusted to memory, instinct, and luck to find the originals. I also used some elementary detective work. Learning after a while that most of the manuscript had been typed on a particular typewriter, I got to the point where I could recognize a song from the book by the type face or the layout style of the typist or the actual typing paper used.

At this point fate lent a helping hand by introducing a minor miracle of coincidence. A second, completely intact copy of the entire manuscript turned up! It was a carbon copy of the original and was brought to us by John Cohen, one of the three mainstays of the New Lost City Ramblers. John got it from his brother, Mike, who in turn got it from Liz Ambellan, who in turn got it from her one-time husband who had a loft downtown in New York City way back when, which used to be a folksinger's hangout. Woody used to stay there often and undoubtedly left a copy of the book behind.

The only problem was that the carbon did not have any of the musical transcriptions. However, using the manuscript as a master guide, we were able to reconstitute ninety per cent of the original -- including the music. Calls went out to various people who might be able to help us with the missing tunes. Pete Seeger remembered some. Jerry Silverman helped with some of the blues. Ellen Stekert helped with Sara Ogan's songs, as did Jim Garland and Sara herself. (None of that great folksinging tribe remain in Kentucky any more. Aunt Molly is dead. Jim lives in Washougal, Washington, and is busy writing songs and stories, as well as collecting. Sara lives in Detroit and has recorded an album of her old songs on the Folk-Legacy label.)

But the biggest contribution was made at this point by Happy Traum, who carefully edited all the music, adapted tunes, transcribed and double-checked many songs, and took over-all musical responsibility for the manuscript.

As the book neared the final stages of production, I realized that there was only one way to illustrate it properly -- with the marvelous pioneering photographs taken in the 1930's under the auspices of the Farm Security Administration. Some of America's finest and most perceptive photographers participated in this vast photographic undertaking which pictorially documented the Depression Years — among them Dorothea Lange, Walker Evans, Ben Shahn, Jack Delano, and Arthur Rothstein.

Accordingly, I enlisted the cooperation of librarians at the Library of Congress in Washington and the Picture Collection at the New York Public Library. I was able to make copies of all the FSA photographs which appear in these pages from their various collections and I wish to thank the directors of these collections for their contribution to this book. In a few cases, pictures other than FSA photos were used, but these, too, are (for the most part) documentary photographs of the period.

For myself, I feel privileged to have worked on this collection and to have been the instrument by which all of the various elements involved have been pulled together.

So, here it is at last -- HARD HITTING SONGS FOR HARD-HIT PEOPLE. It is born more than a quarter of a century after its conception, but perhaps our generation needs the spirit and values inherent in these pages even more than the world of the 1940's did. In fact, it is precisely because the lessons of the 30's increasingly have relevance for our own time, that all of us associated with this book take great personal and collective pride in its publication.

New York City
October 6, 1966

INTRODUCTION   by Woody Guthrie

Howdy Friend:

Here's a book of songs that's going to last a mighty long time, because these are the kind of songs that folks make up when they're a-singing about their hard luck, and hard luck is one thing that you sing louder about than you do about boots and saddles, or moons on the river, or cigarettes a shining in the dark.

There's a heap of people in the country that's a having the hardest time of their life right this minute; and songs are just like having babies. You can take either, but you can't fake it, and if you try to fake it, you don't fool anybody except yourself.

For the last eight years I've been a rambling man, from Oklahoma to California and back three times by freight train, highway, and thumb, and I've been stranded, and disbanded, busted, disgusted with people of all sorts, sizes, shapes and calibres -- folks that wandered around over the country looking for work, down and out, and hungry half of the time. I've slept on and with them, with their feet in my face and my feet in theirs -- in bed rolls with Canadian Lumberjacks, in greasy rotten shacks and tents with the Okies and Arkies that are grazing today over the state of California and Arizona like a herd of lost buffalo with the hot hoof and empty mouth disease.

Then to New York in the month of February, the thumb route, in the snow that blanketed from Big Springs, Texas, north to New York, and south again into even Florida ... Walking down the big road, no job, no money, no home ... no nothing. Nights I slept in jails, and the cells were piled high with young boys, strong men, and old men; and they talked and they sung, and they told you the story of their life, how it used to be, how it got to be, how the home went to pieces, how the young wife died or left, how the mother died in the insane asylum, how Dad tried twice to kill himself, and lay flat on his back for 18 months -- and then crops got to where they wouldn't bring nothing, work in the factories would kill a dog, work on the belt line killed your soul, work in the cement and limestone quarries withered your lungs, work in the cotton mills shot your feet and legs all to hell, work in the steel mills burned your system up like a gnat that lit in the melting pot, and -- always, always had to fight and argue and cuss and swear, and shoot and slaughter and wade mud and sling blood -- to try to get a nickel more out of the rich bosses. But out of all of this mixing bowl of hell and high waters by George, the hard working folks have done something that the bosses, his sons, his wives, his whores, and his daughters have failed to do -- the working folks have walked bare handed against clubs, gas bombs, billys, blackjacks, saps, knucks, machine guns, and log chains -- and they sang their way through the whole dirty mess. And that's why I say the songs in this book will be sung coast to coast acrost the country a hundred years after all nickel phonographs have turned back into dust.

I ain't a writer, I want that understood, I'm just a little one-cylinder guitar picker. But I don't get no kick out of these here songs that are imitation and made up by guys that's paid by the week to write 'em up -- that reminds me of a crow a settin on a fence post a singing when some guy is a sawing his leg off at the same time. I like the song the old hen sings just before she flogs hell out of you for pestering her young chicks.

This book is a song book of that kind. It's a song book that come from the lungs of the workin' folks -- and every little song was easy and simple, but mighty pretty, and it caught on like a whirlwind -- it didn't need sheet music, it didn't need nickel phonographs, and it didn't take nothing but a little fanning from the bosses, the landlords, the deputies, and the cops, and the big shots, and the bankers, and the business men to flare up like an oil field on fire, and the big cloud of black smoke turn into a cyclone -- and cut a swath straight to the door of the man that started the whole thing, the greedy rich people.

You'll find the songs the hungry farmers sing as they bend their backs and drag their sacks, and split their fingers to pieces grabbing your shirts and dresses out of the thorns on a cotton boll. You'll find the blues. The blues are my favorite, because the blues are the saddest and lonesomest, and say the right thing in a way that most preachers ought to pattern after. All honky tonk and dance hall blues had parents, and those parents was the blues that come from the workers in the factories, mills, mines, crops, orchards, and oil fields -- but by the time a blues reaches a honky tonk music box, it is changed from chains to kisses, and from a cold prison cell to a warm bed with a hot mama, and from a sunstroke on a chain gang, to a chock house song, or a brand new baby and a bottle of gin.

You'll find a bunch of songs made up by folks back in the hills of old Kentucky. The hills was full of coal. The men was full of pep and wanted to work. But houses wasn't no good, and wages was next to nothing. Kids died like flies. The mothers couldn't pay the doctor, so the doctor didn't come. It was the midwives, the women like old Aunt Molly Jackson, that rolled up her sleeves, spit out the window, grabbed a wash pan in one hand and a armful of old pads and rags, and old newspapers, and dived under the covers and old rotten blankets -- to come up with a brand new human being in one hand and a hungry mother in the other. Aunt Molly was just a coal miner's wife, and a coal miner's daughter, but she took the place of the doctor in 850 cases, because the coal miners didn't have the money.

You'll find the songs that were scribbled down on the margins of almanacs with a penny pencil, and sung to the rhythms of splinters and rocks that the Winchester rifles kicked up in your face as you sang them. I still wonder who was on the tail end of the rifles. Also in the Kentucky Coal Miner Songs, you'll sing the two wrote by Jim Garland, "Greenback Dollar" and "Harry Simms" -- a couple of ringtail tooters you're bound to like.

Sarah Ogan, she's the half sister of Aunt Molly, about half as old, and a mighty good worker and singer -- she keeps up the spirit of the men that dig for a hamburger in a big black hole in the ground, and are promised pie in the sky when they die and get to heaven, provided they go deep enough in the hole, and stay down there long enough.

Then the next batch of wrong colored eggs to hatch -- out pops the New Deal songs -- the songs that the people sung when they heard the mighty good sounding promises of a re-shuffle, a honest deck, and a brand new deal from the big shots. A Straight flush, the Ace for One Big Union, the King for One Happy Family, the Queen for a happy mother with a full cupboard, the Jack for a hard working young man with money enough in his pockets to show his gal a good time, and the ten spot for the ten commandments that are overlooked too damn much by the big boys.

Next you'll run across some songs called "Songs of the One Big Union" -- which is the same Big Union that Abe Lincoln lived for and fought for and died for. Something has happened to that Big Union since Abe Lincoln was here. It has been raped. The Banking men has got their Big Union, and the Land Lords has got their Big Union, and the Merchants has got their Kiwanis and Lions Club, and the Finance Men has got their Big Union, and the Associated Farmers has got their Big Union, but down south and out west, on the cotton farms, and working in the orchards and fruit crops it is a jail house offence for a few common everyday workers to form them a Union, and get together for higher wages and honest pay and fair treatment. It's damn funny how all of the big boys are in Big Unions, but they cuss and raise old billy hell when us poor damn working guys try to get together and make us a Working Man's Union. This Book is full of songs that the working folks made up about the beatings and the sluggings and the cheatings and the killings that they got when they said they was a going to form them a Working Man's Union. It is a jail house crime for a poor damn working man to even hold a meeting with other working men. They call you a red or a radical or something, and throw you and your family off of the farm and let you starve to death... These songs will echo that song of starvation till the world looks level -- till the world is level -- and there ain't no rich men, and there ain't no poor men, and every man on earth is at work and his family is living as human beings instead of like a nest of rats.

A last section of this book is called Mulligan Stew which are songs that you make up when you're a trying to speak something that's on your mind ... telling your troubles to the blue sky, or a walkin' down the road with your 2 little kids by the hand, thinking of your wife that's just died with her third one -- and you get to speaking your mind -- maybe to yourself the first time, then when you get it a little better fixed in your head, and you squeeze out all of the words you don't need, and you boil it down to just a few that tell the whole story of your hard luck. Then you talk it or sing it to somebody you meet in the hobo jungle or stranded high and dry in the skid row section of a big town, or just fresh kicked off a Georgia farm, and a going nowhere, just a walkin' along, and a draggin' your feet along in the deep sand, and -- then you hear him sing you his song or tell you his tale, and you think, That's a mighty funny thing. His song is just like mine. And my tale is just like his. And everywhere you ramble, under California R.R. bridges, or the mosquito swamps of Louisiana, or the dustbowl deserts of the Texas plains -- it's a different man, a different woman, a different kid a speaking his mind, but it's the same old tale, and the same old song. Maybe different words. Maybe different tune. But it's hard times, and the same hard times. The same big song. This book is that song.

You'll find a section in this book about Prison & Outlaw songs. I know how it is in the states I've rambled through. In the prisons the boys sing about the long, lonesome days in the cold old cell, and the dark nights in the old steel tank and a lot of the best songs you ever heard come from these boys and women that sweat all day in the pea patch, chain gang, a makin' big ones out of little ones, and new roads out of cow trails -- new paved roads for a big black limousine to roll over with a lady in a fur coat and a screwball poodle dog a sniffing at her mouth. Prisoners ain't shooting the bull when they sing a mournful song, it's the real stuff. And they sing about the "man that took them by the arm," and about the "man with the law in his hand," and about the "man a settin' up in the jury box," and the "man on th' judges bench," and the "guard come a walkin' down that graveyard hall," and about the "man with th' jail house key," -- and the "guard a walkin' by my door" -- and about the "sweethearts that walk past the window," and the old mother that wept and tore her hair, and the father that pleaded at the bar, and the little girl that sets in the moonlight alone, and waits for the sentence to roll by. These outlaws may be using the wrong system when they rob banks and hijack the rich traveler, and shoot their way out of a gamblin' game, and shoot down a man in a jewelry store, or blow down the pawn shop owner, but I think I know what's on these old boys minds. Something like this: "Two little children a layin' in the bed, both of them so hungry that they cain't lift up their head ..."

I know how it was with me, there's been a many a time that I set around with my head hanging down, broke, clothes no good, old slouchy shoes, and no place to go to have a good time, and no money to spend on the women, and a sleeping in cattle cars like a whiteface steer, and a starving for days at a time up and down the railroad tracks and then a seeing other people all fixed up with a good high rolling car, and good suits of clothes, and high priced whiskey, and more pretty gals than one. Even had money to blow on damn fool rings and necklaces and bracelets around their necks and arms -- and I would just set there by the side of the road and think ... Just one of them diamonds would buy a little farm with a nice little house and a water well and a gourd dipper, and forty acres of good bottom land to raise a crop on, and a good rich garden spot up next to the house, and a couple of jersey cows with nice big tits, and some chickens to wake me up of a morning, and ... the whole picture of the little house and piece of land would go through my head every time I seen a drunk man with three drunk women a driving a big Lincoln Zephyr down the road -- with money to burn, and they didn't even know where the money was coming from ... yes, siree, it's a mighty tempting thing, mighty tempting.

Now, I might be a little haywired, but I ain't no big hand to like a song because it's pretty, or because it's fancy, or done up with a big smile and a pink ribbon, I'm a man to like songs that ain't sung too good. Big hand to sing songs that ain't really much account. I mean, you know, talking about good music, and fancy runs, and expert music. I like songs, by george, that's sung by folks that ain't musicians, and ain't able to read music, don't know one note from another'n, and -- say something that amounts to something. That a way you can say what you got to say just singing it and if you use the same dern tune, or change it around twice, and turn it upside down, why that still don't amount to a dern, you have spoke what you had to speak, and if folks don't like the music, well, you can still pass better than some political speakers.

But it just so happens that these songs here, they're pretty, they're easy, they got something to say, and they say it in a way you can under- stand, and if you go off somewhere and change 'em around a little bit, well, that don't hurt nothin'. Maybe you got a new song. You have, if you said what you really had to say -- about how the old world looks to you, or how it ought to be fixed.

Hells bells, I'm a going to fool around here and make a song writer out of you. -- No, I couldn't do that -- wouldn't do it if I could. I ruther have you just like you are. You are a songbird right this minute. Today you're a better songbird than you was yesterday, 'cause you know a little bit more, you seen a little bit more, and all you got to do is just park yourself under a shade tree, or maybe at a desk, if you still got a desk, and haul off and write down some way you think this old world could be fixed so's it would be twice as level and half as steep, and take the knocks out of it, and grind the valves, and tighten the rods, and take up the bearings, and put a boot in the casing, and make the whole trip a little bit smoother, and a little bit more like a trip instead of a trap.

It wouldn't have to be fancy words. It wouldn't have to be a fancy tune. The fancier it is the worse it is. The plainer it is the easier it is, and the easier it is, the better it is -- and the words don't even have to be spelt right.

You can write it down with the stub of a burnt match, or with an old chewed up penny pencil, on the back of a sack, or on the edge of a almanac, or you could pitch in and write your walls full of your own songs. They don't even have to rhyme to suit me. If they don't rhyme a tall, well, then it's prose, and all of the college boys will study on it for a couple of hundred years, and because they cain't make heads nor tails of it, they'll swear you're a natural born song writer, maybe call you a natural born genius.

This book is songs like that. If you're too highbrow for that, you can take your pants and go home right now, but please leave the book -- some people might want to look through it.

If you're so rich that you look down on these kind of songs, that's a dam good sign you're a standing on your head, and I would suggest that you leave your pocketbook and wife and ice box and dog and catch out east on a west bound freight, and rattle around over this United States for a year or so, and meet and see and get to knowing the people, and if you will drop me a postal card, and enclose a 3¢ Uncle Sam Postage Stamp -- strawberry or grape, either one, both flavors are good -- why, I'll send you back a full and complete list of the addresses of the railroad bridges that 500,000 of my relatives are stranded under right this minute. (From east coast to west coast, and I ain't a coastin', I mean, I ain't a boasting.) It's the -- it's you wax dummies in the glass cases I'm a roasting. If you are one, you know it already, I don't have to sing it to you, and I don't have to preach it to you, your own song is in your own heart, and the reason you're so damn mixed up and sad, and high tempered and high strung, it's because that song is always a ringing in your own ears -- and it's your own song, you made it up, you added a verse here, and a verse yonder, and a word now, and a word then -- till -- you don't need a book a tellin' about songs, yours is already ringing and singing in your ears.

The only trouble is with you, you hold it back, you hide it, you keep it down, you kick it down, you sing over it, and under it, and off to all four sides, and you get out on limbs and you sing it, and you get lost in so called arts and sciences and all sorts of high fangled stuff like "intellect" and "inspiration" and "religion" and "business" and "reputation" and "pride" and "me" -- and you say, talk, live, breathe, and exercise everything in the world, except that real old song that's in your heart.

Thank heaven, one day we'll all find out that all of our songs was just little notes in a great big song, and when we do, the rich will disappear like the morning fog, and the poor will vanish like a drunkard's dream -- and we'll all be one big happy family, waking up with the chickens, chickens we don't owe nothing on, and a skipping through the morning dew, just as far as you want to skip.

I've got off of the subject 719 times in less than 15 pages. I told you I ain't no good as a writer, but -- well, looks like you're already this far along, and I feel so sorry for you a having to try to wade through my writing like a barefooted kid through a sand-burr patch -- think I'll just thank you for your visit, borrow fifty cents if you got it to spare, and try to throw some sort of trash or weeds or rags or something on this infernal typewriter -- and maybe it'll sort of quit.

True as the average,

WOODROW WILSON GUTHRIE, or just plain old Woody

ABOUT WOODY

You know I been in every town mentioned in John's book "Grapes of Wrath", and in the picture show too. All I know how to write is just sort of what I seen up and down the road.

Left Oklahoma and went out to west Texas. Town called Pampa, Gray County, Santa Fe railroad line. That's right due west of Oklahoma City about 300 miles, and right square in the big middle of the dust bowl.

That's where the wheat grows. Where the Oil Flows. Where the dust blows. And the farmer owes. Where you can see farther and see less, see more trees and less wood, more work and less money, more cows and less milk, more rivers and less water, more crops and less groceries, more cowboys and less work, than most any other place.

Dust some times gets so thick you run your tractor and plows upside down. So dark you can't see a dime in your pocket, a shirt on your back, a meal on your table, or a dadgum thing. Only thing that is higher than that dust is your debts. Dust settles, but debts don't.

I first got work in a jake joint. Jake is another name for alcohol mixed with jamaica ginger for flavor. Then I graduated up to a bootleg whiskey joint next door. Then the same thing across the street. And in most of the alleys around town. Worked there for a dollar a day, 12 to 18 hours a day. Was hired and fired at least 3 times a week, according to how dusty the weather was. I even got married while I was a working there.

My wife was an Oklahoma girl, her folks had just lately come out to the oil boom in the panhandle plains of west Texas. Her family was good hard working farmers. Good natured folks, and they went to the Catholic church. There never was a better girl than Mary, and there never was a better family. She very seldom ever complained and she worked hard all of the time. She could straighten up a house almost as fast as I could litter it up with scrap paper. We had 3 kids, 2 girls, and a boy -- Teeny, Sue, and old Bill. Youngest kids you ever seen. Ain't old enough to vote, but can out vote 99% of the politicians.

We bought a little shack house for $25. It was on her folks lot. We never did pay the last $5 on the house. According to how this book goes. Anyhow, we lived there in our little house in the dustbowl and wondered who in the devil had all of the money. I worked down at the liquor joint some, and walked the streets some. For the first 3 years we was married, we averaged less than $4 a week -- but we got by some how.

Long about that time my dad married a second time. A trained nurse from California, who practiced Magnetic Healing, Fortune Telling, and Cancer Curing, and I found myself hanging around their house most all the time. Such things as this got in my head and just stayed there and we would set up till late hours of the morning and night -- just talking about things of this kind. I asked ten million questions about all of these things. I saw over a hundred people a day come to her house for Magnetic Healing, Readings, and things like that. She done a lot of it free to folks that was broke, but I still figured that she was making a lot better living than me at the whiskey store, or even trying to get started boot-legging on my own hook -- so I saved up all of my nerve for about six months and hung me out a big sign that said Faith Healing, Mind Reading, No Charge.

Well, here they come. I even had a ad in the town paper every day. So here they come -- men, women, and children, everybody, and with more hard luck and troubles than you could shake a stick at -- and more questions. But I stayed in the buggy. I didn't bar nobody, rich or poor, white or black, drunk or sober, and sane or insane. I worked it two ways. One was to let them ask you questions and then pitch in to answer them. The other way was to set them down and guess their question, and then try to answer it. I got pretty good at both.

I read the bible and the life of Jesus almost day and night, and con-centrated on the blue sky in my spare time. I prayed in every known fashion and style, both plain and fancy, and invented no new way that I know of just off handed.

But you'd be surprised how many hundreds of folks come down. They would wake me and my wife up at all hours, and break in on all of our meals. They come and set. They listened and thought. They wept and cried and went into every model of nervous breakdown, including the very latest. They told you everything about their self, and went into their family history 2 or 3 generations back. You waded through all kinds of spider webs and dark corners in their mind, all kinds of stuff they was afraid of, all kinds of things that had done happened in the past, and ought to of been forgot about forty years ago, as well as junk that hadn't happened yet, and cried about things that was going to jump on them some twenty-three years in the future. I learned how to swim through all of this drift wood, and haven't forgot so far. Superstition a thousand feet deep, and something else a million miles across, and a tangle of loco weeds and underbrush that you never could get out of, less you just chucked the whole thing in the creek and forgot it.

Every kind of ism known to mankind hit my door. We had hot debates on all of them, and fought devils and spirits and serpents and corn whiskey all over the place.

Most everybody that come had just recently lost everything they had in the world. The others was fixing to lose it. This caused a lot of fights and feuds to break out between husband and wife, and caused sweethearts to haul off and quit. Kids was at home hungry and nobody could rake up any groceries. The girls was ragged, and nobody to take care of them. A deputy sheriff had a baby by a lady that was out gunning for him. I talked her loose from her shooting iron. The crops was all dried up and the bank was taking the place. You had to hit the road with your wife and kids. The dust pneumonia was killing them off by the hundreds. My relatives took down with it. It looked like there wasn't no hope down here on earth. Everything was haywire and no way to fix it -- nobody got up and told how to fix it -- not even the preachers. Nor the business men, nor the finance men, nor the Ladies Aid outfit. Everything was in a mess. Old man out of work. Ladies wanted jobs to feed their kids. Sombody was down with sugar diabetes, and no money for a doctor. Rotten teeth was poisoning the old lady, and no money for a new set. Sores broke out on the school kids, and no money to doctor it. Would you inherit a million dollars tomorrow or the next day, and if so, from where? Ought I to leave my wife? She's too high tempered to live with. I cain't help it. I looked for a job, but they just dam shore ain't none. Who'll feed the kids if we get a divorce? What does my spirit friend say, not Blue Belle, from the revolution, but try that Indian Guide that starved to death on the desert. He seems to see better than others. Will I be able to get me a p——?

This was the kind of talk that I lived in for about 2 solid years, and then times got so hard that me and the wife couldn't feed the babies -- so folks kept on a coming -- but I decided it would be better to go to California. I kissed the family goodbye and swung on to a cattle car on the Santa Fe, and whistled out down the line.

It was winter time on the Texas plains and colder'n a well digger in Montana -- so I shot south to Amarillo, Hereford, Clovis, Roswell, and to Las Cruces, and Tucson, and Yuma, and Riverside, and on to Los Angeles. Stayed nights in the jails. Days tried to thumb a ride in a car. Night rode the freights to make time. You hate to just sleep all night and not get anywhere. You hate it even worse when a good hot meal is waiting for you at the other end of the line, and you ain't had none in 3 days.

When I hit Tucson, Arizona -- I was really vacant. Dirty, tired, and so hungry I was shaking all over. It was hot there in the Arizona sun -- and I hadn't never hit a back door before -- but I decided to try it -- so I went to about ten of the local churches, offering to do some work for something to eat. I didn't get a bite. One lady, a maid at some church there, said, You better get away from this back door before the parson comes back and sees you -- he don't like for anybody to knock on his back door. At the big Catholic Cathedral on the other side of town, the nun lady said, I'll have to call the father, so he come to the door and said, Sorry, Son, but we're livin on charity our selves, there's nothing here for you. I looked up at the cathedral, every single rock in it cost ten dollars to lay and ten to chop out, and I thought, Boy, you're right -- there's nothing here for me. If piling rocks on top of one another is the top of your religion, I ruther have the railroads and the 'bos. I shook acrost town and back down into the yards -- and set down on a rail and tie, and a big friendly looking Negro boy walked down the track and said, Boy, you looks like you ain't had nuthin' since you was a pup. I said, I'm vacant as a whore house in a ghost town. He said, You's crazy to go hongery. You see them little shack houses right over yondah in the edge o' town? Go on ovah theah an' you'll get somethin' in yo' belly, 'stead o' that preachah talk. So I got up and lit out, and hit the first door. Nobody was at home there. I hit the next one -- a little broke down house -- and the lady come to the door and I offered to work out a meal. She said she didn't have no work to do right then -- but for me to wait -- then out she come with a whole big sack full of stuff to eat. I set down on her door step and poked it down me. Then I started to get up and go back to the yards -- and I first figured I'd ought to hustle up another sack for some of the other boys. This was my first time. I wasn't a virgin no more. And I was liking it. I hit two more houses, and a dog run me off from the first one. The second lady packed me 4 great big juicy sandwiches. So cussed good I et one of them myself, and took the other 3 back to the boys. They gulped once for each sandwich. But they grinned up at me like I wasn't ever grinned at before, with the possible exception of the day I met my wife. I felt like I had learnt the secret of all religion. To give away all of the stuff you can't use. All other baloney is bull.

In the Reno Nevada jail I met a dope fiend. Had been a government doctor. Performed an illegal operation. They took his license. He got on morphine, cocaine, and heroin, and run down to the depot and grabbed up a mail sack with $13,000 in it, and run off into the big high weeds and nobody caught him, till he blowed the money, and got drunk on dope and come into town to cash all of the checks. He got loud and the cops grabbed him. He was in there beating everything up with a gallon bucket, raving and yelling at the top of his lungs, and swearing he was glad to go to the big house. You perform 3000 good operations they don't say nothing. One bad one, and out you go, So take me to the big house -- take me anywhere to get me off of this god dam dope. He would beat all of the cells and bars with his bucket and go hog wild.

A Swedish Lumber Jack got in, beat all to hell, blood running out of his nose and ears, and his mouth cut to pieces. The Reno cops done it. He bought a beer in a gyp joint down in town. Gave the gal a twenty dollar bill. She give him back change for a buck and told him to go to hell. He sailed a mug through the big mirror, and they yelled for the bulls -- they come running in and beat hell out of the Swede, and throwed him in the can with his wages gone and his head beat half off.

A big Indian had found oil in the river bottom. Got drunk to celebrate, and lost a new Ford v-8, a dog, his only son, and had also forgot where the hell the oil well was.

I talked it over with the Indian. He smoked up all of my cigarettes trying to remember ...

They throwed 3 boys with a circus side show in the jug. Asked them what for, and they said it must be because we're in a rich man's town broke. They laughed and joked all night long.

One other boy in that same night was drunk for a couple of weeks. They throwed him in when his last dollar was gone. Not before.

Some man in there was ruptured awful bad. He showed all of us his rupture. And his belt. He moaned half of the night and yelled for a doctor. He was in the steel tank with all of us. He said he couldn't stand the pain any longer, no doctor would come, so he slipped off into his cage and tried to hang his self with his necktie and rupture belt braided into a rope. He fell to the floor when the rope broke, hit his head on the steel, and laid there choking to death. We called the guards. They broke in, cut the slip knot from his neck, rolled him over with the toe of their shoes, and said let the son of a bitch go to hell, dying's too good for the dirty bastard.

In Henderson, Texas Jail they throwed me in with a bunch of slot machines right next to my cell -- with lots of money in 'em. I slid a beer bottle out of the toilet, and hid it aiming to break them glasses and hit about twenty jackpots out of them two bit machines, but -- I didn't. I don't know yet why I didn't.

In Mifflintown, Pennsylvania, the snow was on -- an old man fell off of a freight dadgum near it froze ... we took him up to the jail house, and they let us in. Everybody tells you the whole story of their life while they're a laying there thawing out. The radiator in the cell was too hot, and we couldn't get the window open, and several of the boys took bad colds and headaches from it, and they had to hit the blizzard again next morning. It snowed from Galveston Texas to the North Pole, I left Galveston and come to New York -- and found lots of trees and people breaking down with the snow and ice.

In California I didn't dare to sleep in their jails. I was an Okie full blood, and was afraid I might not get out.

I spent a couple of three years of this rambling, and have been in a lot of states and stranded under all of the important bridges in the country, and generally always packed the old guitar along to entertain myself with, and the 'bos, and maybe pick up a spare nickel with it if it come right handy -- in a saloon or whore house -- or at a house party or square dance, or pie supper, or band standing for some candidate or any damn thing. Even played the other night for a gathering of all women nurses from the Hosspistal down here on Beekman St., New York City ...

* *

The songs in this book come from everywhere, just like I did. Only there was just more and hungrier people. Folks that's really been beat up a lot more than I have by the police and deputies... and folks that's fought a lot harder for a better world to live in. I believe that this is the best book of songs that I ever seen in my whole put togethers. Just forget I had a damn thing to do with it, it's real and it's made up by folks that has had to take 'er the hard way all their life.

I wonder sometimes why you don't ever hear these songs played and sung on the nickel boxes in the saloons and pimp joints, but I guess they belong to some rich guy and he don't want to listen to us poor folks sing. They don't want to even print them on song sheets. I don't know why. But I do know one thing -- and I'll bet my last bottom dollar on it -- these songs come from folks that got beat up for just stepping out in front of the police with their Winchesters, and they'll outlast any ten songs that a rich guy makes up -- 'cause they're just them kind of songs.

There ain't a dam thing sissy about them. That's why I wanted to round them up and make a book out of them. I'm sick and tired of this panty waist crap you hear on the radios and in the saloons, and this book will make them fancy outfits look like a jigger of gin throwed out of a airplane. (They throw everything else out of them).

Woody Guthrie

1 - HARD LUCK ON THE FARM

Hard times and good times. That's what you hear on the farm, and now hard times seems to be about ten laps ahead in the race. When it got tough most folks didn't raise up and raise hell on nobody, they just set down on an old rotten porch with an old broke down banjo or a geed-up guitar and made up some sort of a song to tell you how it was. They're hard fighters, you know, but they ain't trouble raisers. They ain't afraid and they ain't cowards, but they just don't fly off at the handle. Prices up. Prices down. Good crop and bad crop. Always owed more than you ought to, but - it kept on a getting harder and dryer til you had to shoot a shotgun three times at daylight to get the morning glories to wake up. You set around the old eating table when night come and between plates smeared with a few scattered leavings of cornbread crumbs and molasses, you wrote you up a song, and you sung it around at the pie suppers and square dances and it got around the country that way.

The farmer is the man that feeds them all. He's a willing to give you a part, I'd say the biggest part of his crops in return for other stuff he needs, like a car, a fancy ice box, a linen dress, some overalls and work shoes, and a good radio and plenty of eats and drinks - but the hard luck was that you took his crops and you forgot to bring the other stuff down to him. It ain't hard to raise a crop. Ain't hard to miss one on account of dry weather. But when you give your crops and you don't get a dam thing back, well, boy, that's Hard Luck On The Farm.

Arkansas Hard Luck Blues

By George, you know, a feller down in Oklahoma run for state office and used this Arkansas Hard Luck Blues for his campaign literature. I told you that they all sang the same song.

By Lonnie Glossom, on Perfect Record, Matrix C 1543-1. Spoken matter-of-factly with a fast guitar accompaniment.

Now, folks, I'm gonna tell you a little
    something about myself -
You know, I come from down in
    Arkansas.
I live down there on a little farm
    where the land is so poor
You have to put fertilizer around the
    telephone poles
Before you can talk over the wires.
But, nevertheless, it's a fine place to
    be from, folks.

You know, I was born down there in
    Arkansas.
Yeah, and I can remember the first
    day I was born, too.
There was three of us kids -
We was all laying side by side on
    the bed -
I heard the door slam and the old
    man he come in.
He walked up to the bed and he just
    taken one look at us -
He hollered to my maw - she was in
    the kitchen gettin' dinner -
He says, "All right, Lize",
Says, "Come on in here",
Says, "Pick out the one you want",
And says, "We'll drown the rest of
    'em. "

You know, folks, there was just
    seventeen of us kids.
There was eight boys, seven girls,
And two other children.
You know, I had but a little age on me
When the old man said:
"Son, you gonna have to get out and
    make your own livin from now
    on"
He says, "I'm tired of feedin you
    around this place. "

Well, I struck out, folks,
And here's what happened ever since:
You know, I been bawled out and
    bawled up,
Held down and held up,
Bulldogged, blackjacked, walked on
    and chewed,
Squeezed and mooched for war tax,
Excess profits, state, dog and sin
    tax,
Liberty bonds and baby bonds
And the bonds of matrimony.

I've been red crossed, green crossed
    and double crossed, folks,
I've been asked to help the society of
    John the Baptist,
The G. A. R. Women's corpse,
Men's Kiwanis and relief corpse,
I've worked like heck and been worked
    like heck, folks,
I've been drunk and got others drunk,
Lost all I had and part of my
    furniture.

Because I won't go around now and
    spend what I earned,
And go beg, borrow and steal,
I've been cussed and discussed,
Boycotted, talked to and talked about,
Held up and hung up,
And I'm doggoned nigh ruined.
The only reason that I'm sticking
    around now, folks,
Is to see what the heck is a-gonna
    happen next!

Now folks, if that isn't hard luck,
    just tell me what is.

These Old Cumberland Mountain Farms

Some landlords make it so hard on us that we can't stand it any longer. Won't let you live, won't let you die. Won't let you eat, won't let you starve, won't let you work, won't let you rest. It's a sorry place to live in.

Collected by Nicholas Ray for the Resettlement Administration, Skyline Farms, Alabama.

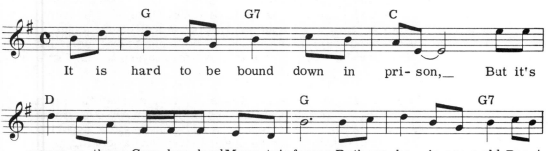

It is hard to be bound down in prison,
But it's worse on these Cumberland
      Mountain farms.
Rather be in some old penitentiary,
Or up in old iron Tennessee.

How weary I've climbed them old
      mountains,
Through the rain and the sleet and
      the snow.
Tip yo' hat when you meet Mister
      Ridges,
Bow yo' head when you meet
      Captain Ross.

Young _____ ___, he run a
      commissary
Mister, you bet he was a thief,
He sold apples at fifty a dozen
And potatoes at fifty cents a piece.

When the Coffee County boys came to
      the mounting,
They expected to get a lot to eat,
But when they called them in to
      dinner,
They got salmon, corn dodgers and
      meat.

It is seventy miles to Chattanooga,
It's a hundred and twenty to Bassell,
It's a thousand miles from here to
      civilization,
But it's only a few steps from here
      to hell.

Young people, you've all heard my
      story
And I hope you don't think it all
      wrong.
If you doubt the words I have told you
See Red Campbell, for he composed
      this song.

The Boll Weevil

The boll weevil was a Homebreaker, and worse than that he was a Home getter. There are certain ways of whispering into the women's ears, certain ways of saying things, certain ways of talking about their hair, their eyes, their red ruby lips and their beauty that some fellers are talented with. These boys are called Home Winners. They win a home with a good warm bed, a bottle of liquor, a new June bride, and all of the good things and heartaches that go with it, but -- all of this, all of your soft words about love and romance, all of your whispers about Home and Fireside and little babies are beat by one old black bug from Mexico. All of your years and your months of hard work, all of your breaking the land, all of your greasing the machinery, all of your oiling the tractor, all of your feeding the team of horses, all of your nights and mornings of back-breaking work are wiped out in one broad sweep by the Little Boll Weevil.

They come in millions, they come in jillions and they blacken the earth and the fields, and the green cotton stalks, and they take away everything you have worked for and dreamed of for years and years---just a looking for a home, just a looking for a home--just like you was a looking for a home.

It's a funny old world when a little black bug as little as the boll weevil can stop and starve and take away the home and the land of a man ---and here's a song that comes from all over the cotton country, from Atlanta to Phoenix, Arizona, all through Texas, back through the whole midwest and all over the nation to prove it. One animal a lookin' for a home can deal another completely out of a home. Sing this one loud and long. But Sing.

Collected and adapted by John A. Lomax and Alan Lomax. © 1934 (renewed) by Ludlow Music, Inc., New York, NY. Used by permission.

The boll wee-vil is a lit - tle black bug, from Mex-i-co they say, Come

all the way to Tex-as, Just a-look-in' for a place to stay.

Chorus:

Gon - na get yo' home,___ gon - na get yo' home.

The Boll Weevil is a little black bug
From Mexico they say -
Come all the way to Texas
Just a lookin' for a place to stay.

Chorus:
Gonna get yo' home.
Gonna get yo' home.
(Repeat after each verse)

The Farmer said to the Boll Weevil,
I see you on the Square.
Yes, sir, said the Boll Weevil,
My whole dam family's there!

The Farmer said to the Merchant,
I want some meat and meal.
Got outta here, you Son of a Gun,
Got Boll Weevil in yo' field!

The Farmer said to the Finance Man,
I'd like to make out a note.
Go to hell, you rascal you,
Gotta Boll Weevil on yo' coat!

Farmer said to the Banker,
I'd like to cash this check.
Get outta here you Clodhopper,
Gotta Boll Weevil down yo' neck!

Boll Weevil said to the Farmer
I'll swing right on yo' gate,
When I git through with yo' cotton,
You'll sell that Cadillac Eight!

Boll Weevil said to the Doctor,
Better put away your pills,
When I git through with the Farmer,
Caint pay no Doctor bills!

Boll Weevil said to the Preacher,
Better close up them church doors,
When I git through with the Farmer,
Caint pay no Preacher no more!

Boll Weevil said to the Business Man,
Boy, drink that cool lemonade.
When I git through with you, boy,
Gonna drag you outta that shade!

Boll Weevil in yo' field, boy,
It's just like shooting dice,
Work the whole dam year round,
But the cotton won't bring no price!

The Boll Weevil knocked on my front
    door,
He said I've come to eat.
I'm gonna starve you plumb to death
And get the shoes right off yo' feet!

The Farmer Is The Man

I believe the best I ever heard this song sung was out there in the cotton strikes in California, around the country mentioned in John Steinbeck's "Grapes of Wrath." Four little girls got up on the stage and sung it together and, you know how it is, when the women folks commence to sing about something, why us men just sort of get to itching or something, just sort of wake up and roll up our sleeves and get ready to go. It's the women that get the men a moving. Something about a bunch of women a singing a song like this that makes you say: "Well, dam my hide, if girls that pretty can sing a song that pretty about something that is so dead right, why, hell's bells, I'll pitch in with the rest of the boys and fight like hell for a good job at honest pay - here at home, and not across the damned ocean."

Men might fight to feed their own faces, but the real fighting don't start til he hears his woman or his kids a whimpering or a crying or a singing about something to eat. Then, you better look out. If you are trying to cheat them out of their home and their clothes and their education and their fair, square share, -- you dam sure better look out. If you are a Chisler that tries to get by without working and just beat these folks out of all they got, boy, you Dam Sure better look out.

Collected by Charles Seeger for the Resettlement Administration.

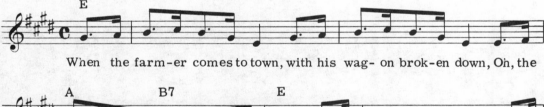

When the farm-er comes to town, with his wag-on brok-en down, Oh, the

farm-er is the man who feeds them all. If you'll on-ly look and see, I ___

think you will a-gree, that the farm-er is the man who feeds them

all. The farm-er is the man, __ the farm-er is the man,

Lives on cred- it till the fall; Then they take him by the hand, and they

lead him from the land, and the mid-dle-man's the one who gets it all.

When the farmer comes to town, with
    his wagon broken down,
O, the farmer is the man that feeds
    them all.
If you'll only look and see, I think
    you will agree,
That the Farmer is the man that
    feeds them all.
The farmer is the man,
The farmer is the man,
Lives on credit til the fall.
Then they take him by the hand
And they lead him from the land,
And the middleman's the one that
    gets it all.

When the lawyer hangs around and
    the butcher cuts a pound,
O, the farmer is the man that feeds
    them all.
And the preacher and the cook go
    a-strolling by the brook,
But the farmer is the man that feeds
    them all.
The farmer is the man,
The farmer is the man,
Lives on credit til the fall;
With the int'rest rate so high,
It's a wonder he don't die,
For the mortgage man's the one that
    gets it all.

When the banker says he's broke,
    and the merchant's up in smoke,
They forget that it's the farmer feeds
    them all.
It would put them to the test if the
    farmer took a rest,
Then they'd know that it's the farmer
    feeds them all.
The farmer is the man,
The farmer is the man,
Lives on credit til the fall:
And his pants are wearing thin,
His condition it's a sin,
He's forgot that he's the man that
    feeds them all.

Down On Roberts' Farm

It's hell to be a renter down on Roberts' farm. That pretty well covers
it. Preachers argue and bite and chew the rag and fight about what Hell
is, and where it is, but to my notion it is right here and right now --
down among the folks that live in hard work and hard times all of their
lives. I think that's why the Fellow Carpenter said, "Thy Will Be Done
On Earth As It Is In Heaven." Which means: you got to fix it here on
earth like you say it is in Heaven, then Heaven can take care of itself.

As sung by B. L. Lunsford who learned it from Calude
Reeves of Little River, Transylvania Co., N. C. He says
Reeves composed this song and wrote of Roberts' farm
from personal experience.

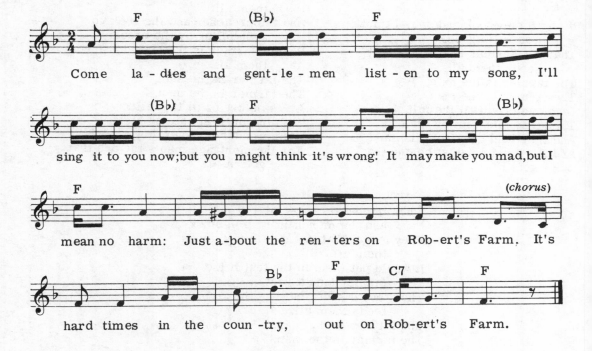

Come la-dies and gent-le-men list-en to my song, I'll
sing it to you now; but you might think it's wrong! It may make you mad, but I
mean no harm: Just a-bout the ren-ters on Rob-ert's Farm. It's
(chorus)
hard times in the coun-try, out on Rob-ert's Farm.

Come ladies and gentlemen, listen to
my song.
I'll sing it to you now but you might
think it wrong!
It might make you mad, but I mean no
harm:
Just about the renters on Roberts'
farm.
It's hard times in the country, out on
Roberts' farm.

You move out to Mr. Roberts' farm,
Plant a big crop o' cotton and a little
crop o' corn.
He'll come around to plan and to plot
Til he gets a chattel mortgage on
everything you got.
It's hard times in the country, down
on Roberts' farm.

34

I moved down to Mr. Roberts' farm,
I worked on a dairy, I worked on a
        farm.
I milked old Brindle and she had one
        horn,
It's hell to be a renter on Roberts'
        farm.
It's hard times in the country, down
        on Roberts' farm.

You go to the field and you work all
        day,
Til way after dark, and you get no
        pay, -
Just a little piece of meat and a little
        turn of corn.
It's hell to be a renter on Roberts'
        farm.
It's hard times in the country, down
        on Roberts' farm.

Roberts' renters, they'll go down
        town
With their hands in their pockets and
        their heads hung down.
We'll go in the store, and the
        merchant will say:
"Your mortgage is due, I'm a-lookin
        for my pay. "
It's hard times in the country, down
        on Roberts' farm.

I went down to my picket with a
        trembling hand:
"I can't pay you all but I'll do what I
        can. "
The merchant jumped to the telephone
        call:
"I'm going to put you in jail if you
        don't pay it all. "
It's hard times in the country, down
        on Roberts' farm.

Mr. Paul Roberts with a big Overland.
He's a little tough luck, you don't
        give a damn.
He'll run you in the mud like a train
        on the track,
He'll haul you to the mountains but he
        won't bring you back.
It's hard times in the country, down
        on Roberts' farm.

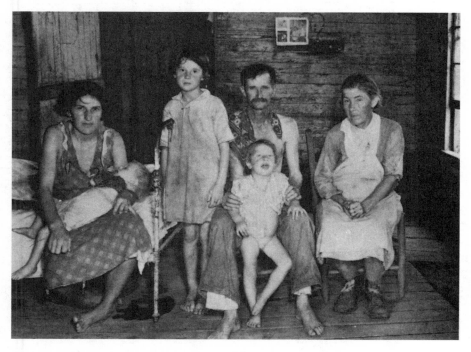

Lynchburg Town

Here's the tale of an old boy that got tied to the whipping post for packing a jug of wine around with him. This is still a common thing in a lot of states. Oklahoma still has Prohibition. You get throwed in the calaboose for having a jug of liquor, but you know god dam well that half the politicians and good people has got twice that much liquor in their houses.

One of the heaviest drinkers I ever saw is now one of the most well known lawyers in Oklahoma. The same is true of lots of southern towns. The same is true of a whole nation in the days when Prohibition was law. Will Rogers once said something like this and I agree with Will: "They tell Jokes. A joke is a law and a law is a joke." But it ain't so funny to us folks that's got to lay out six or eight months or a year and a day on account of some dam fool joke called a law.

Collected, adapted, and arranged by John A. Lomax and Alan Lomax. © 1941 (renewed) by Ludlow Music, Inc., New York, NY. Used by permission.

Times a-gittin' hard, Money's gittin' scarce, Pay me for this to-bac-co,_ and I will leave this place.

Chorus:
Go - in' down to town, Go - in' down to town,
Go - in' down to Lynch-burg Town to take my to-bac-co down.

Times a-gittin' hard,
Money's gittin' scarce,
Pay me for this tobacco,
And I will leave this place.

Chorus:
Going down to town,
Going down to town,
Going down to Lynchburg Town,
To take my tobacco down.
(Repeat after each verse)

I went down to town
To get me a jug of wine.
They tied me to the whipping post
And give me forty nine.

I went down to town
To get me a jug of gin.
They tied me to a whipping post
And give me hell again.

Times a-gittin' hard,
Money's gittin' scarce.
And I'm a-gittin' no fatter here,
So I'm gonna leave this place.

Seven Cent Cotton and Forty Cent Meat

"These blues was composed in nineteen and twenty seven on the condition of the farmers and on the shortness of their cotton. I thought it was very necessary to put out a record of these things. I composed them of the necessity of the farmers. It was very popular among everyone that heard it and became to be well known. The town merchants laughed to think of such a song being composed." --- Sampson Pittman, talking about these cotton farmer blues he made up.

You know the trouble as well as I do. You raise a crop and you don't make enough money out of it to buy the things you need. The big rich men that buy your crops have Organized. They Organized and agreed that they wouldn't give you a fair price for nothing you raise. Or nothing you work at. They got them a Union, and they are a Union of Gamblers, Crooks, Racketeers and Robbers. And songs like Seven Cent Cotton will help to scare them crooked millionaires off your roost.

Words and music by Bob Miller. © by Bob Miller.

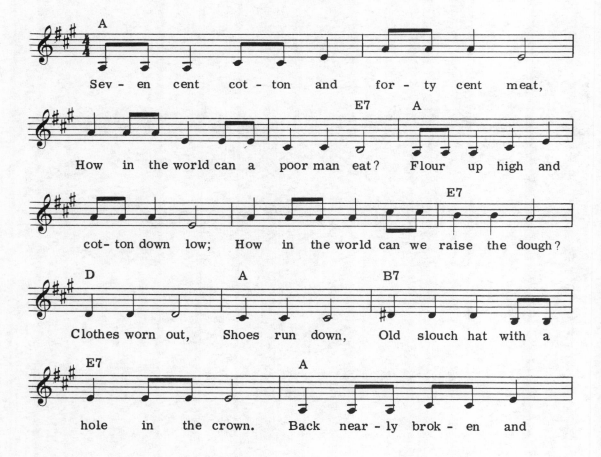

Sev- en cent cot- ton and for- ty cent meat,
How in the world can a poor man eat? Flour up high and
cot- ton down low; How in the world can we raise the dough?
Clothes worn out, Shoes run down, Old slouch hat with a
hole in the crown. Back near- ly brok- en and

fin- gers all   sore,   Cot - ton gone down to   rise no   more.

Seven cent cotton and forty cent
    meat,
How in the world can a poor man eat?
Flour up high and cotton down low,
How in the world can we raise the
    dough?
Clothes worn out, shoes run down,
Old slouch hat with a hole in the
    crown:
Back nearly broken and fingers all
    sore,
Cotton gone down to rise no more.

Seven cent cotton and forty cent meat,
How in the world can a poor man eat?
Mules in the barn, no crops laid by,
Corn crib empty and the cow's gone
    dry.
Well water low, nearly out of sight,
Can't take a bath on Saturday night.
No use talking, any man is beat
With seven cent cotton and forty cent
    meat.

Seven cent cotton and eight dollar
    pants,
Who in the world has got a chance?
We can't buy clothes and we can't buy
    meat,
Too much cotton and not enough to
    eat.
Can't help each other, what shall we
    do?
I can't explain it so it's up to you.
Seven cent cotton and two dollar hose,
Guess we'll have to do without any
    clothes.

Seven cent cotton and forty cent meat
How in the world can a poor man eat?
Poor getting poorer all around here,
Kids coming regular every year.
Fatten our hogs, take 'em to town,
All we get is six cents a pound.
Very next day we have to buy it back,
Forty cents a pound in a paper sack.

*Here's another verse made up by folks
on one of the first New Deal Resettlement projects. 'Course this here part
about Roosevelt can always be changed.
It's a matter of personal opinion.*

We'll raise our cotton, we'll raise
    our meat,
We'll raise everything we eat.
We'll raise our chickens, pigs and
    corn,
We'll make a living just as sure as
    you're born.
Farmers getting stronger every year,
Babies getting fatter all around here.
No use talking, Roosevelt's the man
To show the world that the farmer
    can.

*And here's an added verse with a cer-
tain Oklahoma-California smell about
it. Well, judging from this traffic I see
around New York City, and folks a
running over one another, the payments
are worse back here and so is the
cussing.*

20 cent gasoline, 30 cent oil,
That's what makes my radiator boil.
Engine a missin', payments due,
What in the hell are you gonna do?
Spark plugs cracked, tires all flat,
Collector man is a balling the jack,
Front wheels shimmy and the hind
    ones bump,
Caint git past a garbage dump.
$52 to ride the train,
Git to California and you're out in
    the rain.
$47 to ride the bus,
Make any good man swear and cuss.
You caint ride, gotta walk the street,
Walk the road with blistered feet,
You sure as hell caint eat and sleep
On seven cent cotton, forty cent meat.

40

II - YOU'RE DEAD BROKE

Dead broke, all the way 'round. Takin' her th' hard way, workin' every day, goin' in th' hole worse and worse, bills come due, groceries gone, liquor jug empty, lookin' for work, tryin' to help a carpenter, or move dirt to build a new road, any kind of a job of work to bring in a little money for the stuff I need, and for my folks. What th' hell went wrong, anyhow? Used to have a little money. Aint got a cryin' dam dime. Low down dirty shame. Eat it up quicker with a spoon than I can pack it in with a goddam shovel. Collector men lined up at my door like a thousand relatives a waitin' to use the out house. Got me plumb buffaloed. Ought to be 3 jobs for every single man and woman that wants to work. 'Stead of that, they's a blue jillion piss complected collectors out there --! You take a good man and let him stay out of work for a long time, and he'll go to th' dogs just shore as hell, turn out to be a tramp, or a deputy or a heel of some kind.

Collector Man Blues

Between the Collector Man, the Insurance Man, the Salary Loan Man, the Doctor Man, the Finance Man and just about every other kind of a man that comes around a collecting you just caint hardly get no rest. The Negro people are called on by the relief man about once in a dog's age, but the collector man seems to jump out of every street, alley, brush pile, swamp, ash bank, straw stack, coal pile, dung heap, garbage pile, river bottom, tangle wood, mingle wood, moss forest, piney wood, vacant lot, cow pasture, hog lot, barn yard, sheep dip, seed bin, silo, hen house, hill, holler, house, building, cellar, -- and every place you stick your head. The two following songs help back me up.

As sung by Walter Roland on Melotone M. 13103 B.
(From the collection of Alan Lomax)

Hey, hey,— Some-bod-y knock-in' at my door,
Hey, hey,— some-bod-y knock-in' at my door. Says it
may be a col-lec-tor,— Ba-by I sure don't know.

Hey, hey, somebody knocking at
    my door,
Hey, hey, somebody knocking on
    my door,
Says it may be a collector, baby, I
    sure don't know.

They will try to tear your house
    down, Lord,
And this is what he will say.
They will try to tear your house
    down, Lord,
And this is what he will say:
Says, "I've got to have some
    money, 'cause you didn't give
    me nothing last pay day.

Folks, one thing that I sure can't
    stand,
Folks, one thing that I sure can't
    stand,
Your children can't even play for
    hollin', Daddy, here come that
    collector man!

I say, folks, don't buy nothin, Lord,
    on the installment plan.
I say, folks, don't buy nothin, Lord,
    on the installment plan.
And you will not be worried, Lord,
    by no collector man.

I've begged and borrowed til my
    friends don' want me round,
I'll take old man Depression and
    leave this no-good town.

Depression's here, they tell me it's
    everywhere,
So I'm goin' back to Florida and see
    if Depression's there.

Oh, how it would help if I could just
    explain,
But Depression has me, it's 'bout
    to drive me insane.

Insurance Man Blues

As sung by Sonny Boy Williamson on Bluebird Record
B 8034. (From the collection of Alan Lomax)

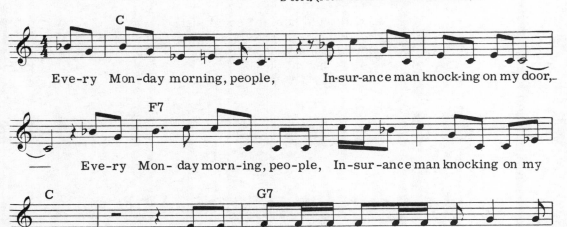

Eve-ry Mon-day morning, people, In-sur-ance man knock-ing on my door,—

Eve-ry Mon-day morn-ing, peo-ple, In-sur-ance man knocking on my

door, Well, I tell him to come back on Tues-day 'Cause

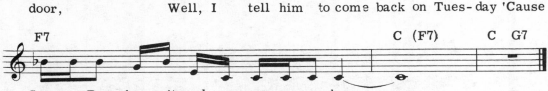

Son-ny Boy has-n't made no mon-ey, you know.——

Every Monday morning, people,
Insurance man knocking on my door,
Every Monday morning, people,
Insurance man knocking on my door,
Well, I tell him to come back on a
 Tuesday
'Cause Sonny Boy hasn't made no
 money, you know.

He say, "But you haven't paid your
 insurance in 2 or 3 weeks, "
He said, "If you don't pay by next
 Wednesday
I reckon I'll have to let your
 insurance drop. "

I say, "Insurance man, please don't
 turn me out,
Lord, I aint got nobody to bury me. "
Well, Lord, I said, "If you don't
 bury me
They'll throw my body in the deep
 blue sea. "

I said, "You know how times is
 nowadays.
Can't no one man find no job. "
I say, "I can't even take care of my
 wife and baby
And I might' near to let my own
 family starve. "

I said, "Please give me two more
 weeks.
Insurance man, please do that for
 me. "
Well, I say, "Don't live up North,
My home is back down in
 Tennessee. "

Depression Blues

Not long ago, on the Will Rogers Highway, the 66 that runs from coast to coast, I walked through the town of Claremore, Oklahoma, and seen a little kid a standing alongside the highway on his way to Florida. He'd been all over the United States and knew all of the numbers of the highways and how to get to any big town or little town you wanted to know about -- since this song is about Florida, it reminded me about that little kid, right young, about fifteen, been on the road for years, and -- was on his way back to Florida. It was snowing that day. It was blowing, too, and I wonder often, since then, where the devil that little kid blowed off to.

As recorded by Tampa Red (The Guitar Wizard) on Vocalion 1656. (From the collection of Alan Lomax)

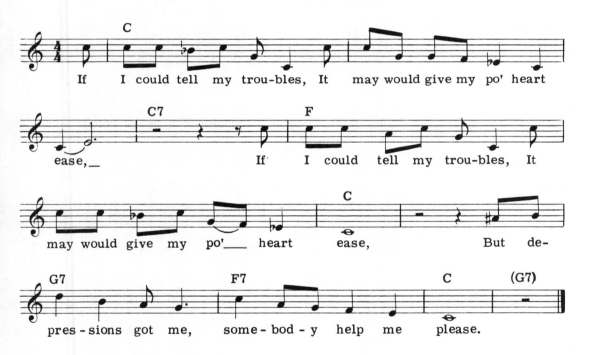

If I could tell my trou-bles, It may would give my po' heart ease,__

If I could tell my trou-bles, It may would give my po'__ heart ease,

But de-pres-sions got me, some-bod-y help me please.

If I could tell my troubles, It would
    give my po' heart ease,
But depression has got me,
    somebody help me please.

If I don't feel no better, than I feel
    today,
I'm gonna pack my few clothes and
    make my getaway.

45

Unemployment Stomp

Mr. President: if you'd like to know what the American people are a thinking, take a gander at that 1st verse.

From the singing of Big Bill Broonzy on Vocalion Record 04378 (C 2159). (From the collection of Alan Lomax)

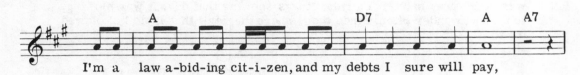

I'm a   law a-bid-ing cit-i-zen, and my debts I   sure will   pay,

I'm a   law a-bid-ing cit-i-zen, and my debts I   sure will   pay.

I hope war don't start and   Un-cle Sam have to send me   a - way.

I'm a law abiding citizen, and my
　debts I sure will pay,
I'm a law abiding citizen, and my
　debts I sure will pay.
I hope war don't start and Uncle Sam
　have to send me away.

I haven't never been in jail, and I
　haven't never paid no fine, baby,
I haven't never been in jail, and I
　haven't never paid no fine, baby.
I wants a job to make my livin',
　cause stealin' aint on my line.

I've knowed a time when I have
　raised my own meat and meal,
I've knowed a time when I have
　raised my own meat and meal.
My meat was in my smokehouse,
　and my meal was in my field.

When Mr. Roosevelt sent out those
　unemployment cards,
Yes, when Mr. Roosevelt sent out
　those unemployment cards,
I just knowed sure that work was
　goin' to start.

Broke up my home 'cause I didn't
　have no work to do,
I broke up my home 'cause I didn't
　have no work to do.
My wife had to leave me 'cause she
　was starvin' too.

No Job Blues

You know, I remember the night I got throwed in the Reno jail for
Vacancy. Well, I don't know -- I didn't know it was against the law.
Hell, every rooming house in town has a sign out in the yard that said:
Vacancy. Try this one in the Skeleton Key.

As sung by Ramblin' Thomas on Paramount 12609-A
(20343). (From the collection of Alan Lomax)

I been walk-in' all day,___ and all night too,
I been walk-in' all_ day___ and all_ night too, 'Cause my
meal tick-et wo-man have quit me,_ and I can't find no work to do.

I been walkin' all day and all night,
    too,
I been walkin' all day and all night,
    too,
'Cause my meal ticket woman have
    quit me
An' I can't find no work to do.

I was pickin' up the newspaper an' I
    was lookin' in it for ads,
I was pickin' up the newspaper and I
    was lookin' in it for ads,
And the policeman come along
And he arrested me for a vag.

Talks:
Now, boys, you oughta see me in my
    black an' white suit.
It won't do.

I said, "Judge, what may be my
    fine?"
Lawd, I asked the judge, "Judge,
    what may be my fine?"
He says, "Git you a pick and shovel
And git thee down in mind."

I'm a poor vag pris'ner, workin' in
    the ice and snow,
I'm a poor vag pris'ner, workin' in
    the ice and snow,
I got to get me a meal ticket woman
So I won't have to work no mo'.

Fifteen Miles from Birmingham

(May look a little silly, printing this second part to sing; it did sound so pretty on the record, though, that I thought I'd try getting it down. Besides, I know that in every community there's always some fellow who fancies himself a great hand at singing tenor parts - let him ease his vocal chords over this one. - Pete)

As sung by the Delmore Brothers, Alton and Rabon, on Bluebird Record B-8301-A. (From the collection of Alan Lomax)

I'm fifteen miles from Birmingham,
I'm looking up, I'm looking down.
Aint got a dime, just killing time,
Can't go to Birmingham,
Can't go to Birmingham.

That little girl in Birmingham,
She thinks I'm up, and I am down.
Can't go to town when I am down,
So I won't hang around,
So I won't hang around.

When a feller's broke he can't
    find a friend,
Nobody's got a dime to lend;
But when he's rich they sit and
    itch,
On him their money spend,
On him their money spend.

So little friend, my love I send.
I'm coming back your heart to win.
So sing a song, it won't be long
Til I'll be back again,
I'll ramble back again.

Just fifteen miles from Birmingham,
Up on a mountain looking down.
My heavy heart is sinking down,
For I can't go to town,
For I can't go to town.

I'm heading back on down the line,
I'm leaving all my love behind.
I'm singing all my blues away,
For me there'll come a time,
For me there'll come a time.

49

Down and Out

Damned if things aint messed worse than a sow's bed. They charge you a year's pay to get borned, seven years pay to live til you're 3, fifteen years pay to hang around til you're 9. You got to work like hell for 45 years to eat til you're 21, and then you go in the hole for falling in love with somebody. They hobble you worse than a blind mule on a rocky pasture. They say you got to give your kids a education 'er go to jail, and they charge you so much to school 'em that you'd of been better off in the jug. They send you to war if you don't marry and to the sweat-shop if you do. They stick you with taxes you can't see and take your money before you ever lay a hand on it. They spend it for you before you git it counted.

Recorded by Kokomo Arnold on Decca 7163, 90317 A.
(From the collection of Alan Lomax)

Says I ain't got no air-plane, Ain't got no aut-o-mo-bile.__ I ain't got no mon-ey guess I have to rob and steal. For when I wake up in the morn-in' I can't eat a de-cent meal, I had bad luck in my fam'-ly,__ I guess you know jus' how I feel.

Says, I aint got no airplane,
Aint got no automobile,
I aint got no money,
I guess I have to rob and steal.

Chorus:
For when I wake up in the mornin'
I caint eat a decent meal,
I had bad luck in my family,
I guess you know jus' how I feel.
(Repeat after each verse)

When I had plenty of money,
And plenty of clothes,
These Chicago women followed me
In big droves.

Says, I asked my mama
To take me back one mo',
She said, "You aint got no money,
Sweet papa, there is the do'."

Now my women standin' on the
    corner,
With their weekly pay,
If they think I want to borry sompen,
They turn and go another way.

When I make this payday,
Get my money in my hand,
You women needn't come
    a-runnin'
You can find another man.

No Dough Blues

Lots of times you go around singing a song in your head and it don't come out at your mouth. You know how that is. Gets on your brain and just goes 'round and 'round like a squirrel up a walnut tree. About a world full of people is a going around these days with a song traveling around in their head.

    That song is the NO DOUGH BLUES
    That song is the NO GROCERIES BLUES
    And the NO HOUSE BLUES
    And the NO CLOTHES BLUES
    And the NO WHISKEY BLUES
    And the NO CAR BLUES
    The NO RADIO or WASHING MACHINE BLUES
    The NO SEWING MACHINE BLUES
    NO SEED BLUES
    NO CROP BLUES
    NO FUN BLUES
    NO MON' BLUES
    NOT A DAM THING BLUES

The No Dough blues has had a litter of pups on the front porch of the White House, and their names are listed above for the benefit of the politicians that look through this book trying to find something new to lie about.

From the singing of Blind Blake on Paramount Record 12723-B (2055), Copyright by Blake. (From the collection of Alan Lomax)

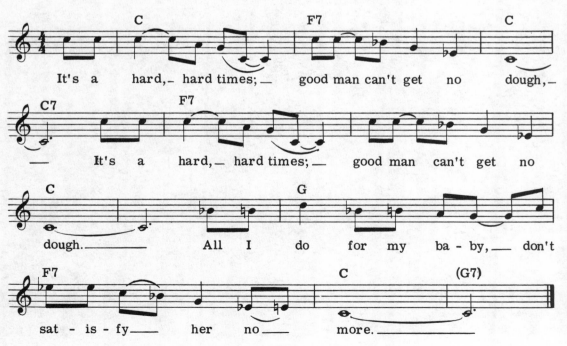

It's a hard,— hard times;— good man can't get no dough,—

— It's a hard,— hard times;— good man can't get no

dough.———— All I do for my ba - by,— don't

sat - is - fy—— her no— more.———

It's a hard times, good man can't
    get no dough,
It's a hard times, good man can't
    get no dough.
All I do for my baby don't satisfy
    her no mo'.

I aint got no job, that's why you
    go'n put me down,
I aint got no job, that's why you go'n
    put me down.
You gonna quit me, baby, for hard
    work in town.

Times is so hard now, maybe
    things will change someday,
Times is so hard now, maybe
    things will change someday.
And if I get me a job, maybe you
    will change your way.

Don't quit me, baby, 'cause I can't
    find no work to do,
Don't quit me, baby, 'cause I can't
    find no work to do.
Lawd, the dirt you done to me is
    comin' back to you.

One Dime Blues

I seen many a time that a dime looked big as a bucket lid, and a two bit piece looked like a wagon wheel and a half dollar was plumb out of sight. I decided while I was a selling whiskey that I'd like to be a preacher, but I kept my ear peeled to what the other preachers said, and I didn't want to say that stuff - just didn't want to scare nobody with crazy notions of hot lead and brimstone and a pit of burning hell. Somehow wanted to yell and talk and sing to folks and tell 'em to get all these notions out of their heads.

I remember there in the Liquor store we use to have a phonograph with a loud speaker tied outside on the hitchin' rack, and one day the boss man sent me to town to get some records and I come back with a armload of good old Negro Blues. Among others, Blind Lemon's ONE DIME BLUES. We played it til we wore it down to a nub.

I use to set back there on a big pile of whiskey cases and play them records over and over, and it made my feet itch, made me want to pick up and light down the road, and to soak up a headful of these songs, and to see the real folks that sung 'em, and to live right with 'em, and work with 'em, and raise a rukus and have a good time with 'em -- somehow, you know, some way or other, I thought I'd get to know everybody better that a way -- and then maybe I could talk or sing or preach something about something -- about stuff that needs a fixing, and things that's wrong, and make it a little better - someway or other, I don't quite know. But I slipped out of that white apron and that white shirt, and I quit that whiskey job and struck out down the road -- just a looking and a listening.

From old Blind Lemon Jefferson, who's dead now. Paramount 12578-B. (From the collection of Alan Lomax)

Ev-'ry-body— gets in hard— luck sometime. _____

I'm broke and I aint got a dime,
I'm broke and I aint got a dime,
I'm broke and aint got a dime,
Everybody gets in hard luck
    sometime.

You want your friend to be bad like
    Jesse James?
You want your friend to be bad like
    Jesse James?
You want your friend to be bad like
    Jesse James?
Just give 'm a six shooter and
    highway some passenger train.

All In and Down and Out Blues

All I got to say is that old Uncle Dave never does miss. He hits the
nail on the head every time. Take her, Dave, and make her happy.

It's hip - pi - ty hop___ to the buck - et shop, I've

lost all my mon - ey and now I have flopped.___

(Chorus)
It's hard times, pi - ty poor boy,___ It's

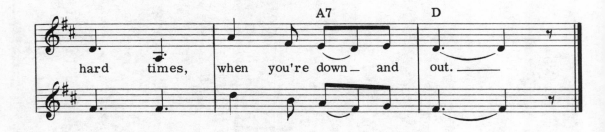

hard times, when you're down___ and out.___

Chorus:
It's hippity hop to the bucket shop
I've lost all my money and now I
  have flopped,
It's hard times, pity poor boy,
It's hard times when you're down
  and out.
(Repeat after each verse)

Now this is the truth and it certainly
  exposes
That Wall Street's proposition is not
  all roses.

I put up my money to win some more,
I lost all I had and it left me so
  sore.

56

I thought I would drink to wear it off,
Bootleg's so high that it left me
worse off.

If they catch you with whiskey in
your car,
You're handicapped, and there you
are.

They'll take you to jail and if you
can't make bond,
Content yourself there, why you're
certainly at home.

I've got no silver and I've got no
gold,
I'm almost naked and it's done
turned cold.

You ask that judge to treat you well,
You offer a hundred dollars he'll
send you to Atlanta.

New Stranger Blues

Po' stranger. I've been a stranger everywhere I go. One day in Glendale, California, a girl friend of mine says, Woody, don't you hoboes get lonesome, bumming around never seeing anybody you know? And I says, Lefty Lou, us hoboes know everybody we see. Sing the first line of this one twice, the last line once, just like the blues - you know - just the damned old blues.

Tampa Red and Georgia Tom on Perfect Record
7-01-67 (20120). (From the collection of Alan Lomax)

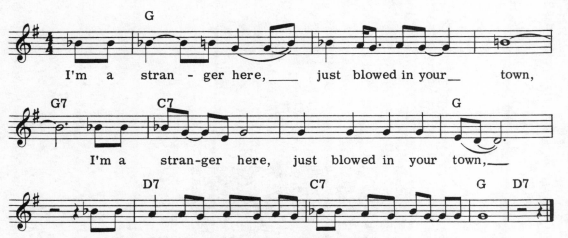

I'm a stran - ger here, ____ just blowed in your __ town,

I'm a stran-ger here, just blowed in your town, ____

Just be-cause I'm a stran-ger, ev'rybod-y wants to dog me a-round.

I'm a stranger here, just blowed in
    your town,
I'm a stranger here, just blowed in
    your town,
Just because I'm a stranger every-
    body wants to dog me around.

Lord, I wonder do my good gal
    know I'm here?
Lord, wonder do my good gal know
    I'm here.
Well, if she do she sure don't seem
    to care.

I wonder how can some people dog
    a poor stranger so,
I wonder how can some people dog
    a poor stranger so.
They should remember they gonna
    reap what they sow.

I would stay up North but there's
    nothing here that I can do,
I would stay up North but there's
    nothing here that I can do,
But hang around this corner and sing
    the "poor stranger" blues.

Mama, I am going back south if I
    wear ninety nine pair of shoes,
Mama, I am going back south if I
    wear ninety nine pair of shoes,
Then I know I'll be welcome and I
    won't have the stranger's blues.

Starvation Blues

"Looked like I had a lapful o' trouble these last few years. A hailstorm destroyed the crop one year, my house and furniture got burnt up; my boy died of pneumonia; the land we paid for had to be mortgaged; I lost my husband. But I keep hopin' for better days." This here letter is a song and a mighty good one at that.

Big Bill and Thomps on Broadway Record 5072-A (20923). (From the collection of Alan Lomax)

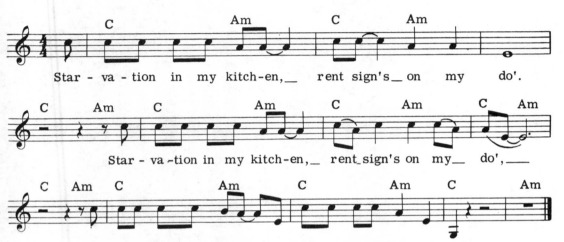

Star - va - tion in my kitch-en,__ rent sign's__ on my do'.

Star - va -tion in my kitch-en,__ rent sign's on my__ do', ___

An if I look down stranger can't see you at my home no mo'.

Starvation in my kitchen, rent sign's on my do', (2 times)
An' if I look down, stranger, can't see you at my home no mo'.

An' I got up this mornin' just about the dawn of day, (2 times)
Then I ain' got no job, I ain' got no place to stay.

Lawd, I walked in a sto', I ain' got a dime, (2 times)
I say, "A dime neckbones," and the clerk don' pay me no min'.

Lawd, Lawd, Lawd, Lawd, Lawd, Lawd, Lawd, Lawd, Lawd,
Lawd, Lawd, mama, some ol' rainy day,
Me an' my luck gwine change an' I don' want to be treated.
thisaway.

60

III - SO YOU GOT TO HIT THE ROAD

"Th' road aint lonesome
It's th' people that's on it."

Hitch Hiking down the lonesome old road, been over that 66 enough to run it up to 6666. Thought maybe I could run onto a job of work. Heard some was openin' up out in Utah. Hell, Utah ain't far. California aint but a hop and a skip, Atlanta Ga., just a small blister in the shoe. Aint far. I dont mind it if I can go to work. Whew, you see a flock of big cars on th' road don't you? Bunch of 'em got plenty of room for me. I wouldn't jump on 'em, er take their dam money. All I want's that job. Hell, if I was a outlaw or a robber like some folks think, I wouldn't rob a guy that treated me right. I aint no heel. God, never seen so many poodle dogs in my life. Women's got fur coats. Hell of a job to try to tell where one quits and the other begins.

66 Highway Blues

You built that Highway and they can put you in jail for thumbing a ride
on it. You built that railroad and they boot you off, shake you down,
search your pockets and make you spend your last red cent to buy a
ticket into the next town. Then the watchmen and cops in the town shove
you out. They get you all rounded up like a herd of sheep heading for
the sledge hammer and drive you off down the road saying, "Take
warning, boys, and don't ever show yourself in this town again..."

In McAlester, Okla., in Haileyville, Okla., in Amarillo, Texas, in Deming,
Tucson, Phoenix, Yuma, Needles, Los Angeles, Frisco, Tracy, Bakers-
field, almost everywhere you can think of, they chase you off the trains
and make you hit the Highway. Sometimes a hundred or more of you,
sometimes fifty or sixty out of a single box car. That means walk.
Root hog or die.

I had part of this tune in my head, but couldn't get no front end for it.
Pete fixed that up. He furnished the engine, and me the cars, and then
we loaded in the words and we whistled out of the yards from New York
City to Oklahoma City, and when we got there we took down our banjo
and git-fiddle and chugged her off just like you see it here. She's a high
roller, an easy rider, a flat wheel bouncer and a tight brake baby with
a whiskey driver.

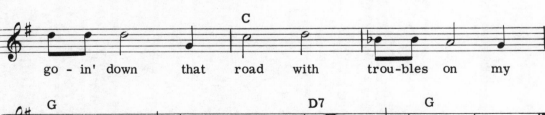

There is a high-way from coast to the coast,
New York to Los An - gel - es, _____ I'm a-
go - in' down that road with trou-bles on my
mind I got them six - ty - six High - way blues. _____

There is a Highway from coast to
   the coast,
New York to Los Angeles,
I'm a goin' down that Road with
     Troubles on my mind,
I got them 66 Highway Blues.

Every old town that I ramble 'round,
Down that Lonesome Road,
The police in yo' town they shove
     me around,
I got them 66 Highway Blues.

Makes me no difference wherever I
     ramble,
Lord, wherever I go,
I don't wanna be pushed around by
     th' police in yo' town,
I got them 66 Highway Blues.

Been on this road for a mighty long
     time,
Ten million men like me,
You drive us from yo' town, we
     ramble around,
And got them 66 Highway Blues.

Sometimes I think I'll blow down a
     cop,
Lord, you treat me so mean,
I done lost my gal, I aint got a
     dime,
I got them 66 Highway Blues.

Sometimes I think I'll get me a gun,
Thirty eight or big forty fo',
But a number for a name and a big
     99,
Is worse than 66 Highway Blues.

I'm gonna start me a hungry man's
     union,
Ainta gonna charge no dues,
Gonna march down that road to the
     Wall Street Walls
A singin' those 66 Highway Blues.

I Ain't Got No Home In This World Any More

This old song to start out with was a religious piece called "I Can't Feel At Home In This World Any More". But I seen there was another side to the picture. Reason why you can't feel at home in this world any more is mostly because you aint got no home to feel at.

Words and music by Woody Guthrie. © 1961 (renewed), 1964 (renewed) by Ludlow Music, Inc., New York, NY. Used by permission.

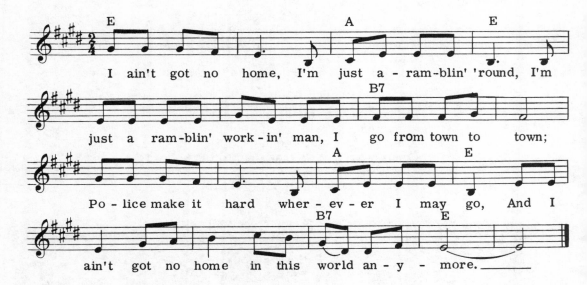

I ain't got no home, I'm just a - ram-blin' 'round, I'm just a ram-blin' work-in' man, I go from town to town; Po - lice make it hard wher - ev - er I may go, And I ain't got no home in this world an - y - more.

I aint got no home, I'm just a
    ramblin' 'round,
I'm just a ramblin' workin' man, I
    go from town to town.
Police make it hard wherever I may
    go,
And I aint got no home in this world
    any more.

My brothers and my sisters are
    stranded on this road
It's a hot and dusty road where a
    million feet have trod.
Rich man took my home, and he
    drove me from my door,
And I aint got no home in this world
    any more.

Was a farming on the shares and
    always I was down,
My debts was so many my pay
    wouldn't go around.
My wife took down and died upon the
    cabin floor,
And I aint got no home in this world
    any more.

Now as I look around it's very plain
    to see
This wide and wicked world is a
    funny place to be,
The gambling man is rich and the
    working man is poor,
And I aint got no home in this world
    any more.

Hitch Hike Blues

The Hall Brothers purty well hit the nail on the head. This sounds like I felt a many a time when I had the Blues of th' worst kind, them old Hitch Hike Blues, them old Holy Shoe Blues.

Hall Brothers on Bluebird Record B-7801-B. (From the collection of Alan Lomax)

Trav'-ling down this lone-some road, Trav'-ling down this lone-some road,

Trav'-ling down this lone-some road, My old_ guit-ar is my load.

Travelin' down this Lonesome Road,
Travelin' down this Lonesome Road,
Travelin' down this Lonesome Road,
My old guitar is my load.

People always pass me by,
People always pass me by,
People always pass me by,
I bow my head and almost cry.

I got them old Hitch Hike Blues,
I got them old Hitch Hike Blues,
I got them old Hitch Hike Blues,
I done wore out my shoes.

I am a thousand miles from home,
I am a thousand miles from home,
I am a thousand miles from home,
I'm out in the western states alone.

I'm a goin' back to Caroline,
I'm a goin' back to Caroline,
I'm a goin' back to Caroline,
To my old home I left behind.

Standin' by the old roadside,
Standin' by the old roadside,
Standin' by the old roadside,
A tryin' my best to catch a ride.

Wanderin'

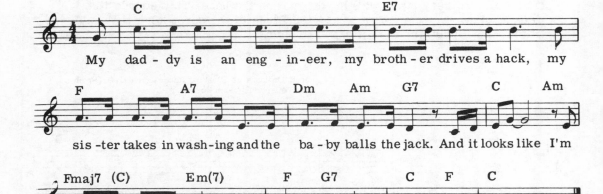

My dad - dy is an eng - in - eer, my broth - er drives a hack, my
sis - ter takes in wash - ing and the ba - by balls the jack. And it looks like I'm
nev - er gon - na cease my wan - der - in'.

My daddy is an engineer,
My brother drives a hack,
My sister takes in washing
And the baby balls the jack,
An' it looks like
I'm never gonna cease
My wanderin'.

I've been a-wanderin'
Early and late,
New York City
To the Golden Gate,
An' it looks like
I'm never gonna cease my wanderin'.

Been a-workin' in the army,
Workin' on a farm,
All I got to show for it
Is the muscle in my arm.
An' it looks like
I'm never gonna cease my wanderin'.

Snakes in the ocean,
Eels in the sea,
Red headed woman
Made a fool out of me,
An' it looks like
I'm never gonna cease my wanderin'.

IV - AND YOU LAND IN JAIL

..........it looks like we're in the jailhouse section all right. Next song book I deal with is gonna have grease smeared all over the jailhouse section and some old black disinfect so's you can open the book in the dark and smell this section when you come to it...........................

..........many's the time you get tossed in the can for something you don't know a dern thing about...

..........a hell of a lot of things goes through your head when you're laid up in a dam filthy jail five or ten years for something you didn't do......

..........the men that wrote the bible had to lay it out in jail...............

..........I believe I'd honestly feel better if all of the jails and prisons was just unlocked and let everybody come a walking out...................

The Old Chain Gang

When I got out of jail th' first thing I made a run for was a bottle of liquor and a pretty woman. I met her in a saloon. I had a couple of shots under my belt and was a rearin' to step. She was one-eyed, but that didn't matter none. I had two eyes. She looked mighty good to me through both of 'em. When I come up out of that jail I felt like a man a steppin' out of the grave. I couldn't think of anything else. I had $71 I'd saved up in the can. I would of blowed $7000 if I'd of had it, just for a crack at that one-eyed girl. That one eye was as pretty as a picture. Man, Howdy!

From the Crowder Brothers on Vocalion Record 03030 (21727). (From the collection of Alan Lomax)

Now hon-ey dear,___ I know you're going to ask ___ Just where I been___ since you saw me last,___ Well, I been down___ where the ham-mers ring. ___ Yes, I been down ____ on the old chain gang.___

Now honey dear, I know you're goin'
 to ask
Just where I been since you saw me
 last.
Well, I been down where the
 hammers ring,
Yes, I been down on the old chain
 gang.

They sent me up on a two year bill.
Well, I soon forgot what it was I
 did.
They chained me down with a
 dozen men.
I can't believe I'm in your arms
 again.

Night and day I didn't get no rest,
Just hold me tight to your lovin'
 breast.
See where the chains they used to
 hang,
Well, that's the mark of the old
 chain gang.

You'd never believe what a life I
 led
On the old chain gang, you're better
 off dead.
I'll never forget those songs we
 sang
While breaking rocks on the old
 chain gang.

That old chain gang is a tough old
 crew,
The boss is hard, I'm telling you.
He drug me to the cellhouse door
And laid me out on the cold stone
 floor.

Now honey dear, if he hits my
 trail
He's going to land me back in jail.
Let's kiss goodbye for a parting
 hand,
Let me go back there on the old
 chain gang.

Crossbone Skully

This is about an actual feller named Bascom Skully that kept a gettin' in jail for holding up people. Well, looks like most of the jails are full running over. Looks like they make up more silly laws every day to get you in. You break the law and you don't know it, cause they pass 'em so fast you can't keep up with 'em.

All I got to say is this, if it keeps up, keeps a goin' that a way, the day and time will soon come when we'll just have to build a big cement wall around the world and all of us go and get in it. Dam near it that a way now.

As I went walking down Peacock Street, no clothes on my back no shoes on my feet; I was hungry and cold, It was late in the fall, I knocked down some old big-shot, took his clothes, money and all. O tell me how long must I wait for a job I don't like to

steal, I don't like to have to rob. _____

As I went walking down Peacock
    Street,
No clothes on my back, no shoes
    on my feet,
I was hungry and cold, it was late
    in the fall.
I knocked down some old big shot,
    took his clothes, money and
    all.

Chorus:
O tell me how long must I wait
    for a job?
I don't like to steal, I don't like to
    rob.
(Repeat after each verse.)

When I took everything this old
    bigshot had,
They called me a robber, yes, they
    called me bad.
They called me a robber, yes, they
    called me bad,
Because misery and starvation
    drove me mad.

They locked me up for a year and a
    day,
For taking that old big shot's money
    away.
Now they turned me out about an
    hour ago
To walk the streets in the rain and
    in the snow.

No clothes on my back, no food to
    eat.
Now a man can't live just walkin'
    the street.
I'd no money for roomrent, no
    place to sleep,
Now a man can't live by just walking
    the street.

Now, a man can't live by just
    walking the street,
I'll be sorry to my heart if I have
    to repeat.
If I knocked down some old big shot
    and take all his kale,
Then they'll put me back in that
    lousy jail.

Hard Times in Cryderville Jail

If the jails I been in was all put together it would make a prison as big as the Capitol Building. But of course your pocketbook would be safer in jail.

Reckon this is one of the best jail house songs I know. There is Birmingham Jail, but it don't say enough. There's the Prisoner's Song, but it don't say much either. There's Moonlight and Skies, but it brags a little too much on the deputies. Lots of officers are honest and straight, we all know that, but there's just a hell of a lot of them that are ten times worse crooks and thieves than the fellers they beat up and throw in jail.

Cryderville Jail aint no Sissy Song. If you can't ride it like you find it, why, just leave it alone. A man will pop up and sing it once in a while and a woman will listen to him, I mean a real man and a real Woman and a real jail.

"O, Mister Turnkey, you old bastard,
  Turn that key, let my man come home,
  Aint had no lovin', Good God knows,
  Since you laid my good man in jail."

Collected, adapted, and arranged by John A. Lomax and Alan Lomax. © 1934 (renewed) by Ludlow Music, Inc., New York, NY. Used by permission.

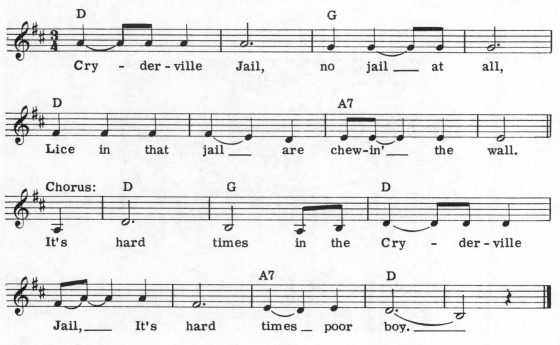

72

Cryderville jail, no jail at all,
Lice in that jail are chewin' the wall.

Chorus:
It's hard times in the Cryderville
jail,
It's hard times, poor boy.
(Repeat after each verse.)

There's a big bull ring in the middle
of the floor,
And a damned old jailer to open the
door.

Your pockets he'll pick, your clothes
he will sell,
Your hands he will handcuff, goddam
him to hell.

And here's to the cook, I wish he
were dead,
It's old boiled beef and old corn
bread.

The coffee is rough and the yards
full of hogs,
And we are guarded by two bull dogs.

Our bed it is made of old rotten rugs,
And when we lay down we are
covered with bugs:

The bugs they swear if we don't give
bail,
We are bound to get busy in
Cryderville jail.

I wrote to my mother to send me a
knife,
For the lice and the chinches have
threatened my life.

And here's to the lawyer, he'll come
to your cell,
And swear he will clear you in spite
of all Hell.

Get all of your money before he will
rest,
Then say, "Plead guilty, for I think
it the best. "

Old Judge Simpkins will read us the
law,
The damndest fool judge that you
ever saw.

And there sits the jury, a devil of a
crew,
They'll look a poor pris'ner
through and through.

And here's to the sheriff, I like to
forgot,
The damndest old rascal we have in
the lot.

Your privileges he will take, your
clothes he will sell,
Get drunk on the money, goddam him
to hell.

And now I have come to the end of
my song,
I'll leave it to the boys as I go
along.

As to gamblin' an' stealin', I never
shall fail,
And I don't give a damn for lying in
jail.

73

You're Bound to Get Lousy
in the Lousy Old Jail

I hollered this song over the microphone in Los Angeles for about twenty months. Not the same song for every day, but, you know, once about every week. I wrote it as a gentle warning to you driving a car, and how easy it is to get in the stir, and how dam lousy it is while you're in there, and how hard it is to get out - without money.

Lousy jails are a shore sign of lousy cops, and lousy cops is a shore sign of Lousy Governors, and Lousy Governors is a dam shore sign of Lousy Presidents...

Take it lousy.

..........some cops are as Lousy as the people they take to the jail. And some jails are full of leeches. I said that and I stick to it...

You drunk-en driv-ers come lis-ten to my tale, __ Your drink-in' and a driv-in's gon-na get you in jail, __ __ You've got to stay sob-er to drive at the wheel 'cause you're bound to __ get lous-y in the lous-y old jail. __

You drunken drivers come listen to
my Tale,
Your drinkin' and a drivin's gonna
git you in Jail.
You've got to stay sober to drive at
the Wheel,
'Cause you're bound to git Lousy in
the Lousy Old Jail.

You Reckless Drivers come Listen
to my Tale,
Your Reckless Drivin's gonna git
you in Jail,
They'll fine you and slam you way
back in a cell,
You're bound to git Lousy in the
Lousy Old Jail.

You Sweethearts and Lovers, come
listen to my Tale,
Your one-handed Drivin's gonna git
you in Jail,
Keep yo' mind on yo' business, and
boy, if you fail,
You're bound to git Lousy in the
Lousy Old Jail.

You Speed Demon Drivers come
listen to my Tale,
Your dam fool Speedin's gonna git
you in Jail,
You got to slow down if you want to
go free,
You're bound to git Lousy in the
Lousy Old Jail.

You Smart Aleck Drivers come
listen to my Tale,
Your Smart Aleck wise cracks will
git you in Jail.
One crack to the Cop and you land
in the Cell,
You're bound to git Lousy in the
Lousy Old Jail.

You Lousy Drivers come listen to
my Tale,
Your Lousy Drivin's gonna git you
in Jail.
If the Bedbugs don't git you, the
Cockroaches will,
You're bound to git Lousy in the
Lousy Old Jail.

Lord, It's All, Almost Done

When you hear the songs of the poor folks' troubles you see for yourself that they always manage to say "It's Almost Done" – because they
know very well that the crooks and racketeers that have stole their money
and taken away their lands and homes and caused their families to break
up, sweethearts to quit, boys to go rambling and friends to part forever --
those crooks are almost done.

Collected, adapted, and arranged by John A. Lomax and Alan
Lomax. © 1941 (renewed) by Ludlow Music, Inc., New York, NY.
Used by permission.

Take these stripes, stripes from
    around my shoulder,
Take these chains, chains from
    around my leg.
Lord, these stripes, stripes sure
    don't worry me,
But these chains, these chains gonna
    kill me dead.

  Chorus:
   Lord, it's all, almost done,
   Lord, it's all, almost done,
   Lord, it's all, almost done,
   An' I aint gonna ring those yellow
    women's do' bells.
   (Repeat after each verse.)

On Monday I was arrested,
On Tuesday I was locked up in jail.
On Wednesday my trial was attested,
On Thursday nobody wouldn't go my
   bail.

On Friday me an' my baby was
   a-talkin',
On Saturday she throwed me out
   o' do's.
On Sunday me an' my baby was
   a-walkin',
On Monday she pawned all my
   clothes.

Midnight Special

Well, I've put out about 4 song books now, and good old Midnight Special has been corraled for every round up. It is the story of the boys in jail. The song of the men behind the bars. They hope and pray to get out. They talk and sing about getting out.

If you never been in jail, with not a single friend to your name, and stood around there like a lost dog in a hard rain, why, then you won't get the full meaning out of any jail house song, nor any chain gang song, nor any sweat shop, road gang, steel mill, factory, department store, farm gang, pipe liners -- which is the only reason that rich folks' songs are mainly about little tassles, ribbons, frills, and fancies that fizzle out over night.

But in jail is worst of all. Waiting for the big, bright midnight light to shine her ever loving light on you. Waiting for the big headlight of the midnight passenger train that would carry you away from that jail house - or bring your mother or your sweetheart to see you with a sheet of paper in her hand - a pardon that would turn that key and let you leave them bars behind.

New words and new music adaptation by Huddie Ledbetter. Collected and adapted by John A. Lomax and Alan Lomax. © 1936 (renewed) by Folkways Music Publishers, Inc., New York, NY. Used by permission.

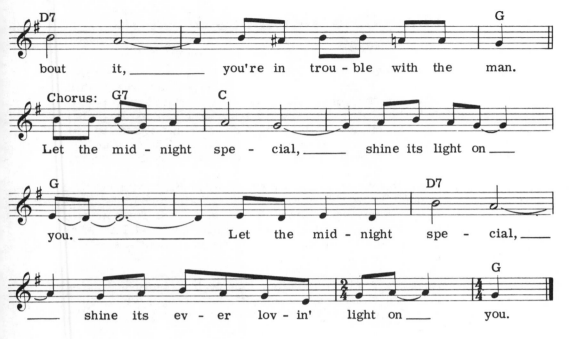

bout it, _____ you're in trou - ble with the man.

Chorus: Let the mid - night spe - cial, _____ shine its light on ____

you. _____ Let the mid - night spe - cial, ____

____ shine its ev - er lov - in' light on ____ you.

Well, you wake up in the mornin',
    hear the ding dong ring,
Go marchin' to the table, see the
    same dam thing.
Knife and folk are on the table,
    nothin' in my pan,
An' if you say anything about it,
    you're in trouble with the man.

    Chorus:
    Let the Midnight Special shine its
    light on you.
    Let the Midnight Special shine its
    ever-lovin' light on you.

If you ever go to Houston, you
    better walk right,
You better not stagger and you
    better not fight,
Or Sheriff Benson will arrest you,
    he will carry you down.
If de jury finds you guilty, you'll be
    penitentiary bound.

Yonder comes Miss Rosie--how in
    the worl' do you know?
I can tell her by her apron and de
    dress she wo'.
Umbrella on her shoulder, piece o'
    paper in her hand.
Well, I heard her tell the captain,
    "I want my man."

I'm gwine away an' leave you, an'
    my time aint long.
De man is gonna call me an' I'm
    a-goin' home.
Then I'll be done all my grievin',
    whoopin', hollin' and
    a-cryin',
Then I'll be done all my studyin'
    'bout my great long time.

Well, de biscuits on de table just
    as hard as any rock.
If you try to swallow dem, break a
    convict's heart.
My sister wrote a letter, my
    mother wrote a card:
"If you want to come and see us,
    you'll have to ride the rods."

Lonesome Jailhouse Blues

Hard enough to be broke and be a hobo, even if you're a white man. But the Negroes have got it ten times tougher. In a box car load of white men and colored men the police found a couple of white girls. Lots of girls rode the trains. With the railroad bulls so tough and the police so mean, you are suspicioned all of the time, and investigated to boot for everything that goes wrong. Something happened. The cops and the girls had some words. The girls was a little scared and a little nervous.

The police accused these nine Negro boys of rape. At first the girls said yes, then no. I don't know if they ever made up their minds. The girls admitted it was a frame up against the colored boys. The boys was proved innocent. But they would not let them out of jail. At last, after several years, they let five of the boys go. The other four are still in jail singing the Lonesome Jailhouse Blues.

I can't figure that out. I believe the other four ought to be turned loose. When you're in jail for something you done, it's bad enough. When you're in there for something you didn't do, boy, that's enough to give the whole country the Blues.

"She hollered 'Rape.' Nine of us went to jail over it. She changed her mind and said we was innocent, but they wouldn't let us out."

(Olen Montgomery, one of the Scottsboro Boys)

A
All last night I walked in my cell and cried,

A7 D7
All last night I walked in my cell and

A   E7
cried. Be-cause this old jail-house got lone-some, and

D7(+9)   A   (E7)
I just can't be sat - is - fied.

All last night I walked my cell and
  cried (2)
Because this old jailhouse got lonesome and I just can't be
  satisfied.

I tried to eat my breakfast this
  morning, but I couldn't for
  shedding tears, mama (2),
It almost breaks my heart to think
  of those five long years.

Oh Lord, Oh Lord, what am I going
  to do? (2)
I have walked around in this old jail
  so long I can't even wear my
  shoes.

I wouldn't even treat a dog like these
  people treats poor me, (2)
They treats me just like I'm some
  kind of an animal they aint
  never seen.

I don't know anything about Alabama,
  'cause it's not my home. (2)
But ever since I been here I have
  regretted the day I was born.

I'm singing this song because I
  wants everybody to know (2)
How a poor boy feels when he is
  down so low.

81

Ruben

I learned this off of Willie Johnson who says it's the story of a pore old colored boy down in Mississippi, whom they tried to lynch, but he escaped. Can't remember any more verses than just these two.

New words and new music by Willie Johnson and Alan Lomax.
© 1962 (renewed) by Ludlow Music, Inc., New York, NY. Used by permission.

When ol' Rub-en left home, he was jus' nine days old, When he came back he was a full grown man, O Lord, when he came back he was a full grown man.

Chorus:
Cry-ing Ru-ben, cry-ing Ru-ben, Cry-ing where have you been so long?

When old Ruben left home,
He was jus' nine days old,
When he come back he was a
    fullgrown man, O Lord,
When he come back he was a
    fullgrown man.

Chorus:
Crying Ruben,
Crying Ruben,
Crying, where have you been so
    long?

O they got old Ruben down and
They took his watch and chain.
It was all the poor boy ever had,
    O Lord,
It was all the poor boy ever had.

You Kick and Stomp and Beat Me
(Jumpin' Judy)

Collected, adapted, and arranged by John A. Lomax and Alan Lomax. © 1934 (renewed) by Ludlow Music, Inc., New York, NY. Used by permission. From the singing of Huddie Ledbetter.

Jumpin' Judy Jumpin' Judy
Jumpin' Judy Jumpin' Judy
Jumpin' Judy Jumpin' Judy
All over dis world, all over dis
world.

Well you kick and stomp and beat
me (3 times)
Da's all I know, da's all I know.

Yonder come my captain (3 times)
Who has been gone so long, who has
been gone so long.

Gonna tell him how you treat me
(3 times)
So you better git gone, so you better
git gone.

83

Take This Hammer

Words and music adapted and arranged by John A. Lomax and
Alan Lomax. © 1941 (renewed) by Ludlow Music, Inc., New York,
NY. Used by permission.

Take this ham - mer (wah!) Car - ry it to the Cap - tain
(wah!) Take this ham - mer (wah!) And car - ry it to the Cap - tain
(wah!) Take this ham - mer (wah!) And car - ry it to the cap -
tain___ you tell him I'm gone___ (wah!) You tell him I'm gone. (wah!)

Take dis hammer, carry it to the
    captain. (3 times)
Tell him I'm gone,
Tell him I'm gone.

If he asks you was I runnin',
    (3 times)
Tell him I was flyin',
Tell him I was flyin'.

If he asks you was I laughin',
    (3 times)
Tell him I was cryin'
Tell him I was cryin'.

They wanna feed me cornbread and
    molasses, (3 times)
But I got my pride,
Well, I got my pride.

Take this hammer, carry it to my
     captain, (3 times)
Tell him I won't scab
Tell him I won't scab.

If he asks you where he can find me
     (3 times)
Say, on the picket line,
Say, on the picket line.

If he asks you how I'm feelin'
     (3 times)
Well, I'm feelin' fine,
Well, I'm feelin' fine.

I won't work when my buddy aint
     working (3 times)
He's got to eat, too,
He's got to eat, too.

And if he asks you what's my union
     (3 times)
It's the C. I. O. ,
It's the C. I. O.

Things About Comin' My Way

Think in some ways this has just about the best tune in the whole book...
After I lost my farm, I lost my job, my home, my gal, my money, my
health, my friends -- after all my hard travelling -- things is 'bout
coming my way.

Recorded by Tampa Red, Vocalion 1637. (From the
collection of Alan Lomax)

Lost all my mon-ey ____ ain't got a dime ____
____ Giv-in' up this whole world, __ Leav-in' it behind ____ But af-ter all ____ my hard
trav-'lin' ____ Things is 'bout com-in' my way. __

Los' all my money, aint got a dime,
Givin' up this whole world, leavin'
    it behind.

Chorus:
But after all, all my hard
    travelin',
Things is 'bout comin my way.
(Repeat after each verse)

When I was sick, down on my bed,
My friends forgot me, thought I was
    dead.

Boys, aint it hard when you aint got
    a frien',
Just to keep on travelin', they'll
    need yo' help agin.

I'm always pleased. I'm never mad,
Thinkin' 'bout the bad luck I once
    have had.

Now take me, baby, just as I am,
Aint got no money, I'm in a jam.

She told my neighbors and all my
    friends,
That I was a mistreater, she didn't
    want me back again.

V - SOME FROM THE OLD WOBBLIES

The I. W. W. was the Industrial Workers of the World. They wanted to get control of all of the farms and factories, mines, mills and railroads. They wanted to get good wages, short hours and better treatment all the way 'round. But they steered clear of politics. They tried to get the things that money will buy without going to the folks that's got all of the money. I think they even wanted to start a coupon system to take the place of money. That sure would be a joke on all of the rich boys to wake up some morning and find out we was using a new color of money. The I.W.W. folks sprung up amongst the migratory workers, fruit, farm and harvest workers. They rode the rods and walked the ties, and spread their gospel everywhere. They got to be called the I Won't Work folks.

They had different ways of fighting for their rights, but they didn't quite have the right politics, so they washed out. There's a good word for them in the pages of history, but you just can't outwit these people that's got the money unless you blast away in their face with politics, votes, petitions, letters, unions, speeches and meeting halls running full blast. The rich folks got your money with politics. You can get it back with politics. Politics is how you vote. What Union you belong to. If you're in debt, uncertain, broke, out of work or running behind, take a good purgative and come out behind the Farmer-Labor folks. That is your only chance to win. The I.W.W. worked up some mighty good songs. They rambled everywhere and sang and worked and made speeches. Their song was worth about an even dozen sermons.

Pie in the Sky

THE PREACHER AND THE SLAVE

Some fellers seem to say that if you work good and hard down here on earth you'll get a dam good meal when you're dead, too dead to enjoy it. Well, for me, I would ruther have my pie here while I can still taste it. I don't care nothin' about it after I'm so dead and rotten that maggots will be a pickin' my teeth.

Some of the preachers that promise you hamburgers in the hereafter get on my nerves; what I'd really like to do part of the time is to give 'em a hunk of blackberry pie right in the face.

Preachers can go hungry if they think it helps, but I know when I was drivin' a tractor on Bill Phillips' Farm down in Jericho, Texas, well, I needed groceries right that minute and I says to myself: "What good does it do to grease a Tractor after the cussed thing has wore out and fell apart?" Same way with a hard workin' man, you give him groceries to take care of his stomach and his soul will take care of itself. If your soul is eternal, it won't git lost, and if it's everlasting, it won't git hungry...Groceries now is what I believe in.

Words by Joe Hill
Music: "Sweet Bye and Bye"

Long-haired preach - ers come out ev - 'ry night, Try to

tell you what's wrong and what's right; But when asked how 'bout some-thing to

eat, they will ans - wer in voic - es so sweet: You will

Chorus:
eat, bye and bye, in that glo - ri-ous land a-bove the sky; work and

pray, live on hay, you'll get pie in the sky when you die. (That's a lie!)

Long-haired preachers come out
 every night
And they tell you what's wrong and
 what's right,
But when you ask them for something
 to eat,
They will answer in voices so sweet:

 Chorus:
 You will eat, bye and bye,
 In that glorious land above the sky.
 Work and pray, live on hay,
 You'll get pie in the sky when you
 die.
 (Repeat after each verse)

Oh, the starvation army they play
And they sing and they clap and they
 pray,
Til they get all your coin on the
 drum
Then they'll tell you when you're on
 the bum:

Holy Rollers and Jumpers come out
And they holler, they jump and they
 shout:
"Give your money to Jesus", they
 say,
"He will cure all diseases today. "

If you fight hard for children and
 wife
Try to get something good in this
 life,
You're a sinner and a bad man, they
 tell,
When you die you will sure go to
 Hell.

Workingmen of all countries, unite
Side by side we for freedom will
 fight,
When the world and its wealth we
 have gained
To the grafter we will sing this
 refrain:

Last Chorus:
You will eat bye and bye
When you've learned how to cook
 and to fry.
Chop some wood, 'twill do you
 good,
And you'll eat in the sweet bye
 and bye.

The Tramp

The old "wobblies" roared at this one when the boys would get together
around meal time, or around a jungle fire down by the railroad yards.
All of the 'bos would cock their ears to one side and listen and grin.
This business of doing all of your living, loving, eating, drinking out
yonder in the blue sky somewhere, is a joke to everybody that has had
his religion hammered into his head with a policeman's club.

Words by Joe Hill
Music: "Tramp, Tramp, Tramp, The Boys Are
Marching"

If you all will shut your trap, I will tell you 'bout a chap that was
broke and up a-gainst it too for fair; He was not the kind to shirk, he was
look-ing hard for work, But he heard the same old sto-ry ev-'ry - where.

Chorus:

Tramp, tramp, tramp and keep on tramp - ing, Noth-ing do-ing here for
you. If I catch you 'round a - gain, you will
wear the ball and chain, Keep on tramp-ing that's the best thing you can do.

If you all will shut your trap,
I will tell you 'bout a chap
That was broke and up against it,
    too, for fair.
He was not the kind to shirk,
He was looking hard for work
But he heard the same old story
    everywhere.

Chorus:
Tramp, tramp, tramp keep on a
    tramping,
Nothing a doing here for you.
If I catch you 'round again,
You will wear the ball and chain.
Keep on tramping, that's the best
    thing you can do.
(Repeat after each verse)

He walked up and down the street
Til his shoes fell off his feet,
In a house he spied a lady cooking
    stew
And he said, "How do you do.
May I chop some wood for you?"
What the lady told him made him
    feel so blue:

Down the street he met a cop
And the copper made him stop
And he asked him, "When did you
    blow into town?"
To the judge the poor boy went
But he didn't have a cent,
So the judge he said, "You needn't
    come around."

Finally came the happy day
When his life did pass away,
He was sure he'd go to heaven when
    he died.
When he reached the pearly gate,
Old Saint Peter, mean old skate,
Slammed the gates of heaven in his
    face and cried:

...try scraping out this chorus....

Scratch, scratch, scratch, the bugs
    are biting,
Cheer up, comrades, they will
    come,
But beneath the fingernail
You can grab him by the tail,
And put him in his everlasting
    home.

91

Casey Jones

Here's old Casey Jones gone plumb Loco. I mean he had to go through Heaven and Hell to learn about it. You got to go a long ways to find out some things. And this shows you how Casey didn't like the UNION down here on Earth, so he had a wreck and got killed and went up to Heaven and the Angels, you see, they was Union, 'cause they believed in you STICKING TOGETHER, you know, like the Good Book said, let me see: "All Become One." Well, when you all do that, why, that's a UNION. That's all a Union is. But the police beat the living daylights out of some folks for a trying to JOIN UP and have a BIG UNION, and Casey he thought he knowed it all, but when he got to Heaven, the Angels said; "Boy, you don't fit in 'round here" and they kicked his tail out. If you like Rich Men better than you do the Poor Men, you can't never get to Heaven, and if you was to manage to sneak in, they'd kick you out the minute they found out, 'cause, boy, they're REALLY ORGANIZED up there. Same way it ought to be down here. You been hungry too long.

Words by Joe Hill

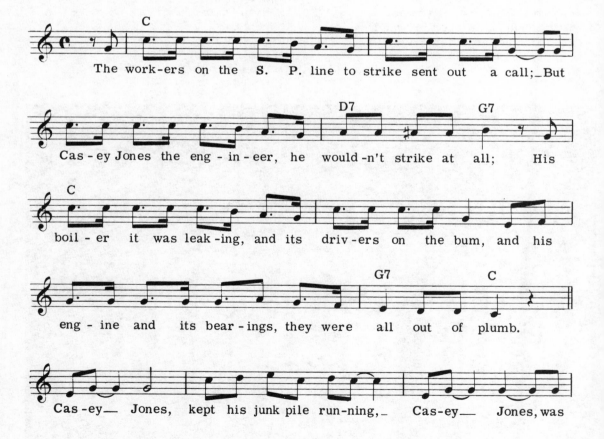

The work-ers on the S. P. line to strike sent out a call;_But
Cas-ey Jones the eng-in-eer, he would-n't strike at all; His
boil-er it was leak-ing, and its driv-ers on the bum, and his
eng-ine and its bear-ings, they were all out of plumb.
Cas-ey_ Jones, kept his junk pile run-ning,_ Cas-ey_ Jones, was

92

work-ing dou-ble time; Cas-ey_ Jones got a wood-en me-dal,_ for

be - ing good and faith - ful on the S. P. Line.

The workers on the S. P. Line to
  strike sent out a call
But Casey Jones, the engineer, he
  wouldn't strike at all:
His boilers they were leaking and
  his drivers on the bum,
And his engine and its bearings they
  were all out of plumb.

  Casey Jones kept his junk pile
    running
  Casey Jones was working double
    time.
  Casey Jones got a wooden medal
  For being good and faithful on the
    S. P. Line.

The workers said to Casey, "Won't
  you help us win this strike?"
But Casey said, "Let me alone;
  you'd better take a hike. "
Then someone put a bunch of railroad ties across the track,
And Casey hit the river with an
  awful crack.

  Casey Jones hit the river bottom;
  Casey Jones broke his blooming
    spine.
  Casey Jones was an Angelino,
  He took a trip to heaven on the
    S. P. Line.

When Casey Jones got up to heaven
  to the Pearly Gate,
He said: "I'm Casey Jones, the guy
  that pulled the S. P. freight. "
"You're just the man", said Peter,
  "Our musicians are on strike,
You can get a job a-scabbing any
  time you like. "

  Casey Jones got a job in heaven,
  Casey Jones was going mighty
    fine,
  Casey Jones went scabbing on the
    angels
  Just like he did to workers on the
    S. P. Line.

The angels got together and they
  said it wasn't fair
For Casey Jones to go around
  a-scabbing everywhere.
The Angels Union No. 23, they sure
  were there,
And they promptly fired Casey down
  the Golden Stair.

  Casey Jones went to hell a-flying.
  Casey Jones, the devil said, "Oh
    fine.
  Casey Jones, get busy shovelling
    sulphur,
  That's what you get for scabbing
    on the S. P. Line. "

Beans, Bacon and Gravy

Unless you working folks get together and work together, the bean is going to get to be about the best known thing in the country. Fact it will be about all you do know. During the first war when Hoover was food commissioner, they used to say, "Eat every bean and pea on the plate."

I was born long a-go,— in eight-een-nine-ty-four, and I've
seen man-y a pan-ic I will own, I've been hun-gry, I've been cold, and
now I'm grow-ing old, but the worst I've seen is nine-teen thir-ty-nine.

Chorus:
Oh those beans, ba-con and grav-y,— They al-most drive me cra-zy,— I
eat them till I see them in my dreams. (in my dreams) When I
wake up in the morn-ing— and an-oth-er day is dawn-ing,— I
know I'll have an-oth-er mess of beans.

I was born long ago, in 1894,
And I've seen a many a panic I will
    own:
I've been hungry, I've been cold,
And now I'm growing old
But the worst I've seen in 1939.

Chorus:
Oh, those beans, bacon and
    gravy,
They almost drive me crazy.
I eat them til I see them in my
    dreams, in my dreams.
When I wake up in the morning
And another day is dawning,
Yes, I know I'll have another
    mess of beans.

We congregate each morning
At the country barn at dawning
And every one is happy so it seems.
But when our work is done,
We file in one by one,
And thank the Lord for one more
    mess of beans.   (Chorus)

*.....here's some more verses also
sung by a young Negro delegate to the
Washington Hunger March in 1932..*

We have Hooverized on butter,
For milk we've only water,
And I haven't seen a steak in many
    a day.
As for pies, cakes and jellies,
We substitute sow-bellies,
For which we work the country road
    each day.

If there ever comes a time
When I have more than a dime,
They will have to put me under lock
    and key,
For I've been broke so long
I can only sing this song
Of the workers and their
    misery.

95

The Mysteries of a Hobo's Life

Words by T-Bone Slim
Music: Girl I Left Behind Me

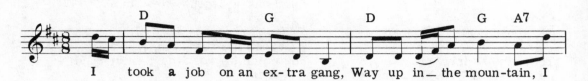

I took a job on an ex-tra gang, Way up in the moun-tain, I

paid my fee and the shark shipped me, And the ties I soon was count-ing. The

boss put me to driv-ing spikes And the sweat was e-nough to blind me, He

did-n't seem to like my pace, So I left the job be-hind me.

I took a job on an extra gang,
Way up in the mountain,
I paid my fee and the shark shipped
me
And the ties I soon was counting.

The boss put me to driving spikes
And the sweat was enough to blind
me.
He didn't seem to like my pace,
So I left the job behind me.

I grabbed ahold of an old freight
train
And around the country traveled,
The mysteries of a hobo's life
To me were soon unraveled.

I traveled east and I traveled west
And the "shacks" could never find
me.
Next morning I was miles away
From the job I left behind me.

I ran across a bunch of "stiffs"
Who were known as Industrial
Workers,
They taught me how to be a man,
And how to fight the shirkers.

I kicked right in and joined the
bunch
And now in the ranks you'll find me,
Hurrah for the cause, To hell with
the boss!
And the job I left behind me.

96

The Commonwealth of Toil

Words by Ralph Chaplin
Music: "My Darling Nellie Grey"

In the gloom of might-y cit-ies, mid the roar of whirl-ing wheels, we are toil-ing on like chat-tel slaves of old, —— And our mas-ters hope to keep us ev-er thus be-neath their heels, and to coin our ve-ry life blood in-to gold. —— But we have a glow-ing dream of how fair the world will seem, when each man can live his life se-cure and free.—— When the earth is owned by la-bor and there's joy and peace for all in the com-mon-wealth of toil that is to be.——

They would keep us cowed and beaten,
  cringing meekly at their feet.
They would stand between each worker
  and his bread.
Shall we yield our lives up to them
  for the bitter crusts we eat?
Shall we only hope for heaven when
  we're dead?
    (Cho.)

They have laid our lives out for us
  to the utter end of time.
Shall we stagger on beneath their
  heavy load?

Shall we let them live forever in
  their gilded halls of crime
With our children doomed to toil
  beneath their goad?
    (Cho.)

When our cause is all triumphant
  and we claim our mother earth,
And the nightmare of the present
  fades away,
We shall live with love and laughter,
  we who now are little worth,
And we'll not regret the price we have
  to pay.
    (Cho.)

.......at the time we're writing this, we aren't through the book yet but we know for sure there's going to be a lot of misspellings and mistakes of a sort like that. But you don't need grammar to know you're hungry, and it don't matter whose language you're speaking, when it's the truth.

VI - OLD TIME SONGS FROM ALL OVER

This next bunch of songs come from the sweat shops and hell holes of the mines, mills, factories, prairies and oceans. They are both old and new, inasmuch as long hours of hard work at low wages has made these hell holes what they are today, and not all of the songs that come out of these people were very gay ones. They're sad, and they're boiling hot and they're the very sweat that is the salt of the earth.

I don't guess you could find a big radio station that's willing to make these songs very famous. There's a little bunch of fellers that twist a cool million dollars out of the sweat and blood of the folks that made up these songs. If they was given a half, even a fourth, of a chance these songs would strike a light in the heart of the people that would spread like a prairie fire on a dry, windy day. And because in the days to come, and who knows when, the grafters, slave drivers, hate spreaders, and money worshippers will be wiped out and destroyed in the fire of their own damned greed. They will start that fire, and they'll fan it twenty four hours a day and tamper with it and blow it and tease it and then - when it leaps up into a flame as high as the sky - and starts roaring across the pastures, they'll fall back and run and jabber and yell that somebody else caused the whole thing.

There wouldn't be much trouble on this earth if it wasn't for the rich man's greed. But he will try his best to throw the poor folks in jail as fast as they talk, write or sing about That.

The Buffalo Skinners

An Indian used to scalp his enemies. They say a white man skins his friends. Lots of folks don't want you for a friend 'less they can skin you once or twice a day. You are their friend only as long as you are able to make money for them. They sent you everywhere to make money for them, and they patted you on the back and smiled as long as you brought them gold from up out of the mines, coal from back under the hills, copper from over under the mountains, cotton from out of the patch, fruits from your trees, groceries from your garden, oil from the middle of the earth, and even hides, skins, and furs from Alaska, the frozen north and the buffalo hides from the wild and woolly plains.

This song just goes to show you what happened to one boss who forgot to pay up once too often. It shows you that the fellers that was doing the hard work knew all of the time that the boss was a gypping them, but they got sick and tired of his crooked work and left his bones to whiten in the sun that comes up every morning to see something like this, somewhere in this world.

Collected and adapted by John A. Lomax and Alan Lomax. © 1934 (renewed) by Ludlow Music, Inc., New York, NY. Used by permission.

on the range of the buf-fa - lo.

'Twas in the town of Jacksboro in the
    spring of Sev'nty three,
A man by the name of Crego came
    stepping up to me,
Saying, "How do you do, young
    fellow, and how would you like
    to go
And spend one summer pleasantly
    on the range of the buffalo?"

"It's me being out of employment,
    this to Crego I did say:
"This going out on the buffalo range
    depends upon the pay.
But if you will pay good wages and
    transportation, too,
I think, sir, I will go with you to the
    range of the buffalo. "

"Yes, I will pay good wages, give
    transportation, too,
Provided you will go with me and
    stay the summer through:
But if you should grow homesick,
    come back to Jacksboro,
I won't pay transportation from the
    range of the buffalo. "

It's now our outfit was complete -
    seven able-bodied men, **
With navy six and needle gun - our
    troubles did begin:
Our way it was a pleasant one, the
    route we had to go,
Until we crossed Pease River on
    the range of the buffalo.

It's now we've crossed Pease River,
    our troubles have begun.
The first dam tail I went to rip,
    Christ! how I cut my thumb!
While skinning the dam old stinkers
    our lives they had no show,
For the Indians watched to pick us
    off while skinning the buffalo.

**Two to kill, four to skin and one to cook.

He fed us on such sorry chuck I
    wished myself most dead,
It was old jerked beef, croton
    coffee and sour bread.
Pease River's as salty as hell fire,
    the water I could never go -
O God! I wished I had never come
    to the range of the buffalo.

Our meat it was buffalo hump and
    iron wedge bread,
And all we had to sleep on was a
    buffalo robe for a bed:
The fleas and graybacks worked on
    us, O boys, it was not slow,
I'll tell you there's no worse hell on
    earth than the range of the
    buffalo.

Our hearts were cased with buffalo
    hocks, our souls were cased
    with steel.
And the hardships of that summer
    would nearly make us reel.
While skinning the damned old
    stinkers our lives they had no
    show.
For the Indians waited to pick us off
    on the Hills of Mexico.

The season being near over, old
    Crego he did say,
The crowd had been extravagant,
    was in debt to him that day,
We coaxed him and we begged him
    and still it was no go -
We left old Crego's bones to bleach
    on the range of the buffalo.

Oh, it's now we've crossed Pease
    River and homeward we are
    bound,
No more in that hell-fired country
    shall ever we be found.
Go home to our wives and
    sweethearts, tell others not to
    go,
For God's forsaken the buffalo range
    and the damned old buffalo.

The Old Chisholm Trail

Be purty hard to find a song that's got a better reputation than the Old Chisholm Trail. "Went to the Boss to draw my roll, figured me out $9 in the hole..." The damned old cuss.

Collected, adapted, and arranged by John A. Lomax and Alan Lomax. © 1938 (renewed) by Ludlow Music, Inc., New York, NY. Used by permission.

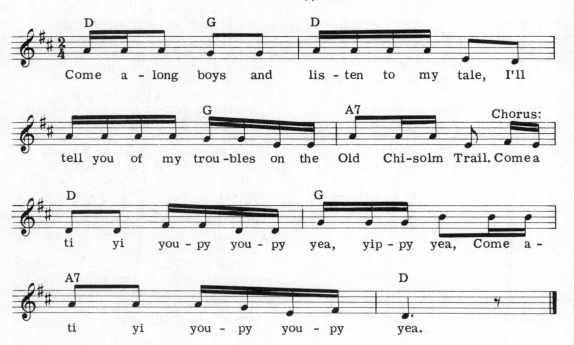

Come a-long boys and lis-ten to my tale, I'll tell you of my trou-bles on the Old Chi-solm Trail. Come a ti yi you-py you-py yea, yip-py yea, Come a- ti yi you-py you-py yea.

Come along, boys, and listen to my tale,
I'll tell you of my troubles on the old Chisholm trail.

Chorus:
Come a ti yi youpy, youpy yea, youpy yea,
Come a ti yi youpy, youpy yea.
(Repeat after each verse)

I'm up in the mornin' afore daylight
And afore I sleep the moon shines bright.

Oh, it's bacon and beans most every day,
I'd as soon be a-eatin' prairie hay.

No chaps, no slicker, and it's pouring rain.
And I swear, by God, I'll never night-herd again.

My slicker's in the wagon and I'm gittin mighty cold,
And these longhorn sons-o-guns are gittin' hard to hold.

The wind commenced to blow, and the rain began to fall,
It looked, by gosh, like we was goin' to lose 'em all.

Saddle up, boys, and saddle up well,
For I think these cattle have scattered to hell.

I don't give a damn if they never do stop:
I'll ride as long as an eight day clock.

Foot in the stirrup and hand on the horn,
Best damned cowboy ever was born.

I herded and I hollered and I done very well,
Til the boss said, "Boys, just let them go to hell."

I went to the boss to draw my roll,
He had it figgered out I was nine dollars in the hole.

I went up to the boss and we had a little chat,
I slapped him in the face with my big slouch hat.

Oh, the boss says to me, "I'll fire you,
Not only you, but the whole darn crew."

I'll sell my outfit just as soon as I can,
I won't punch cattle for no damn man.

I'll sell my horse and I'll sell my saddle:
You can go to hell with your longhorn cattle.

Fare you well, old trail-boss, I don't wish you any harm.
I'm quittin' this business to go on the farm.

No more cow-puncher to sleep at my ease,
'Mid the crawlin' of the lice and the bitin' of the fleas.

Drill Ye Tarriers Drill

An old tune from the west where it was originally sung by the Irish workers on the railroad. It became so popular that it was sung on vaudeville stages all over the country. "Tarriers" were the rock drillers.

Words and music by Thomas Casey (circa 1880), popular as a vaudeville stage song. Learned from the singing of Earl Robinson.

Ev - 'ry morn-ing at sev-en o'-clock, There's twen-ty tar - ri - ers work-ing at the rock. And the boss comes a - long and he says, "Kape still", and come down heav-y on the cast ir-on drill, and

Chorus:

drill ye tar - ri - ers, drill. And drill ye tar - ri - ers, drill. For it's work all day for the sug - ar in your tay, Down_ be - hind_ the rail - way, and drill ye tar - ri - ers, drill, and fire, and blast.

Every morning at seven o'clock
There's twenty tarriers working at
    the rock.
And the boss comes along and he
    says, "Kape still",
And come down heavy on the cast
    iron drill,

Chorus: (Repeat after each verse)
And drill, ye tarriers, drill.
And drill, ye tarriers, drill.
For it's work all day for sugar in
    your tay,
Down behind the railway,
And drill, ye tarriers, drill,
And fire.   And Blast.

Now our new foreman was Gene
    McCann,
By God, he was a blame mean man.
Last week a premature blast went
    off
And a mile in the air went big Jim
    Goff.

Next time payday came around,
Jim Goff a dollar short was found,
When asked, "What for", came this
    reply,
"Yer docked for the time you was
    up in the sky. "

The boss was a fine man down to the
    ground,
And he married a lady six feet
    round.
She baked good bread and she baked
    it well,
But she baked it hard as the holes of
    hell.

Skinnamalinkadoolium

Whim, wham, and the mule throwed Tony. The blind hog found an acorn
and Jonah swallowed the whale. This song about explains itself. The
moral to this song is that all of us poor folks is headed straight to
heaven, 'cause we're so stony broke, seems like. Seems like some of
the loudest preachers you hear has got plenty of money.

There was a rich man and he lived
   in Jerusalem,
Glory, hallelujah hei–ro–je–rum.
He wore a silk hat and his coat was
   sprucium,
Glory hallelujah hei–ro–je–rum.

Chorus:
Hei–ro–je–rum, hei–ro–je–rum,
Skinamalinkadoolium
Skinamalinkadoolium
Glory hallelujah hei–ro–je–rum.
(Repeat after each verse)

And at his gate there sat a human
   wreckium
Glory hallelujah hei–ro–je–rum,
He wore a bowler hat and the rim
   was round his neckium,
Glory hallelujah hei–ro–je–rum.

That poor man asked for a piece of
   bread and cheesium,
Glory hallelujah hie–ro–je–rum.
The rich man answered, "I'll call
   for a policeium,
Glory hallelujah hei–ro–je–rum.

The poor man died and his soul went
  to heavium,
Glory hallelujah hei-ro-je-rum.
And he danced with the saints til
  quarter past ellevium.
Glory hallelujah hei-ro-je-rum.

And there he dwelt in Abraham's
  bosium,
Glory Hallelujah hei-ro-je-rum.
Fraternizing there with scores of
  other Jewseum,
Glory hallelujah hei-ro-je-rum.

The rich man died but he didn't fare
  so welleum,
Glory hallelujah hei-ro-je-rum.
He couldn't go to heaven so he had
  to go to helleum,
Glory hallelujah, hei-ro-je-rum.

The rich man asked for to have a
  consolium,
Glory hallelujah hei-ro-je-rum.
The devil only answered, "Come
  shovel on the coalium."
Glory hallelujah hei-ro-je-rum.

The moral of this story is that
  riches are no jokium,
Glory hallelujah hei-ro-je-rum.
We will all go to heaven because we
  are stony brokium,
Glory hallelujah hei-ro-je-rum.

John Brown's Body

Well, I be dam. Here's old John Brown's Body - lays a moulding in th'
grave - but I suppose we all got a little plain and fancy moulding to do
sometime. I don't see how you could keep from a moulding in these here
New York Slums, or in Chicago, or Birmingham, or San Francisco.
And you know I really think the folks that do all of the hard work is a
going to find their way out of them slippery slums one of these days...
and it'll be songs like that they'll be a singing on the day they pull the
Big Walk Out.

John Brown's Body lies a mould'ring
   in the grave (3 times)
But his soul goes marching on.

The stars above in heaven are
   looking kindly down (3 times)
On the grave of old John Brown.

America's working folks are all
   remembering the spot (3 times)
It's the grave of old John Brown.

John Brown died that the slave
   might be free (3 times)
But his soul goes marching on.

He captured Harpers Ferry with his
    nineteen men so true,
And he frightened old Virginia til
    she trembled through and
    through.
They hung him for a traitor,
    themselves the traitor crew,
But his soul goes marching on.

Now has come the glorious jubilee,
Now has come the glorious jubilee,
Now has come the glorious jubilee,
When all mankind shall be free.

.......there's a lot of things we wanted to say in the introduction to this book, but we know most people never read introductions, anyway, so we broke it up and scattered the introduction far and wide through the pages. Reads better that way, anyhow ....

Johnnie Woncha Ramble

This here is an old slave song and I think it speaks for itself. When the boss's back was turned and the colored folks were just singing to theirselves, why, this is one of the songs they'd sing. Mighty rare to find a song like this nowadays down in print.

Collected, adapted, and arranged by John A. Lomax and Alan Lomax. © 1941 (renewed) by Ludlow Music, Inc., New York, NY. Used by permission.

I looked up on the hill ___ and spied old mas - ter rid - ing, John - ny wont - cha ram - ble, ___ hoe, hoe, hoe. I looked up on the hill ___ and spied old mas - ter rid- ing, ___ John - ny wont- cha ram - ble, ___ hoe, hoe, ___ hoe.

Had a bull whip in one hand, cow hide in the other,
Johnnie wontcha ramble, hoe, hoe hoe:
Had a bull whip in one hand, cow hide in the other,
Johnnie wontcha ramble, hoe, hoe, hoe.

Pocket full of leather strings to tie your hands together,
Johnnie wontcha ramble, hoe, hoe, hoe;
Pocket full of leather strings to tie your hands together,
Johnnie wontcha ramble, hoe, hoe, hoe.

Ole Mastah, dont you whip me, I'll give you half a dollar,
Johnnie wontcha ramble, hoe, hoe, hoe;
Ole Mastah, don't you whip me, I'll give you half a dollar,
Johnnie wontcha ramble, hoe, hoe, hoe.

No, no, Bully Boy, I'd ruther hear you holler,
Johnnie wontcha ramble, hoe, hoe, hoe;
No, no, Bully Boy, I'd ruther hear you holler,
Johnnie wontcha ramble, hoe, hoe, hoe.

Jesse James and His Boys

Here's a song about Jesse James I wrote one day when I lost the song-book it was in. I couldn't remember it the other way so I set down and hoed this one out. In some respects it's pretty fair. I got some of the ideas from the picture show. It showed the life of Jesse James and his boys a raising Sam Hill down through the Missouri Mountains and the Kansas Badlands and all over the country.

(I was on a CBS broadcast here a while back called "The Pursuit Of Happiness" with Burgess Meredith, Franchot Tone, Walter Huston and a big orchestra – they put on the life of Jesse James. It showed how Jesse robbed a stage coach and gathered up all of the watches, and then turned right square around and give them to a little girl that was crying. That was Old Jesse. Mighty tough hombre, they said, but a little kid a crying because it's hungry or scared or something like that will cause the worst of outlaws to turn soft – or the tenderest father to turn out-law... getting a shade mushy here, myself, just thinking about it... dadgum it...)

It was the Railroad buyers that sent the bullies down to push folks off of their farms in the country that the new railroad was a coming through, but some folks just naturally don't push so easy. Jesse James and Frank was them kind of men. You just didn't drive them around like cattle. Yeah, and we still sing about Frank and Jesse. There wasn't a sissy bone in their body. They never drew a scared breath. They drew some fast ones, but they wasn't scared.

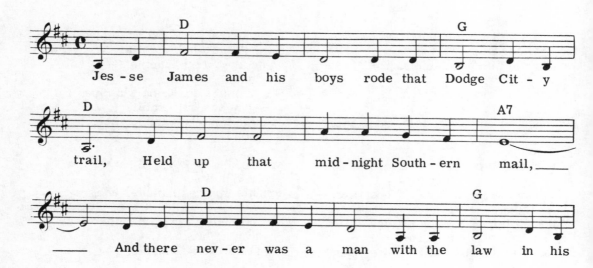

Jes - se James and his boys rode that Dodge Cit - y trail, Held up that mid-night South-ern mail, _____ And there nev - er was a man with the law in his

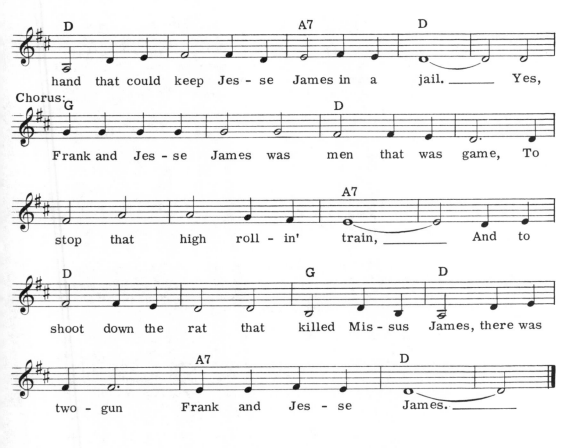

hand that could keep Jes - se James in a jail. _____ Yes,

Chorus:
Frank and Jes - se James was men that was game, To

stop that high roll - in' train, _____ And to

shoot down the rat that killed Mis - sus James, there was

two - gun Frank and Jes - se James. _____

Jesse James and his boys rode that
  Dodge City Trail,
Held up that Midnight Southern Mail,
And there never was a man with the
  law in his hand
That could keep Jesse James in jail.

It was Frank and Jesse James that
  killed a many a man,
But they never was outlaws at
  heart -
I wrote this song to tell you how it
  come
That Frank and Jesse James got
  their start.

They was living on a farm in the
  old Missouri Hills
With a silver-haired mother and a
  home.
Now the Railroad bullies come to
  chase them off their land,
But they found that Frank and
  Jesse wouldn't run.

Then a Railroad scab he went and
  got a bomb
And he throwed it at the door
And it killed Mrs. James a sleeping
  in her bed,
So Jesse grabbed a big fourty four.

Chorus:
Yes, Frank and Jesse James was
  men that was game,
To stop that high rollin' train,
And to shoot down the rat that
  killed Mrs. James,
There was "2-Gun Frank and
  Jesse James. "

Now a bastard and a coward called
  little Robert Ford
He claimed he was Frank and
  Jesse's friend,
Made love to Jesse's wife and took
  Jesse's life
And he laid poor Jesse in his grave.

(Continued on next page)

The people was surprised when
    Jesse lost his life,
Wondered how he ever come to fall.
Robert Ford it's a fact, shot Jesse
    in the back,
While Jesse hung a picture on the
    wall.

They dug Jesse's grave and a
    stone they raised,
It says, "Jesse James lies here.
Was killed by a man, a bastard and
    a coward,
Whose name aint worthy to appear. "

Pretty Boy Floyd

Charles (Pretty Boy) Floyd was borned and raised right down in there where I was. I talked to lots of folks that knowed him personal. Said he wasn't much of a bad feller. Fact, some of 'em respected him lots more than they did the sheriff and his deputies.

Something went haywire and Pretty Boy took to outlawing. Still he had more friends than any governor Oklahoma ever had. He went to packing shooting irons, blowing his way into the banks where the peoples money was. Grabbed big sacks of it up and took it out and strewed and scattered it everywhere, and give it to the poor folks all up and down the country. He had the right idea but he had the wrong system.

The Outlaw is in his grave today. So is Jesse James. So is Billy, the Kid, so is Cole Younger, and Belle Starr...but we still sing about them. You hear songs everywhere springing up about these fellers, springing up like flowers in the right early spring.

One night the deputies thought sure as hell they had Pretty Boy hemmed up down there in the Rock Island Freight Yards in Oklahoma City. Supposed to be riding in on a freight. Me and my uncle was on that same freight. Riding with a guitar and a fiddle, his fiddle. Pretty Boy was about my uncle's size and weight and he was reported to be riding that freight train with a sub-machine gun hid in a fiddle case.

We rolled into the yards, it was black as tar, long after midnight, and we looked up and seen a whole flock of flashlights a coming right straight at us through the dark. We'd been used to railroad bulls and their lanterns, but not quite so many. Here they come like a flock of airplanes lit up, and they yelled at me and my uncle and said, "Hey, boys, you gonna hafta leave here. Too dangerous from here on." And so we set there about a minute. It so happened that we was a setting out on one of these flat cars, gondola or some dern kind, and so I reached over and slung onto my guitar and slipped off alongside the car, aiming to climb back on after I'd run a little ways along side of the train. So my uncle says, "All Right, Boys, I'll get off". Yes, and he reached down to grab his fiddle and case up under his arm, and when he did - when he raised up - brother and sister, me and my uncle went one direction, and 6 jillion streaks of light went the other.

This song is one I fixed up about Pretty Boy. It tells of tales I heard concerning his life and what kind of a man he was, and as I said before I spoke, we ain't never had a governor down there that was half as popular as Pretty Boy. He tried and done it wrong. The governor won't even try.

If you'll gath-er 'round ———— me, chil-dren, ———— A sto - ry I will tell, ———————— A - bout Pret-ty Boy Floyd, an out - law, ———————— Ok - la - ho - ma knew him well.————

It was in the town of Shawnee on a
  Saturday afternoon
His wife beside him in the wagon as
  into town they rode.
There a deputy sheriff reproached
  him in a manner rather rude
Using vulgar words of anger, and
  his wife she overheard.

Pretty Boy grabbed a log chain, the
  deputy grabbed his gun,
And in the fight that followed, he
  laid that deputy down.
Then he took to the trees and timber
  and lived a life of shame,
Every crime in Oklahoma was added
  to his name.

Yes, he took to the river bottom
  along the river shore,
And Pretty Boy found a welcome at
  every farmer's door.
The papers said that Pretty Boy had
  robbed a bank each day,
While he was setting in some
  farmhouse 300 miles away.

There's many a starving farmer the
  same old story told
How the outlaw paid their mortgage
  and saved their little home.
Others tell you 'bout a stranger that
  come to beg a meal
And when the meal was finished left
  a thousand dollar bill.

It was in Oklahoma City, it was on
  Christmas Day,
There come a whole carload of
  groceries with a note to say:
"You say that I'm an outlaw, you
  say that I'm a thief.
Here's a Christmas dinner for the
  families on relief. "

Yes, as through this world I ramble,
  I see lots of funny men,
Some will rob you with a 6 gun, and
  some with a fountain pen.
But as through your life you'll travel,
  wherever you may roam,
You won't never see an Outlaw drive
  a family from their home.

Matthew Kimes

Washington, D.C. was where this song come from. It was at the house of Mr. and Mrs. Alan Lomax, two mighty good friends of mine. I believe that feller knows as much, if not more, about the real pure-dee red blood songs of the American people than any other person I ever met. And I've drunk with a many a one.

Feller over there asked me who Matthew Kimes was, well, there's a little piece about him like this: Matthew Kimes was undoubtedly Oklahoma's fanciest jailbreaker, and I remember how he broke every jail they laid him in. I was still too young to recall all of the detail, but when any living creature walks out of a jailhouse, I like it. It's wrong to be in it and it's right to be out.

I was a shining shoes in Okemah, Okla., in the Meadors Hotel, right acrost the street from our brand new 5-story court house and jail, when they had the trial of Matthew Kimes. Matthew had so many friends on the outside that he walked out of jail about as fast as they could turn the key. He used all kinds of tricks, too, to get the locks open and sometimes turned everybody else out of jail, and left funny notes and letters on the jailers desk or pillow. This song was wrote about Matthew.

Words and music by Woody Guthrie. © 1966 (renewed) by Ludlow Music, Inc., New York, NY. Used by permission.

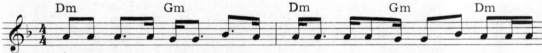

Matt-hew Kimes he got in bad, I'll tell you a-bout the scrapes he had, It's a

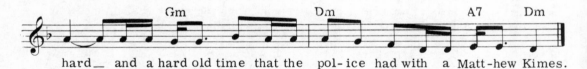

hard— and a hard old time that the pol-ice had with a Matt-hew Kimes.

Matthew Kimes he got in bad
I'll tell you about the scrapes he had.

Chorus:
It's a hard and a hard old time
That the police had with-a
　Matthew Kimes.
(Repeat after each verse)

He robbed some banks and he killed
　some men
And I'll tell of the jails that they
　laid him in.

I was shining shoes in the old hotel
When they locked him up in his jail
　house cell.

He bet the jailer that chained him
　down
That he would beat him to the edge
　of town.

They shut his door and turned the
　key,
In fifteen minutes Mr. Kimes was
　free.

As fast as they could lock him up,
Matthew Kimes would get back out.

In old Okemah they locked his door
But he escaped just the same as
    before.

He wrote a note and the note did say:
"There aint a jail house made that
    can hinder me. "

He polished his guns and he robbed
    his banks
And on the deputies he played his
    pranks.

He could rob a bank and get in jail
And get away and hit the trail.

He walked through every jail house
    wall
He'd laff and smile and the wall
    would fall.

As fast as they turned that lock of
    the pen
He'd laff and walk right out again.

He used string and nails and knives
    and soap
And secret keys to the doors to open.

But they got him down on the
    government road
And they shot him down like a dirty
    dog.

When The Maid Comes To Town

Well, all I know about maids is what I heard in a Union meeting over in Harlem. They was all taking turns about getting up and telling how hard they used to work and how much better it was now that they'd joined the Union. A testimonial service was what they called it.

Reminded me of the hundreds and hundreds of testimonial services I've went to in the Gospel Missions and the Little Tent Churches around over the country. That Union Testimony service was something new on me. I just set there and soaked every bit of it up. You just couldn't set through one of them meetings without coming out a Union Maid or Union Man.

'Course I was Union when I went in. I come out with two coats. I don't mean the women's coats. I mean two good thick coats of Union Paint. That still sounds a little leery. What I really mean is that when I come out I knew who it is that keeps you rich folks houses so nice and clean. I have no doubt that some friend of the maids built the house that she keeps so clean. What I caint hardly figure is just exactly what the mistress does.

Same tune as "Farmer is the Man." (Page 32)
Words by Social Club of Cleveland, Ohio, Branch YWCA.

When the maid she comes to town
With her arches broken down,
Oh, the maid she is the one who
    works the most.
If you'll only look and see
We think you will agree
That the maid she is the one who
    works the most.

Chorus:
The maid she is the one
The maid she is the one
Works all hours of the day.
Then she goes to the gloom
Of her lonely little room
While the rest of the world goes
    by. (Sing this line slowly)
(Repeat after each verse)

Oh, the mistress hangs around
While the maid's about her work.
Oh, the maid she is the one who
    works the most.
If you'll only look and see,
We think that you'll agree
That the maid is the one who
    works the most.

The chauffeur and the cook
Go strolling by the brook,
And the maid is the one who works
    the most.
If you'll only look and see,
We think that you'll agree
That the maid is the one who works
    the most.

When the mistress goes to town
And the babies whine and frown,
Oh, the maid she is the one who
    works the most.
Even tho' she tries her best
Just to get a little rest,
There is no way to quiet them
    down.

Longshoreman's Strike

Rich folks say they'll give you a little money to keep you from starving, you know, quick as they find some way to give you some without subtracting from what they've got, or quicker even, if they could only invent some way to toss you a buck and get two back. Whistle and sing.

(Question department: what size helmet does the president wear?)

From a New York Strike more than 50 years ago, as it appears in an old songster. (From the collection of Alan Lomax)

I am a de-cent la-bor-ing man that works a-long the shore, To

keep the hun-gry wolf a-way from the poor long-shoreman's door.

I am a decent laboring man that
    works along the shore
To keep the hungry wolf away from
    the poor longshoreman's door.
I work all day in the broiling sun on
    ships that come from the sea.
From broad daylight til late at night
    for the poor man's family

Chorus:
Give us good pay for every day,
That's all we ask of ye.
Our cause is right, we're out on
    strike,
For the poor man's family.
(Repeat after each verse)

The rich man's gilded carriages
    with horses swift and strong,
If a poor man asks for a bite to eat
    they'll tell him he is wrong.
Go take your shovel in your hand and
    come and work for me,
But die or live, they've nothing to
    give to the poor man's family.

They bring over the 'Talians and
    Naygurs from the South,
Thinking they can do the work, take
    beans from out our mouth.
The poor man's children they must
    starve but we will not agree,
To be put down like a worm in the
    ground and starve our families.

Cotton Mill Colic

Fat back meat is called a lot of things. Salt pork, sow belly, sow bosom. About as cheap a meat as you can buy when you can buy it. But folks in the cotton mill work long hours at low pay. You make the clothes. Somebody else wears 'em.

It's a shame and a pity, people that does the hard work ain't never got a dam thing. Folks that never hit a lick of useful work in their lives owns everything, and they don't know where it come from, who made it, or what to do with it and when you go to them to get a little of it for your own use, why, they turn their nose away up in the air toward the evening star and they call it "charity"

But - down in the cotton mills you work from can til can't. Every day you work you make $100 worth of goods. Some boss man comes along, takes the goods, sells 'em, and mails the money to some dam fool body up in New York City and they don't even know where the money come from. Just own some stock somewhere, they don't know where, they don't know how come, they don't know nothing. They pay more out of every week on a poodle dog than it would take to support 2 or 3 workers in the cotton mills. But they can't see it.

They can't see. Eyes but they can't see. Ears but they can't hear. Fingers but they can't write. Mouth but they can't talk. Lips but they can't sing. All they can do with a face is paint it up so you can't tell whether its a rich man's daughter or a new model car a coming down the street.

Cotton Mill Colic is a song about hard times in the mills, and is one of my favorite songs. You can tell by the way its wrote up that it aint 'put on' -- I mean its the real thing.

Arranged by John A. Lomax and Alan Lomax. © 1941 (renewed) by Ludlow Music, Inc., New York, NY. Used by permission.

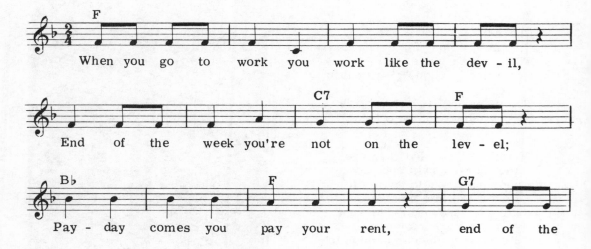

When you go to work you work like the dev-il,

End of the week you're not on the lev-el;

Pay-day comes you pay your rent, end of the

week you ain't got a cent to buy fat - back meat,____ pin - to beans,__ cook up a mess of turn - ip greens. No use to col - ic, when ev - 'ry day at noon, Kids get to cry - in' in a dif - f'rent tune.

Chorus:

I'm a - gon - na starve__ and ev - 'ry - bod - y will, 'Cause you can't make a liv - in' in a cot - ton mill.

When you go to work you work like
    the devil
End of the week you're not on the
    level;
Payday comes you pay your rent,
End of the week you aint got a cent
To buy fat-back meat, pinto beans,
Cook up a mess of turnip greens.
No use to colic when every day at
    noon,
Kids get to crying in a different
    tune.
    I'm a gonna starve and everybody
    will
    You can't make a living in a
    cotton mill.

Patches on my britches, hole in my
    hat,
Aint had a shave since my wife got
    fat.
No use to colic, we're all that way,
Can't get the money to move away.
Twelve dollars a week is all we get.
How in the hell can we live on
    that?
I got a wife and fourteen kids,
All we got is two bedsteads.
    I'm a gonna starve and everybody
    will,
    Cause you can't make a living in
    a cotton mill.

(Continued on next page)

When you buy clothes on Easy Terms,
Collector treats you like a measly
    worm.
One dollar down and then Lord
    knows,
If you can't make a payment they
    take your clothes.
When you go to bed you can't sleep,
You owe so much at the end of the
    week.
No use to bellyache we're all that
    way,
Collectors at our door til they get
    our pay.
    I'm a gonna starve and everybody
    will,
    Cause you can't make a living in
    a cotton mill.

They run a few days and then they
    stand,
Just to keep down the working man.
We'll never make it, we never will,
As long as we work in a 'Rounding
    Mill.
The poor getting poorer, the Rich a
    getting rich,
If we don't starve, I'm a son of a
    bitch.
No use to bellyache, no use to rave,
We'll never rest til we're in our
    grave.
    If we don't starve, nobody will,
    Can't make a living in a cotton
    mill.

Cotton Mill Blues

Same tune as "Cotton Mill Colic." From the singing of Lester (The Highwayman) on Decca 5559-A. Composed by L. P. Blivens. © by L.P. Blivens. (From the collection of Alan Lomax)

Come all you good people, I'll tell
   you somep'n true.
When you work in a cotton mill,
   what you gonna do?
You get up before daylight,
Labor all day until it gets night.
Then you work a few days, get pale
   in the face,
Stand so long in the same dam
   place,
Long comes the boss, as hard as
   he can tear,
Wants you to think he's a grizzly
   bear.
   Ashes to ashes, dust to dust,
   Let the rich man live and the poor
   man bust.

When dinner time comes you'll have
   to run;
They'll blow the whistle before
   you're done.
Payday comes, you aint got a penny,
'Cause when you pay your bills, you
   got so many.
Sometimes you rattle like a
   peckerwood,
Merchants outside tryin' to sell
   their goods.
Merchants' hair, just about gray,
Figgering how to get the poor man's
   pay.
   Ashes to ashes, dust to dust,
   Let the rich man live and the poor
   man bust.

When winter time comes there's hell
   to pay,
If you see the boss you'll have to
   say:
"I want a load of wood and I want a
   ton of coal,
Take a dollar out a week - I'll go in
   the hole. "
I'll have to buy merchandise at some
   chain store;
You can't afford to pay any more.
If you don't starve I'm a son-of-a-
   gun,
Can't buy beans without any mon'.
   Ashes to ashes, dust to dust,
   Let the rich man live and the poor
   man bust.

You go to the store and the clerk
   won't speak,
Go downstairs, grab a little piece
   of meat.
You can work all week, you can work
   your best,
Can't buy your wife a ten cent dress.
   Ashes to ashes, dust to dust,
   Let the rich man live and the poor
   man bust.

Hard Times in the Mill

You ain't seen no Hard Times til you come over some time and see my Hard Times.

Everybody seems to think that they're a having a Hard Time; even some of these Poodle Dog Paraders along 5th Avenue, New York, they think they really got a load of trouble on their chests. Only thing that keeps some of 'em on an even keel is that pooch hound to guide 'em down the road.

Mill People do the work of a making your clothes, but it's hard for them to even own a new layout of duds ... just like most barbers aint got no hair. Just like a mechanic will fix 456 of the world's best cars every month and drive around in some old broke down rattle trap.

The old boys and the girls that hit the Heavy in the Southern cotton mills come home with the seat of their pants a dragging their tracks out -- if you want to know about Hard Work and Hard Times, just take a gander down there and see. 'Course I know you might be a workin' so dam hard right where you're at that you don't have to take a trip to see -- but it ought to be a state law that these idle moneyed folks ought to have to set and watch us poor folks while we work - 16 hours a day - then they'd get tired of just a settin' on their fanny, and they'd shorten them hours.

Sung by Lessie Crocker, worker in Columbia, S.C. knitting mills, and now a member of Local 252 of her union. "This song was composed by my mother and some old spoolers in the mill 40 years ago."

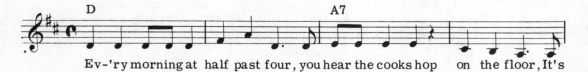

Ev-'ry morning at half past four, you hear the cooks hop on the floor, It's

hard times in the mill, my love, hard times in the mill.

Every morning at half past four,
You hear the cooks hop on the floor.

Chorus:
It's hard times in the mill, my love,
Hard Times in the mill.
(Repeat after each verse)

Every morning just at five,
You gotta get up, dead or alive.

Every morning right at six,
Don't that old bell make you sick.

The pulley got hot, the belt jumped off,
Knocked Mr. Guyon's derby off.

Old Pat Goble thinks he's a hon,
He puts me in mind of a doodle in
    the sun.

The section hand thinks he's a man,
And he aint got the sense to pay off
    his hands.

They steal his ring, they steal his
    knife,
They steal everything but his big
    fat wife.

My ropen's all out, my ends all
    down,
The doffer's in my alley and I can't
    get around.

The section hand's sweepers standing
    at the door,
Ordering the sweepers to sweep up
    the floor.

Every night when I go home,
A piece of cornbread and an old
    jaw bone.

Aint it enough to break your heart,
Hafta work all day and at night it's
    dark.

No More Shall I Work in the Factory

Now here's a pretty little gal with the right idea in her head. She wants to get the devil out of them factories. She wants to marry a country boy before the year is 'round. She wants to get loose from the noise and the wheels. She's done layed her time out down there in the factory. She don't want to lay there all her life. She's sick and tired of it, she wants a sweetheart to pack her away to the country – and take her into a little house, and cover her in the early fall with a good warm blanket and a couple or three quilts, not to mention a couple of good strong arms. Sure she wants it. She's dam sure got it a coming to her. She has earned it a hundred times. She has worked for a long time and now she wants to be married and loved and to have a home with a big tribe of boys and girls that all look exactly like ma and pa...out yonder somewhere in the hills and down under the trees away from the old black smoke of that big old factory.

Collected, adapted, and arranged by John A. Lomax and Alan Lomax. © 1934 (renewed) by Ludlow Music, Inc., New York, NY. Used by permission.

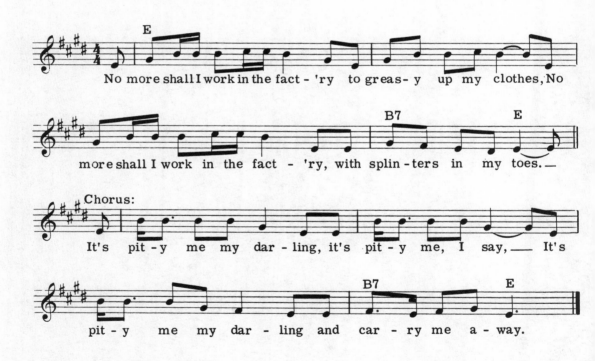

No more shall I work in the factory
To greasy up my clothes,
No more shall I work in the factory
With splinters in my toes.

Chorus:
It's a pity me, my darling,
It's a pity me, I say,
It's a pity me, my darling,
And carry me away.
(Repeat after each verse)

No more shall I hear the bosses say,
"Boys, you'd better daulf,"
No more shall I hear those bosses
say,
"Spinners, you had better clean off."

No more shall I hear the drummer
wheels
A-rolling over my head;
When factory girls are hard at work,
I'll be in my bed.

No more shall I hear the whistle
blow
To call me up so soon:
No more shall I hear the whistle
blow
To call me from my home.

No more shall I see the super come,
All dressed up so fine:
For I know I'll marry a country boy
Before the year is round.

No more shall I wear the old black
dress,
Greasy all around;
No more shall I wear the old black
bonnet,
With holes all in the crown.

Winnsboro Cotton Mill Blues

Lots of kinds of blues is worse than the Alcoholic Blues, and one of them is the Greed Hog Blues. I don't guess they got a song by that name, but there's one that comes out of a cotton mill down south -- tired and all fagged out, no money for a good time on, no money to buy decent clothes on, even when you hit the heavy, heavy, in a clothing mill.

Old man Sar-gent, sit-ting at the desk, the damn'd old fool won't give us no rest.__ He'd take the nick-els off a dead man's eyes to buy a Co-ca-Co-la and a Po-mo pie.__

Chorus:

I got the blues, I got the blues, I got the Winns-b'ro cot-ton mill blues.__ Lord-y, Lord-y, spool-in's hard: You know and I know, I don't have to tell, you work for Tom Wat-son, got to work like hell,_ I got the blues, I got the

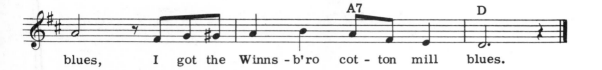

blues, I got the Winns-b'ro cot-ton mill blues.

Old man Sargent sitting at the desk,
The damned old fool won't give us no
  rest.
He'd take the nickels off a dead
    man's eyes,
To buy a Coco=cola and a Pomo Pie.

Chorus:
I've got the blues,
I've got the blues,
I've got the Winnsboro Cotton Mill
  blues.
Lordy, lordy, spoolin's hard.
You know and I know, I don't have
  to tell:
Work for Tom Watson, got to
  work like hell.

I've got the blues,
I've got the blues,
I've got the Winnsboro Cotton Mill
  blues.
(Repeat after each verse)

When I die, don't bury me at all,
Just hang me up on the spoolroom
    wall.
Place a knotter in my hand,
So I can spool in the Promised Land.

When I die, don't bury me deep,
Bury me down on 600 Street.
Place a bobbin in each hand,
So I can dolph in the Promised Land.

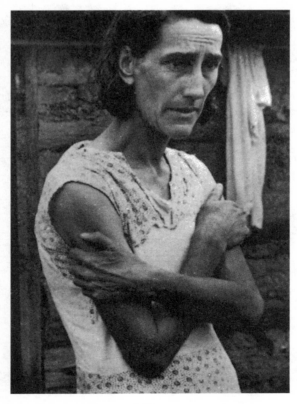

129

Weave Room Blues

By Dorsey Dixon. © Dorsey Dixon. From the singing
of the Dixon Brothers on Bluebird Record, B-6441-B.
(From the collection of Alan Lomax)

Work-ing in a weave room, fight-ing for my life,

Trying to make a liv-ing for my kid-dies and my wife,

Some are need-ing cloth-ing, and some are need-ing shoes, But

I'm get-ting noth-ing but them weave_room blues. I've got the

blues,____ I've got the blues,____ I've got them aw - ful ___

weave_room blues.____ I've got the blues, _____ the

(yodel)

weave _____ room _ blues. _____

Working in a weave room, fighting
    for my life,
Trying to make a living for my
    kiddies and my wife,
Some are needing clothing and some
    are needing shoes,
But I'm getting nothing but them
    weave room blues.

Chorus:
I've got the blues, I've got the
    blues,
I've got them awful weave room
    blues.
I've got the blues, the weave room
    blues.
(Repeat after each verse)

When your loom's a-slamming,
    shackles bouncing on the floor,
And when you flag a fixer, you can
    see that he is sore.
I'm trying to make a living but I'm
    thinking I will lose,
For I'm going crazy with them
    weave room blues.

The harness eyes are breaking with
    the double coming through,
The Devil's in your alley and he's
    coming after you.
Our hearts are aching, let us take a
    little booze,
For we're going crazy with them
    weave room blues.

Slam, break out, makeouts by the
    score.
Cloth all rolled back and piled up on
    the floor.
The bats are running into strings,
    they are hanging to your shoes,
I'm simply dying with them weave
    room blues.

Weaver's Life

Something about this song that gets me. You could take this and sing it easy as falling off a log. This comes from way down south in the mills, and shows you that the Weavers are looking forward to better times, somewhere, some day. Everybody seems to be a looking for a better shore. You can best ride to that better shore on a Union Bus.

By Dorsey Dixon. © Dorsey Dixon. Recorded by the Dixon Brothers on Bluebird 7802-A. Tune of "Life Is Like A Mountain Railway." (From the collection of Alan Lomax)

Weav-er's life is like an eng-ine, com-ing round the moun-tain steep; We've had our ups and downs a-plen-ty and at night we can-not sleep; Ver-y of-ten flag your fix-er, when his head is bend-ing low, You may

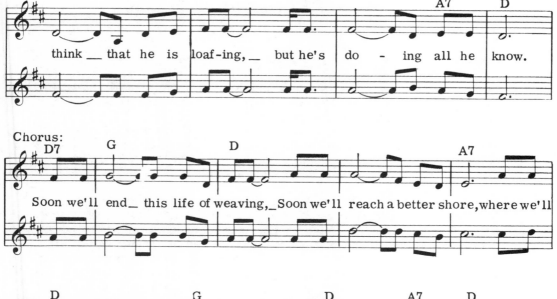

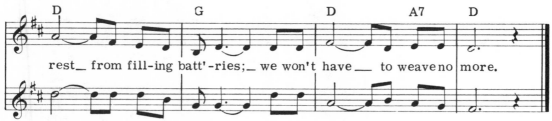

Weaver's life is like an engine
Coming around the mountain steep;
We've had our ups and down a
    plenty
And at night we cannot sleep.
Very often flag your fixer
When his head is bending low
You may think that he is loafing
But he's doing all he knows.

    Chorus:
Soon we'll end this life of weaving
Soon we'll reach a better shore,
Where we'll rest from filling
    batteries
We won't have to weave no more.
(Repeat after each verse)

Very often meet a partner
Who would like to learn to weave,
And we feel it is our duty
We are bound that to believe,
Show him all those break outs
For he'll have them by the score
When the conversation's over
He won't want to weave no more.

Very often have a break out
That will surely make you sweat,
Maybe you're feeling blue and
    drowsy,
They will almost make you quit.
Very often have a headache
When our looms are running bad
When we frown and snap the lever
You can bet your life we're mad.

Silicosis Is Killin' Me

You get the silicosis a working in hard rock tunnels.

Dust is deadly poison. One woman said, "As sure as there's a God in Heaven, the men that killed our boys will suffer eternal torments. It broke my heart to see the boys dying like flies. I can't count the hundreds that passed on. They came into the dining hall covered with dust. We didn't know the dust was worse than poison. The company is glad to bring us up from the south so cheap. But now they're through with us, they cast us off, and we are lower than animals..."

She was Mrs. Raines, the cook in the Gauley Bridge Construction Camp. It killed an average of a man a week on rock drilling jobs in New York City. Sixteen Union men died in 4 months from it. No masks to keep it out of your lungs. They'd set off the dynamite and then make you go right in; the law says you got to wait thirty minutes for the dust to settle. To hell with the law, the big shots figured, and they hired spies to stand in the mouth of the tunnel and holler when a inspector was a coming, so's they could hide their illegal tools, the ones that makes so much dust.

Wanted: More and bigger and better Cuss Words to tell what I think of a man that would do a thing like this just to squeeze a extry dollar out of a working man's dead body.

Tune: "Insurance Man Blues," or any 3-line blues. Recorded by Pinewood Tom on Perfect Record 6-05-51 (18733). (From the collection of Alan Lomax)

I said, "Silicosis, you made a
  mighty bad break of me. "
"Oh, Silicosis, you made a mighty
  bad break of me.
You robbed me of my youth and
  health.
All you brought poor me was
  misery. "

Now, silicosis, you a dirty robber
  and a thief,
Robbed me of my right to live,
And all you brought to me was grief.

I was there diggin' that tunnel for
  six bits a day,
Didn' know I was diggin' my own
  grave.
Silicosis eatin' my lungs away.

I says, "Mama, mama, mama, cool
  my fevered head. "
I says, "Mama, mama, cool my
  fevered head,
I'm gonna leave my Jesus, God
  knows I'll soon be dead. "

Six bits I got for diggin', diggin' that
  tunnel hole,
Take me away from my baby,
It sho' done wrecked my soul.

Now tell all my buddies, tell all my
  friends you see,
I'm going away up yonder.
Please don't weep for me.

It's Hard Times in These Mines

In New York you go down in the hole to build a subway. In Arkansas you go down in the hole to get lead. In Oklahoma you go down in the hole to get zinc. Missouri you go down to get coal. Kansas you go down to get zunk. Texas you go down in your cellar to get out of the dust. Arizona you go down to get copper. California to get away from the coppers. If you ever get anything from the rich guys you got to go in the hole.

Tune: "Cryderville Jail." Collected by Alan Lomax and Mary Elizabeth Barnicle from the singing of Finley Donaldson, Bell County, Kentucky.

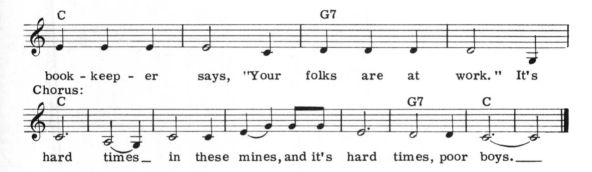

You go to tne office and you go in a
  flirt,
The bookkeeper says, "Your folks
  are at work. "

Chorus:
It's hard times in these mines,
And it's hard times, poor boys.
(Repeat after each verse)

The women they go to the office and
  grin,
The bookkeeper says, "Here you
  come again. "

O' the bread that we eat is short
  number 2,
A dollar a sack is the best we can
  do.

Well, you go to the mines with a
  frown on your face,
You're a rarin' an' cussin' 'cause
  you got no place.

Well this set of miners is the
  meanest of all,
They'll bum yer tobaccer and steal
  yer oil.

There's Wes McBridge, the biggest
  blow of all,
He swears you'll get rich if you half
  work at all.

The Hard Working Miner

"You go to work in the morning and you leave your wife and children, but the mines you go into are not the safe and sanitary mines you used to go into. You go into the mines to slave for one dollar or eighty cents a day. You eat pea beans and corn beans. You go into bed in a bag of rags but the hell bound Criminal Syndicalist law forbids you to speak. Miners today are worse off than slaves during slave times." Finaly (Red Ore) Donaldson, 1932.

Come on, boy, go down in the hole. Maybe th' last time, I don't know. Four or five gets their leg hung in a log chain, or some kind of a pulley or swivel, the hoist slips, and the loose coal falls...and lots of 'em go down that don't come out so good...and they got a big ambulance sets over on yonder hill to carry 'em off in, so's nobody won't know about what happened. They got ways of a keepin' it a secret. Th' government don't never hear about it. They think it's honey and pie down there in th' goddam mines, but it's hell, pure dee hell's all it is.

Collected, adapted, and arranged by John A. Lomax and Alan Lomax. © 1934 (renewed) by Ludlow Music, Inc., New York, NY. Used by permission.

To the hard work-ing min-er the dan-ger is great,_ So man-y while min-ing have met their sad fate, While do-ing_ their du-ty as all min-ers do,_ Shut out from the day-light and their dar-ling ones too.

To the hard working miner the
    danger is great,
So many while mining have met
    their sad fate,
While doing their duty as all miners
    do,
Shut out from the daylight and their
    darling ones, too.

Chorus:
He's only a miner killed down in
    the ground,
He's only a miner and one more
    is gone.
He's killed by an accident, there's
    no one can tell,
His mining's all over, poor miner
    farewell.

He leaves his dear wife and darling
    ones, too,
To earn them a living as all miners
    do,
But while he is working for them that
    he loves,
The boulder that struck him
    comes down from above

With our heart full of sorrow, we
    bid him farewell.
How soon we may follow, there's no
    one can tell.
God pity poor miner, protect him
    from harm,
Shield him from danger with Thy all
    tried arm.

Chorus:
He's only a miner killed down in
    the ground,
He's only a miner and one more
    is gone.
There's no one that seen him,
    there's no one can say,
But now this poor miner must
    sleep in the clay.

Roll On Buddy

..........this song was so good I just had to run me off a batch of verses.
Didn't aim to bootleg them, just buried them down here in the holler
so's you'd be sure to run onto them...

Sung by a section hand on the L & N Railroad when it first cut
through the mountains in Kentucky. Additional words by Woody
Guthrie. © 1967 (renewed) by Woody Guthrie Publications, Inc.
All rights reserved. Used by permission.

I been a working ten years on the
L & N Road
I can't make enough for to pay my
board.
O, roll on Buddy, and make up your
time,
I'm so weak and hungry that I can't
make mine.

O, roll on, Buddy, don't you roll
so slow,
I'm so weak and hungry, I can't roll
no mo'.
I went to the boss and I asked for my
time,
What do you reckon he said? I owed
him a dime.

I looked at the sun and the sun looked
low,
I looked at my woman and she said,
"Don't go. "
I looked at the sun and the sun looked
high,
I looked at my woman and I said
good-bye.

Some of these days and that before
long
You're gonna call my name and I'll
be gone.
Yes, some of these days, you're
gonna look for me,
And I'll be gone to Tenne-seeeee.

Some of these days, and that before
long,
You gonna holler "frog" and I aint
gonna jump.
About 2:30, this summer or fall,
You gonna call my name, boss, and
I won't come.

VII - HELL BUSTS LOOSE IN KENTUCKY

Aunt Molly was born in the mountains around Harlan, Kentucky. Some Cherokee and English blood in her veins. She grew up to be the herb doctor, mid wife, and best ballad singer in the whole country.

In 1929 the coal strike hit the mountains. Men worked all of the time but couldn't make enough money to feed their kids and raise a family. Couldn't pay for a doctor when a baby was born. Aunt Molly took the place of several doctors. She done the best she knew how, and helped to bring over a hundred little babies into the world.

When she saw these little babies starving to death like flies all around her, Aunt Molly got interested in good wages for their dads. She got up in front of the miners, sung them songs, made them speeches, yelled at them to lay down their tools and wait till the boss raised the pay. She tells of the meetings they had. How the winchester rifle bullets use to kick the gravel up in your face while you was out making a talk about the rich coal operators and the poor hungry miners. In a year Aunt Molly told more truth than the politicians could bear to hear, so it got too hot for her down in Kentucky.

She lives in New York City now.* Over on the east side. In the slums and tenements. Where filth and starvation and disease is just as bad, only thicker, than anywhere in Kentucky. She's still one of the nation's best ballad singers and can say for herself, "I can sing all day and all night every day for a month, and never sing the same song twicet." (All ballad singers can.)

I know Molly well. She's strong and she's good, and she aint afraid of the police. She says what she thinks when she thinks it. The big guys call her a red. Well, Molly, it looks like if you always say just exactly what you think is right, they'll jump up and say you're a red.

Some folks just aint quite got the nerve to say what they think is right. But some day they'll wish they had. You aint a scared of nobody, Molly. I know it. I've been around you enough to know that. And you can't stay around Molly for even a few minutes, but what she'll speak out something that is so good, so true, and so honest, that it'll stick in your head as long as you live.

This section of our book is turned over to Aunt Molly. In most cases, her own words are ten times better than any I could put there. In some cases, I've added a word or two. I figure it a pretty big honor to introduce you now to one of America's best native ballad singers, the one and only, Aunt Molly Jackson...

* In 1941, Aunt Molly Jackson was living in NYC.

140

Lonesome Jailhouse Blues

"It originated from a bunch of 'em a-gettin' mad at me because that I participated in the strike, and they framed me and had me put in jail. This was in Clay County, three miles above Manchester, up on Horse Creek. This happened in '31. I picked the melody, and then composed the words to fit the melody." -- Aunt Molly Jackson.

Listen friends and comrades,
I have some very sad news,
Your Aunt Molly's locked up in
    prison
With the lonesome Jail house blues.

You may find someone will tell you
The jail house blues aint bad.
They're the worst kind of blues
Your Aunt Molly ever had.

I joined the miner's union,
That made them mad at me,
Now I am locked up in prison,
Just as lonesome as I can be.

I am locked up in prison
Walking on the concrete floor,
When I leave here this time,
I don't want to be here no more.

Because I joined the union
They framed up a lot of lies on me,
They had me put in prison,
I am just as lonesome as I can be.

I am locked up in prison,
Just as lonesome as I can be,
I want you to write me a letter
To the dear old I. L. D.

Tell them I am in prison,
Then they will know what to do,
The bosses had me put in jail,
For joining the N. M. U.

This N. M. U. means union,
Many thousand strong,
And if you will come and join us,
We will teach you right from
    wrong.

I Am A Union Woman

"When I was organizing the miners around Bell and Harlan Counties in 19 and 31, I sang this song. I used it in my organizational work; I always sung this before giving my speech. In those days it was 'Join the NMU.' But later on, John L. Lewis started a real democratic organization, so I changed it to 'Join the CIO.'"--Aunt Molly Jackson.

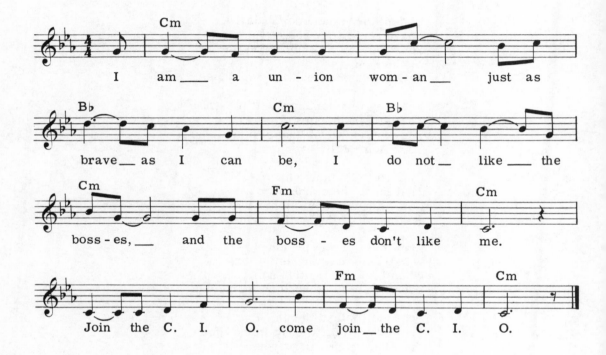

I am a union woman,
Just as brave as I can be,
I do not like the bosses
And the bosses don't like me.

Refrain:
Join the CIO
Come join the CIO.

I was raised in old Kentucky,
In Kentucky borned and bred,
And when I joined the union,
They called me a Rooshian Red.

This is the worst time on earth
That I have ever saw,
To get killed out by gun-thugs,
And framed up by the law.

When my husband asked the boss for
        a job,
This is the words he said:-
"Bill Jackson, I can't work you, sir,
Your wife's a Rooshian Red."

If you want to join a union,
As strong as one can be,
Join the dear old CIO,
And come along with me.

We are many thousand strong
And I am glad to say,
We are getting stronger
And stronger every day.

If you want to get your freedom,
Also your liberty,
Join the dear old CIO,
Also the ILD.

The bosses ride big fine horses,
While we walk in the mud,
Their banner is the dollar sign,
And ours is striped with blood.

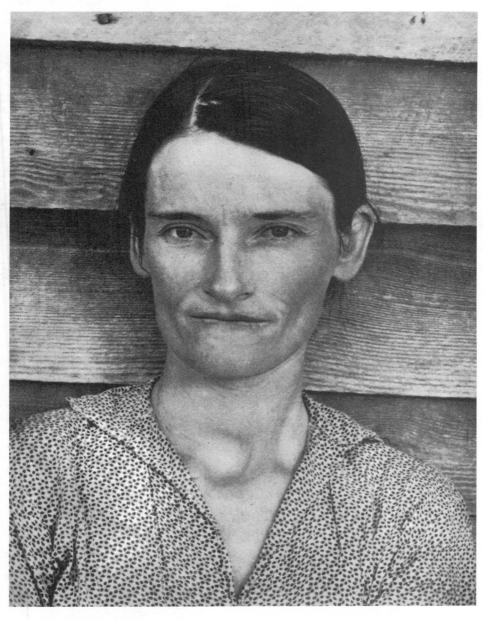

Kentucky Miner's Wife's Hungry, Ragged Blues

"I composed this song one morning a few months after that the miners wages had been cut down so low that the children was a starving like flies, and dying like flies. We had to put up a soup kitchen to put everything that we had out of the houses into the soup kitchen and make soup to try to save their lives. Some of them hadn't had anything to eat for two days. - This song came out of my head - not from the point of a pen."

- Aunt Molly Jackson

Best sung unaccompanied

I'm sad and I'm wea-ry,— I got those hun-gry, rag-ged blues. I'm

sad and I'm wea-ry, ___ I got those hun-gry, rag-ged blues. Not a

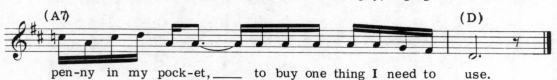

pen-ny in my pock-et, ___ to buy one thing I need to use.

I'm sad and I'm weary, I got those
    hungry, ragged blues.
I'm sad and I'm weary, I got those
    hungry, ragged blues.
Not a penny in my pocket to buy one
    thing I need to use.

I woke up this morning with the
    worst blues I ever had in my
    life.
I woke up this morning with the
    worst blues I ever had in my
    life.
Not a bite to cook for breakfast, a
    poor coal miner's wife.

When my husband works in the coal
    mine he loads a car most every
    trip
When my husband works in the coal
    mine he loads a car most every
    trip
Then he goes to the office that eve-
    ning and gits denied of scrip.

Just because it took all he made
    that day to pay his mine ex-
    pense.
Just because it took all he made
    that day to pay his mine ex-
    pense.
A man that'll work for Coal, Light
    and Carbide aint got a lick of
    sense.

All the women in this coal camp are
    a-sitting with bowed down heads.
All the women in this coal camp are
    a-sitting with bowed down heads.
Ragged and barefooted and their
    children a-crying for bread.

This mining town I live in is a sad
    and dreary place.
This mining town I live in is a sad
    and dreary place.
Where pity and starvation are pic-
    tured on every face.

O don't go under that mountain with
    the slate a-hanging over your
    head.
O don't do under that mountain with
    the slate a-hanging over your
    head.
And work for just Coal, Light and
    Carbide and your children a-
    crying for bread.

Some coal operator might tell you
    the hungry blues are not bad
Some coal operator might tell you
    the hungry blues are not bad
They're the worst kind of blues this
    old woman ever had.

O listen, friends and comrades,
    please take a friend's advice.
Listen, friends and comrades,
    please take a friends advice.
Don't load no more, don't put out
    no more till you git a living
    price.

I Love Coal Miners, I Do

"I composed this song in 1931, two weeks after I started on my tour, collectin' finance for the miners children in Kentucky, when I begin to feel blue and lonesome and homesick for home." -- Aunt Molly Jackson.

Best sung unaccompanied

I'm nine hun - dred miles a - way from home, I'm nine hun - dred miles a - way from home, I'm nine hun - dred miles a - way from my home, I love coal min - ers, I do.

Chorus:

I love coal min - ers, I do. I love coal min - ers, I do. I've lived a - mong them all their lives, With their chil - dren and their wives, I dear - ly love a coal min - ing man.

I'm 900 miles away from home,
I'm 900 miles away from home,
I'm nine hundred miles away from
    my home,
I love coal miners, I do.

    I love coal miners, I do,
    I love coal miners, I do,
    I've lived among them all their
        lives,
    With their children and their
        wives,
    I dearly love a coal mining man.

My father was a coal mining man,
My father was a coal mining man,
Then it oughta be plain for you to
    understand
Just why I love a coal mining man.

    I love coal miners, I do,
    I love coal miners, I do,
    I've lived among them all their
        lives,
    With their children and their
        wives,
    And I'll love 'em 'til the day I die.

I have two brothers dead and gone,
I have two brothers dead and gone,
One was killed by the slate a-fallin'
    down,
I love coal miners, I do.

    I love coal miners, I do,
    I love coal miners, I do,
    I've lived among them all their
        lives,
    With their children and their
        wives,
    And I'll love them till the sea
        runs dry.

Fare Ye Well Old Ely Branch

"Old Hughes, the coal operator up at Ely Branch, been expecting a strike for two weeks back pay, so he didn't order nothing for the commissary. There was nothing left but dried beef and canned tomatoes.

"Now, my husband liked a lot to eat, and since you can't buy food nowhere else excepting at the commissary, he decided we got to leave. He was a machinist and was missed more than any other one of the men. Also, we had just moved into our first new house. It was all nice and wall-papered up, and golly, I felt sorry to leave.

"So I composed this poem and went down and dropped it by the spring where all the woman had to go get water, so that it'd get around without no one knowing who wrote it.

"But Mrs. Burrow, she saw me, and said, 'What's that you dropping down? - A love letter?'

"So I showed it to her and told her, 'Don't you say nothing about who wrote it!'

"But Jack Welch's wife, she knew my handwriting 'cause I written some letters for her and pretty soon up to my house come John Yager, the bookkeeper down at the store. He says, 'I'll give you five dollars if you make up a tune to that.'

So I sat right down and sang out a tune right off. Later, after we moved to B———, old Hughes met me and said, 'You didn't do me no harm by that song. I printed it up and made fifty dollars selling copies at twenty cents apiece to the men.'" -- Aunt Molly Jackson.

Fare ye well, old Ely Branch,
Fare ye well, I say,
I'm tired of living on dried beef and
  termaters
And I'm a-goin away.

When we had a strike in Ely this
  spring
Those words old Hughes did say,
"Come along boys, go back to work,
We'll give you the two weeks pay."

When they put on their mining
  clothes,
Hard work again they tried,
And when old pay-day rolled around,
They found ole Hughes had lied.

When Hughes thinks his mines was
  going to stop,
A sight to see him frown,
They's gas enough in old Hughes
To blow these mountains down.

Oh take your children out of Ely
  Branch
Before they cry for bread,
For when old Hughes debts is
  payed,
He won't be worth a thread.

Hughes claims he owns more
  mines than these,
He says he's got money to lend,
And when old pay-day rolls around
He can't pay off his men.

I'd rather be in Pineville Jail,
With my back all covered in lice,
Than to be here in old Hughes coal
  mines
Digging coal at Hughes price.

Fare ye well old Ely Branch
Fare ye well, I say.
I'm tired of living on dried beef and
  termaters,
And I'm a-going away.

Kentucky Miners' Dreadful Fate

By Aunt Molly Jackson. © 1967 (renewed) by Stormking Music, Inc. All rights reserved. Used by permission.

Dear Comrades, listen to my song, A story I'll relate, About the old Kentucky hills, And the miners' dreadful fate.

Dear Comrades, listen to my song,
A story I'll relate
About the old Kentucky hills,
And the miners' dreadful fate.

The coal operators have robbed the
      miners,
Of their food and daily bread,
And then they send their gun thugs
      'round
To shoot and kill us dead.

The gangsters rove from town to
      town,
They went from place to place,
Until they came on comrade Tom
And also comrade Grace.

They drove them onto a mountain
      top,
"Get out of this car," they said.
"We know you both are union men,
And we aim to kill you dead."

At first they beat up comrade Tom,
Bruised up his head and face,
And left him on the spot to die,
Then turned on comrade Grace.

And when they turned on comrade
      Grace,
"Your time is next," they said.
They also beat this comrade up,
And left him there for dead.

Both comrade Tom and comrade
      Grace
Was placed in a lousy jail.
And the gangsters told them to their
      face
They could not have no bail.

So then the union miners said,
"Our comrades must go free."
So they sat down and wrote a
      letter
To the dear old I. L. D.

The I. L. D. sets prisoners free
And takes them out of jail.
Now they are out of the gun thugs
      hands
For they don't need no bail.

150

Last August at the W. I. R.
  kitchen
The gun thugs drove up to the door
They shot and killed our comrade
  Baldwin,
And also comrade Moore.

So when the miners' children
  starved
And deprived of feeds and bread
The operators send their gun thugs
  'round
To fill them full of lead.

So, comrades, you have heard my
  song,
And every word is true.
Why don't you miners come along
And join the N. M. U. ?

Join the dear old ILD
As well as the NMU
And we'll whoop and yell and fight
  like hell
Just what we ought to do.

The East Ohio Miners' Strike

By Aunt Molly Jackson. © 1967 (renewed) by Stormking Music,
Inc. All rights reserved. Used by permission.

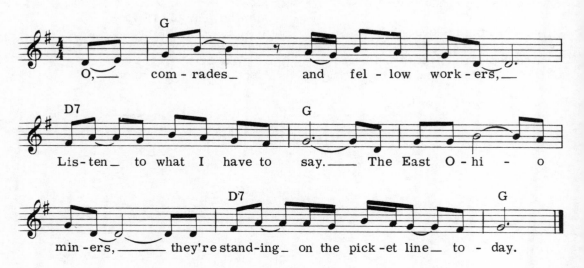

O,___ com - rades___ and fel - low work - ers,___
Lis - ten_ to what I have to say.___ The East O - hi - o
min - ers,_____ they're stand - ing_ on the pick - et line_ to - day.

O, comrades and fellow workers,
Listen to what I have to say.
The East Ohio miners,
They're standin' on the picket line
    today.

They're fighting starvation wage
    cuts,
Listen to what the operators done:
They cut the poor miner's wages
    down
To twenty-three cents a ton.

Then the miners told them
Just what they aimed to do.
We'll fight starvation wage cuts
By joining the N. M. U.

The N. M. U. is a miner's union,
They're fighting hand in hand,
Against starvation wage cuts,
Bread and freedom is our demand.

O these operators wives,
They wear their gold diamond rings.
The miners' wives and children,
They wear just any old thing.
Yes, we wear just any old thing.

While the miners are striking,
They're struggling hand in hand.
It is our duty, fellow workers,
To help them all we can.

Their children are all hungry,
And O, how sad I feel,
Will you help us, fellow workers,
And view our loud appeal?

The Coal Creek Explosion

Come my friends__ and near re - la - tions, And I'll tell__ you if I can, What a sad__ and great oc - cur - rence That has hap - pened in__ our land.

Come my friends and near relations
And I'll tell you if I can
What a sad and great occurrence
That has happened in our land.

It was on one Monday morning,
Of the eighteenth day of May,
Yes, three hundred coal miners round us
They left their homes and marched away.

They went to labor for their families
And for those they dearly love.
All at once a sad occurrence
...... chanced to meet them ......

Up and down that lonesome valley
Cries was heard from side to side.
Wives they cried to see their husbands,
And some of them done crossed the tide.

Some was killed without a moment's warning.
Some did last an hour or two.
Some said they would soon be in heaven
O, just think if that could be true.

Note: When I got word that the trapped miners had scribbled notes of love and farewell to their wifes, children, and fellow Union Members, I took the liberty of adding the eight lines to this song, I hope Aunt Molly nor Jim don't care. I know they won't. (W.G.)

The miners that was trapped there
Was doomed to meet their Fate
They wrote their last love letters
Upon the coal mine slate.
Goodbye to Wife and Children
To the Union Members All
We write God Save Our Union
Upon this coal mine wall.

The Story of Sara Ogan

Sara Ogan is the half sister to Aunt Molly Jackson. She's a housewife, and more than a housewife. A mother and more than a mother. She's worked and slaved and fought to save the children of her own home, and to keep her own house, and she was so full of the Union Spirit that she found time to get out in the wind and rain and the hail of bullets from the deputies guns, and make up her own songs and sing them to give nerve and backbone to the starving men that slaved in the coal mines.

Somehow, something has always protected Sara. In all of her adventures, rifle balls have bounced off of her like golf balls off of a mountain. You better not start a taking the groceries away from Sara's children. You better not try to take the roof from over their heads. You better not even try to cheat her friends, 'cause Sara's heart is big enough to include all of the folks she knows. Reminds me of this old song, ''My waist it may be slender, My fingers they are small, but I've got a heart that's big enough, love, to face that rifle ball, Lord, to face that rifle ball.''

Sara's father is dead. Sara's husband is dead. Her little baby boy is dead. The dust from the coal mines gave them that deadly disease called, ''Silicosis'' -- gets your lungs.

Sara knows what's wrong with this old world. She knows how it needs a fixing. She has paid the price, and has seen the show, and it was terrible, and awful!!!! But Sara Ogan knows.

Sara Ogan's homemade songs and speeches, made up from actual experience, are deadlier and stronger than rifle bullets, and have cut a wider swath than a machine gun could. She sings about the Union...the One Big Union that has got to come...when the farmers and the working folks all over everywhere get together, shake hands, and stand side by side, and back to back, a fighting hell out of the big rich guys that say they own all of the land, all of the hills, all of the crops, and all of the coal and iron and gold that's down under the ground.

They claim they own all of this stuff. Sara says they don't. Sara says it belongs equal and alike to all of us. I say Sara is right. It damn shore don't belong to no one special feller, nor no one special family, nor no few special families. It belongs equal and alike to all of us. Me, and you. Us.

We might be right and we might be wrong, but we got several fellers on our side that said that same thing. Abe Lincoln said it. And one more man said it...and they killed him for a saying it. His name was Jesus Christ.

Sara sings the songs of Jesus. She sings them better than a lot of folks do because she sings with the Union Spirit of her dead father, her dead husband, and her little baby boy that died just to rake more and more money into the pocketbooks of the big rich men -- the coal operators.

Sara, there aint a man a living that can give you as good a write up as you need...nor tell the love and the hate that is a beating in your heart. I done my best. I'm just a praying and a hoping that your songs will "mow them rich guys down" -- and I know they will.

Rich folks ain't afraid of bullets. They're more afraid of words. And more of "songs like Sara Ogan made up."

Let me introduce now the woman, Sara Ogan, and some of her songs....

I Am A Girl Of Constant Sorrow

Sara's a girl of constant sorrow. Well, my heart beats the same as yours, Sara. I been weary all of my life. When you write a song from the real old honest to goodness bottom of your heart, the words will be almost exactly the same as everybody you meet on the street.

In this song you'll hear a girl of constant sorrow a saying 'goodbye' to the place of her troubles. But she sings a song of parting, and tells of the sorrows she's a leaving.

But -- no matter where you go to, or where you turn, or which a way you travel, you'll see on every side people of every color, people of every size, description, and kind, and all you'll see is more 'Constant Sorrow.'

Sara Ogan has caught the complete spirit of all of the hard working people in this song, and we could say as Sara says, We are Folks of Constant Sorrow.

If all of the Sorrowful Folks would join hands and form a big Union -- for no other reason at all, just that we are Sorrowful, it would be the biggest and strongest Union on earth.

The big rich guys are miserable and nervous and half crazy with worry, and greed and fear, but they won't admit it. If they was to write a song out of the bottom of their own heart, it would be "I'm a Rich Man of Constant Sorrow."

Well, all I got to say is this old world's brimming full of girls of Constant Sorrow, Boys of Constant Sorrow, Mothers of Constant Sorrow, Dads of Constant Sorrow, and Neighbors, and Friends, and Relations of Constant Sorrow and Constant Empty Pocketbooks, so you go to the store and you can't buy a single solitary thing.

You just got to get bounced around a little bit before you really know what it's all about. You might be so scared that you ain't got out to stick your nose into a few things to see who's a causing all of this Hard Luck and Hard Times and Hard Get By, but don't worry, friend, you might be next.

Ain't but one goddam thing that makes trouble and sorrow in this country and that's somebody's greed. And the running of the country ought to be took out of the greedy man's hands. And then, dam my hide to hell, we'd have working folks and honest folks in there a running the works, and they wouldn't be no more hard times, and no more fights and wars to kill you off.

Sara's come through the mill. She knows. Ask her. Sing her song, and sing it loud and long like a railroad train.

Traditional tune with new words by Sarah Ogan
Gunning. © 1965 by Folk Legacy Records, Inc.

I am a girl of constant sorrow,
I've seen trouble all my days,
I bid farewell to old Kentucky,
The place where I was borned and
    raised.

Goodbye, my friends, I hate to
    leave you,
It grieves me so that we must part,
For I know we all are hungry,
Oh, it almost breaks my heart.

My mother, how I hated to leave
    her,
Mother dear, now is dead,
But I had to go and leave her
So my children could have bread.

Perhaps, dear friends, you are
    a-wondering,
What the miners eat and wear,
This question I will try to answer
For I'm sure that it is fair.

For breakfast we had bulldog gravy,
For supper we had beans and bread,
The miners don't have any dinner
And a tick of straw they call a bed.

Well, our clothes are always
    ragged,
And our feet are always bare,
And I know if there's a heaven
That we all are going there.

Well, we call this Hell on earth,
    friends,
I must tell you all goodbye,
Oh, I know you all are hungry.
Oh, my darling friends, don't cry.

157

I'm Thinking Tonight of an Old Southern Town

Didn't Jimmie Rodgers sing a song like that, too? I think so. But his sounds blank and empty and all vacant compared to this one that Sara Ogan sings from the graves of her loved ones that sacrificed their lives at the feet of the Rich Coal Operators.

Words by Sarah Ogan Gunning, adaptation of melody.
© 1965 by Folk Legacy Records, Inc.

I'm think- ing to-night of an old south-ern town, And the loved ones that I left be - hind.____ I know they are nak - ed and hun - gry, too, And it sure_ does wor - ry my mind.____ Oh poor lit - tle chil - dren, so hun - gry and cold, The rich might - y cap - i - ta - list, so big and so bold, They stole all our land and they stole all our coal; We get star - va -tion and they get the gold. I

know how it feels to be lone - ly, _____ And I know how it feels to be blue,__ And I know how it feels to be nak - ed,_____ And I sure_ been hun - gry too. _____

I'm thinking tonight of an old
  Southern town,
And the loved ones that I left behind.
I know they are naked and hungry
  too,
And it sure does worry my mind.

Oh, poor little children so hungry
  and cold,
The rich, mighty capitalists so big
  and so bold,
They stole all our land and they
  stole all our coal;
We get starvation while they get the
  gold.

I know how it feels to be lonely,
And I know how it is to be blue,
And I know how it is to be naked,
And I sure been hungry too.

I'm thinking of brother and sister,
From the loved ones whom I have to
  part;
I'm thinking of their little children
Who is so near to my heart.

I'm thinking of the heart-aches and
  starvation
That the capitalists have caused me
  and mine,
I'm thinking of brother and sister
And the loved ones that I left behind.

Now, if I had the rotten capitalists
Where the capitalists has got me,
What I wouldn't do to them bastards
Would be a shame to see.

Long, Long Ago

My grandfather was a rich farmer, and my family didn't need money, because the whole year around we didn't need to buy much, but just usually traded what we had for what we needed. Then when the coal operators came along and offered to buy our land, we thought we were getting a lot of money at the time.

Where is the land that our grand-fa-thers owned Long, long a-

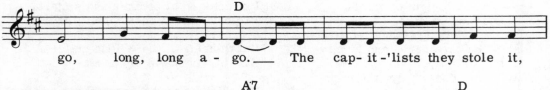

go, long, long a-go.___ The cap-it-'lists they stole it,

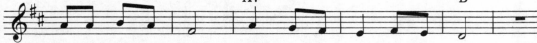

now we have no home, Long, long a-go, long a-go.

Where is the land that our grand-
 fathers owned,
Long, long ago, long long ago?
The cap'talists they stole it; now we
 have no homes,
Long, long ago, long, long ago.

Our Grandfathers was farmers, and
 owned all the land,
Long, long ago, long, long ago.
It was stole away by the capitalist
 band,
Long, long ago, long, long ago.

Now we are ragged, hungry and
 cold,
The operators made millions on our
 grandfathers coal.

The farmers in our country were
 doing very well,
Till they stole all our land, now
 the living is hell.

Ten dollars an acre, that's all that
 they payed,
Now they have gun thugs to drive us
 away.

We slave under the land that is really
 our own,
Diggin and loading and pushing the
 cars.

So it's left up to us, and now we've
 got the fight,
And take back part of our own
 birthright,
That they stole away, long, long
 ago.

Win It

Words by Sarah Ogan Gunning. Music: Traditional. © 1967 (re-newed) by Stormking Music, Inc. All rights reserved. Used by permission.

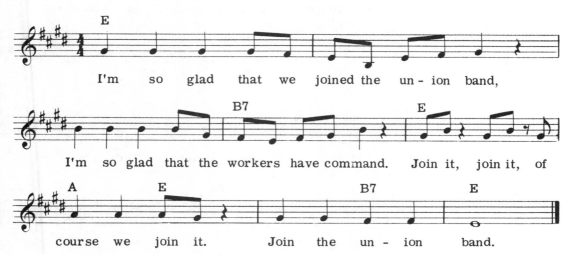

I'm so glad that we joined the un - ion band,

I'm so glad that the workers have command. Join it, join it, of

course we join it. Join the un - ion band.

I'm so glad that we joined the union
 band,
I'm so glad that the workers have
 command.
Join it, join it,
Of course we join it.
Join the union band.

March on, for the workers lead the
 way,
March on, and we win better pay.
Win it, win it,
Of course we win it.
We will win the day.

Some folks wonder why we workers
 fight.
Just because we know that we are
 right.
Wonder, wonder,
Of course they wonder
Wonder why we fight.

Some folks wonder why we scream
 and holler.
Just because we haven't got a
 dollar.
Wonder, wonder, of course they
 wonder.
Why we scream and holler.

Some folks wonder why we
 demonstrate
Just because starvation's at the
 gate.
Wonder, Wonder,
Of course they wonder.
Why we demonstrate.

Some folks wonder why we have a
 picket line
Just because we haven't got a dime.
Wonder, wonder,
Of course they wonder
Why we have a picket line.

I'm so glad that the workers have
 command.
I'm so glad that we win our
 demands.
Win it, win it,
Of course we win it.
We win our demands.

161

They Tell Us To Wait

"This was composed about a neighbor of mine, and her family, and it's a true story. She used to live down on the East Side. But she died last month in Kings County Hospital."

By Sarah Ogan Gunning. © 1967 (renewed) by Stormking Music, Inc. All rights reserved. Used by permission.

In this land of the brave and home of the free, So full of_ star - va - tion and mis - er - y, Four lit - tle chil - dren, and a grand-moth - er, sev - en - ty - eight, starv - ing to death,_and they tell them to wait.

Chorus: Wait, wait, wait, that's all we can hear,_ as we slow - ly starve to death, year af - ter year.

In this land of the brave and home
  of the free,
So full of starvation and misery,
Four little children, and a
  grandmother, seventy-eight,
Starving to death and they tell them
  to wait.

Chorus:
Wait, wait, wait, that's all we can
  hear
As we slowly starve to death year
  after year.
(Repeat after each verse)

No work for the father, because he's
  sick yet.
Two months ago they stopped their
  check.
Four little children, the old one
  eight,
Crying for bread and still they must
  wait.

One of the oldest families in the
  United States,
Starving to death and they tell them
  to wait.
The father a veteran - he went over
  the sea,
Fought for his country, for you and
  for me.
And what do they do - they show him
  the gate
And tell him plainly that he has to
  wait.

The loving old mother with hair so
  grey
Worked hard all her life and is
  starving today.
She tries to figure out, but she can't
  understand
Why she's starving to death in this
  plentiful land.

Wait, wait, wait, it rings in our
  ears.
As we sit naked and hungry, in
  misery and in tears.
Just wait, wait, wait till we're laid
  in our grave,
And bid farewell to this land of the
  brave.

The little children are starving,
  please listen to me
And fight for our right in this land
  of the free.
My blood is boiling and I'm mad as
  hell.
- Wait, wait, wait - like the tone of
  a bell.

We waited so long now, we have to
  fight
And show these big shots that we
  stand for our right
With these thoughts my friends, I
  bid you farewell.
Wait, wait, wait, like the tone of
  a bell.

- from another of Sara Ogan's songs.

"We'll chase the capitalists around
  the stump
And give them a kick at every
  jump.
We'll make them pay for the blood
  they've shed,
And for the way our babies have
  been fed.
The workers are a-movin', movin',
  movin',
The workers are a-movin', and I'm
  so glad.
The workers are a-movin', movin',
  movin',
The workers are a-movin' and I'm
  so glad. "

163

I Hate The Capitalist System

Sara ain't a "puttin' on" when she says what she hates. Sara don't get no pay for her singing. She just sings from what she's went through with. Just sings out of the trouble she's had. She knows what caused the trouble. Hard work and no money. Last night at a house full of ritzy people -- folks that don't work much, and folks that don't know what it is to go hungry, Sara said, "All I can sing about is what trouble I been through, me and my kids, and my husband..."

She sings that good old honest way. Thank God she never took no lessons. Folks that sing too much what teachers tell 'em to sing, seldom ever sing anything they've really went through their self.

I like it the hard way, and I like it the honest way. That's how Sara talks. That's how she lives. And she'd starve to death before she'd turn scab, snitch, or heel.

Sara loved her husband. He's dead from hard work in the mines. She loved her baby that died. She loves the 2 she's still got, and she hates the system that wrecked her family. Hates the set up that robbed her kids mouths. Hates the guns of war that aim at her sons and daughters. Hates all of these big Crooks and Greedy Rich Folks, reason is because she Loves what She Loves, and she'll fight to protect her Home.

This song was composed by Sara Ogan and every word is true.

Tune: "Sailor on the Deep Blue Sea." New words by Sara Ogan Gunning. © 1965 by Folk Legacy Records, Inc.

I hate the Cap't-list sys-tem, I'll tell you the rea-son why, They caused me so much suff-'ring, And my dear-est friends to die.

I hate the capitalist system,
I'll tell you the reason why,
They caused me so much suffering
And my dearest friends to die.

Oh yes, I guess you wonder
What they have done to me
Well, I am going to tell you --
My husband had T. B.

Brought on by hard work and low
     wages
And not enough to eat,
Going naked and hungry,
No shoes on his feet.

I guess you say he's lazy
And did not want to work;
But I must say you're crazy,
For work he did not shirk.

My husband was a coal-miner,
He worked and risked his life
To try to support three children,
Himself, his mother, and wife.

I had a blue-eyed baby,
The darling of my heart,
But from my little darling
Her mother had to part.

The rich and mighty capitalists,
They dress in jewels and silk;
But my darling, blue-eyed baby,
She starved to death for milk.

I had a darling mother,
For her I often cried,
But with these rotten conditions
My mother had to die.

"Well, what killed your mother?"
I hear some capitalist say,
'Twas the debt of hard work and
     starvation
My mother had to pay.

"Oh, what killed your mother?
Oh, tell us if you please. "
"Excuse me, it was pellagra
That starvation did breed. "

They call this a land of plenty,
To them I guess it's true;
But that's to the rich old
     capitalists,
Not workers like me and you.

"Oh, what can you do about it,
To these men of power and might?
I tell you Mr. Capitalist,
I'm going to fight, fight, fight.

Come All You Coal Miners

By Sarah Ogan Gunning. © 1967 (renewed) by Stormking Music,
Inc. All rights reserved. Used by permission.

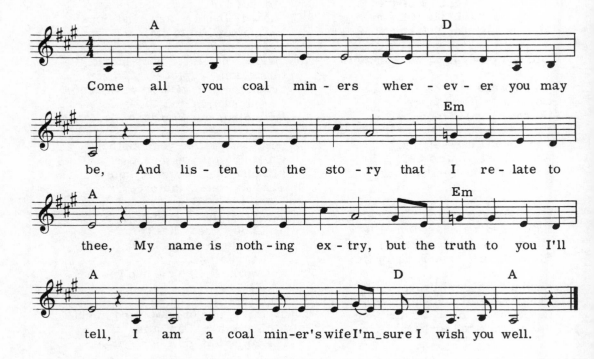

Come all you coal min-ers wher-ev-er you may be, And lis-ten to the sto-ry that I re-late to thee, My name is noth-ing ex-try, but the truth to you I'll tell, I am a coal min-er's wife I'm sure I wish you well.

Come all you coal miners wherever
   you may be
And listen to the story that I relate
   to thee,
My name is nothing extry, but the
   truth to you I'll tell
I am a coal miner's wife, I'm sure
   I wish you well.

I was born in old Kentucky, in a
   coal camp born and bred,
I know all about the pinto beans,
   bulldog gravy and cornbread,
And I know how the coal miners
   work and slave in the coal mines
   every day,
For a dollar in the company store,
   for that is all they pay.

Coal mining is the dangerousest
   work in our land today
With plenty of dirty slavin' work but
   very little pay.
Coal miner won't you wake up and
   open your eyes and see
What the dirty capitalist system is
   doing to you and me.

They take our very life blood, they
   take our children's lives,
Take fathers away from children
   and husbands away from wives,
Coal miners, won't you organize,
   wherever you may be
And make this a land of freedom
   for workers like you and me.

Dear miners, they will slave you
        till you can't work no more
And what will you get for your labor
        but a dollar in the company
        store?
A tumble-down shack to live in, snow
        and rain pouring through the top,
You'll have to pay the company rent,
        your paying never stop.

I am a coal miner's wife, I'm sure
        I wish you well
Let's sink this capitalist system in
        the darkest pits of Hell.

That Old Feeling

By Sara Ogan Gunning. © 1965 by Folk Legacy Records, Inc.

I went to bed last night, I had that old feel- ing, My
sup - per was so light I had that old feel - ing.

I went to bed last night,
I had that old feeling
My supper was so light
I had that old feeling
I got up this morning
With that old feeling,
I was so hungry
I was rocking and reeling.
The workers' children are crying
From that old feeling
Some of them are dying
From that old feeling;

The capitalists is to blame
For this old feeling,
I tell you it's a shame
About that old feeling;
We workers see the light
About that old feeling;
And we are going to fight
That old feeling;
The capitalists, they are fat,
They don't have that old feeling;
The workers' stomachs are flat,
We have that old feeling;
Mr. Capitalist, we are through,
With that old feeling.

Come On Friends and Let's Go Down

Sara told me that she sung this song to the folks around town and they all got up and walked with her down to the railroad tracks that run down to the mine.

The hired thugs and deputies and scabs come down the tracks after a little bit, and when they heard the workers a singing this song, the thugs, duputies, guards, and the whole dam litter turned tail and run like a striped ass zebra.

By Sara Ogan Gunning. © 1965 by Folk Legacy Records, Inc.

Come on friends and let's go down, Let's go down, Let's go down, Come on friends and let's go down, Down on the pick-et line. As I went down on the pick-et line, To keep them scabs out of the mine, Who's a goin' to win the strike, Come on and we'll show you the way.

Verse:
Went out one morn-ing be-fore day-light, And I was sure we'd

have a fight, But the cap - it - 'list scur - vy __ had

run a - way, __ But we __ went back the ver -y next day.

Chorus:
Come on you friends and let's go
    down,
Let's go down, let's go down,
Come on you friends and let's go
    down,
Down on the picket line.

As I went down on the picket line,
To keep them scabs out of the
    mine,
Who's a going to win the strike,
Come on and we'll show you the
    way.
(Repeat after each verse)

Went out one morning before day-
    light,
And I was sure we'd have a fight,
But the capitalist scurvy had run
    away
But we went back the very next day.

We all went out on the railroad track
To meet them scabs and turn them
    back,
We win that strike I'm glad to say
Come on, and we'll show you the
    way.

169

The Murder of Harry Simms

"Harry Simms was a young Jewish organizer who was murdered on Brush Creek, Knot County. He was walking along the railroad track with another fellow - they were going down to meet some writers who came to Bell County to study the conditions of the miners - when the gun thugs shot him. They took him and the other fellow back to town. They put the other fellow in jail. They left Harry sitting on a rock in front of the town hospital with a bullet in his stomach. He sat there on that rock an hour or more with his hands on his stomach bleeding to death. He was sitting there because the hospital wouldn't take him in till somebody guaranteed to pay his bill. After a while a man said he would pay the bill so they took Harry in. But it was too late. This song was composed right after that in 1932 by me and my brother Jim Garland." -- Aunt Molly Jackson.

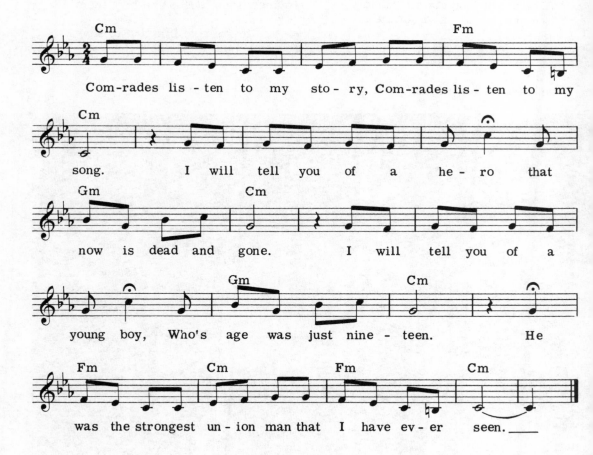

Com-rades lis-ten to my sto-ry, Com-rades lis-ten to my song. I will tell you of a he-ro that now is dead and gone. I will tell you of a young boy, Who's age was just nine-teen. He was the strongest un-ion man that I have ev-er seen.

Comrades, listen to my story,
Comrades, listen to my song.
I'll tell you of a hero
That now -- is dead and gone.
I'll tell you of a young boy,
Who's age was just nineteen
He was the strongest Union Man
That I have ever seen.

Harry Simms was a pal of mine,
We labored side by side,
Expecting to be shot on sight,
Or taken for a ride.
By the dirty capitalist gun thugs
That roam from town to town,
To shoot and kill our Comrades,
Wherever they may be found.

Harry Simms and I were parted
At five o'clock that day,
Be careful, My dear Comrade,
To Harry I did say.
I must do my duty,
Was his reply to me.
if I get killed by gun thugs,
Don't grieve after me.

Harry Simms was walking up the
            track
This bright sunshiny day,
He was a youth of courage,
His step was light and gay.
We did not know the gun thugs
Were hiding on the way,
To kill our dear young Comrade
This bright sunshiny day.

Harry Simms was killed on
            Brush Creek
In nineteen thirty-two,
He organized the Y. C. L.,
Also the N. M. U.
He gave his life in struggle,
That was all that he could do.
He died to save the Union,
Also for me and you.

Comrades we must vow today,
This one thing we must do.
Must organize all the miners
In the dear old N. M. U.
And get a million volunteers,
Into the Y. C. L.
And sink this Rotten System
In the deepest pits of Hell.

Welcome the Traveler Home

"This was composed by me in 1932. I was run out of Kentucky with indictments over strike trouble, where I was a member of the strike committee in the strike of coal miners in Kentucky in 1932. I was going back after being in the North for a period of three months. These indictments were still against me, although they were later dropped, because there was no evidence that I'd ever broken a law. I was expectin' to be put in jail. For that reason before going back, I composed this song." -- Jim Garland.

I guess if the coal operators hated Jim, it was an even break.

Chorus:

For to wel-come the tra-vel-er home,____ For to wel-come the tra-vel-er home, The_ gun thugs_they_ are wait - ing to___ wel - come the tra-vel-er home. There's the old judge_ of Bell Count - y, His_ nose is_ big and long, And the son_ of a gun is a- wait - ing for to wel-come the tra-vel-er home.

172

Chorus:
For to welcome the traveler home,
For to welcome the traveler home,
The gun thugs they are waiting,
To welcome the traveler home.
(Repeat after each verse)

There's the old judge of Bell County,
His nose is big and long,
And the son-of-a-gun is a-waiting
For to welcome the traveler home.

There's Walter B. Smith and
    Garvey,
And he's got Gils and Combs,
And the son-of-a-gun is a-waiting,
For to welcome the traveler home.

The beans and potatoes are ready
For to feed the traveler home,
And the jailhouse cell is a-waiting
For to welcome a red-neck home.

Here's these old chinches and
    graybacks
They say "We're glad you've
    come.
For we know we'll have our dinner,"
They welcome a red-neck home.

When I get back to Kentucky,
And I get my 45's on
I'll give them a little tea party
If they try to welcome the traveler
    home.

173

The Greenback Dollar
(I DON'T WANT YOUR MILLIONS, MISTER)

Lots of rich guys would have you shot down like a dirty dog over a measly greenback. Guy like that aint fit to boss nobody. I hate dictators especially if they're the rich and greedy kind like the Bible cusses from cover to cover.

I don't want your millions, mister. I don't want your diamond ring. All I want is the right to live mister. Give me back my job again.

Chorus:
I don't want your millions, mister.
I don't want your diamond ring.
All I want's just live and let live,
Give me back my job again.
(Repeat chorus after each verse)

I don't want your Rolls Royce, mister,
I don't want your pleasure yacht.
All I want is food for my babies,
Now give to me my old job back.

We worked to build this country, mister,
While you enjoyed a life of ease.
You've stolen all that we've built, mister,
Now our children starve and freeze.

Yes, you have a land deed, mister,
The money is all in your name.
But where's the work that you did, mister?
I'm demanding back my job again.

Think me dumb if you wish, mister,
Call me green or blue or red.
There's just one thing that I know, mister,
Our hungry babies must be fed.

We'll organize together, mister,
In one big united band,
And with a Farmer-Labor party
We will win our just demands.

Take the two old parties, mister,
No difference in them I can see.
But with a Farmer-Labor party,
We will set the workers free.

Which Side Are You On?

"This song was composed in 19 and 31 by the two children of Sam Reece, two little girls. They're grown up now but one was nine and the other eleven then. It was made up from the condition of their father, who was organizer in Harlan County for the U.M.W. of A...One night during the big Harlan Strike their home was raided by company thugs, and after that they composed this song."

Maybe you're a hell of a good song writer and don't know it. You see ads in all of the magazines a saying they got schools that can teach you the plain and fancy ways of writing songs, and you see ads a telling you to mail your songs into some outfit and they'll get it copyrighted for twenty-five bucks. But maybe you could write songs so fast the rich folks would think Heaven had cut a loose -- if only you was a holding out for Union Pay and Union Hours, and was a setting out on the side of the road a waiting for the big boys to make up their one track mind, and then all at once a car load of pistol packing papas sailed up in a big black sedan, and chased you into your house, and raided it, and tore hell out of everything, and took you for a ride in the hills, and beat your head in like a Thanksgiving Punkin, and -- maybe if they even done this to your brother or your neighbor or some of your folks, -- maybe you could write a song. That's where songs come from.

Lord pity these two-bit drug store sissies that write up some kind of a song that goes on for about forty seven verses and don't tell a single thing. Lord pity the scabs, the ginks, the hooded Lizards, and Great Gizzards, that jump on the working folks and beat these songs out of 'em.

Come all of you good workers,
Good news to you I'll tell,
Of how the good old union
Has come in here to dwell.

Refrain:
Which side are you on?
Which side are you on?
(Repeat after each verse)

We've started our good battle,
We know we're sure to win,
Because we've got the gun thugs
A-lookin' very thin.

They say they have to guard us
To educate their child
Their children lives in luxury,
Our children's almost wild.

With pistols and with rifles
They take away our bread,
And if you miners hinted it,
They'll sock you on the head.

If you go up to Harlan County
There is no neutral there,
You'll either be a union man
Or a thug for J. H. Blair.

Oh gentlemen, can you stand it?
Oh tell me how you can?
Will you be a gun thug
Or will you be a man?

My daddy was a miner,
He is now in the air and sun, *
He'll be with you fellow workers,
Until the battle's won.

*Blacklisted and without a job.

177

Come All You Hardy Miners

You goddam, lowlife, sneakthief, scabs ain't got guts enough to take up
for your own rights...cowardly bastards, yellow bellied skunks...like
to be slaves 'cause you dont have to fight and stand up for your rights.
Ain't got brains enough to do your own thinking and do your own livin'...
and love your own women and drink your own whiskey...so you just leave
it up to the rich sonsabitches to do all of this for you.

If you're a real he man or a real she woman, there ain't nothing on
earth you hate worse than a goddam lowlife stool pigeon, stooge, tattle
tale of a scab.

Gather around me, all you Scabs, and listen to a real red-blooded,
American song -- not a song of cowards and sissies, but a song that
roars out of a thousand foot shaft like a mountain lion with his leg in a
steel trap. And brother, take warning!

Collected by Alan Lomax and Mary Elizabeth Barnicle
as sung by Finlay "Red Ore" Donaldson, Bell County,
Kentucky.

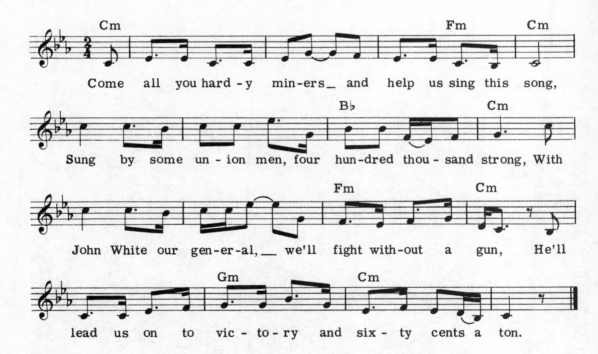

Come all you hard-y min-ers_ and help us sing this song,
Sung by some un-ion men, four hun-dred thou-sand strong, With
John White our gen-er-al,_ we'll fight with-out a gun, He'll
lead us on to vic-to-ry and six-ty cents a ton.

Come all you hardy miners and help
    us sing this song,
Sung by some union men, four
    hundred thousand strong,
With John White our general we'll
    fight without a gun,
He'll lead us on to victory and
    sixty cents a ton.

Come all you hardy miners and
    help us sing this song,
On the twenty first day of April we
    struck for sixty cents a ton.
The operators laughed at us and
    said we'd never come
Out in one body and demand that
    sixty cents a ton.

Come out, you scabs and blacklegs
    and join the men like one,
Tell them that you 're in the fight
    for the sixty cents a ton,
There now in old Virginia they're
    scabbing right along,
But when we win they're sure to try
    for the sixty cents a ton.

Come all you hardy miners, let's
    try to do our best,
We'll first get old Virginia,
    Kentucky, and then we'll get the
    rest,
There's going to be a meeting, right
    up in this land,
When we reach across the river and
    take them by the hand.

The Striking Miners

By Hershel Phillips of Crossville, Tennessee

There's a call from old Kentucky and
    it rings to Tennessee
To the union of the country for to
    set the miners free.
In their homes, all pinched and
    hollow,
At the mercy of the foe,
Men and women, little children,
    fight on bravely, all alone.

O I've .... in Dixie land, or must
    know the reason why,
That them miners all are starving,
    Let us ring their battle cry.
For a right to join a union,
That our children may be free,
In the mountains of Kentucky, and
    the hills of Tennessee.

Chief Aderholt

Ella May Wiggins was shot through the heart on her way to a Union Meetin' in Gastonia, North Carolina. Died September the 14th. It was an armed mob of gun-totin' killers sent out by the big rich guys that ramrod the mines and take the money.

She'd had 9 children. 4 of them died all at once with the whooping cough. "I was working nights and nobody to do for them, only Myrtle. She's eleven, and a sight of help. I asked the super to put me on day shift so I could 'tend 'em, but he wouldn't. I dont know why. So I had to quit my job and then there wasn't any money for medicine, so they just died. I never could do anything for my children, not even keep 'em alive, it seems. That's why I'm for th' Union, so's I can do better for them..." said Ella May.

She never had much schoolin', but she knowed People. That's a heap better than a knowin' books.

She had Faith in th' Union. It was her Religion. It was her Sermon and the poor people was her Church. It was the only Power that promised her a better Life. It was the Only Power that would give her kids some groceries to eat and clothes to wear.

Faith without Works is Dead. Ella knowed that. So she Worked. She went out and talked the Union. She said, Poor Folks, You got to get together. So's we can wear good clothes and live in a better house.

Who put that bullet in her heart? Why did they shoot her down? Why did they nail Jesus on a cross?

That kind of stuff has got to be stopped. And the Union is the only power on earth that'll put a stop to it, a Farmer-Labor Union. Ella May died for her Union. They sung her songs over the red earth of her fresh dug grave. You'll sing 'em all over the world.

This is Ella May's best known song. Tune is Floyd Collins. Beats 100 speeches and 9 sermons throwed in.

By Ella May Wiggins

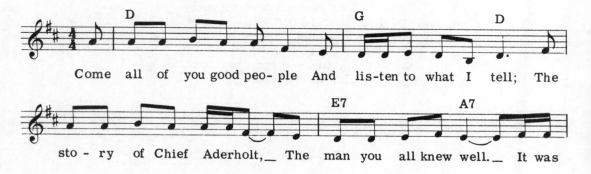

Come all of you good peo- ple And lis-ten to what I tell; The sto - ry of Chief Aderholt,__ The man you all knew well.__ It was

on one Fri-day eve-ning. The sev-enth day of June, He

went down to the un-ion ground And met his fa-tal doom.

Come all of you good people, and
    listen to what I tell;
The story of Chief Aderholt, the
    man you all knew well.
It was on one Friday evening, the
    seventh day of June,
He went down to the union ground
    and met his fatal doom.

They locked up our leaders, they
    put them in jail,
They shoved them in prison, refused
    to give them bail.
The workers joined together, but
    this was their reply:
We'll never, no we'll never let our
    leaders die.

They moved the trial to Charlotte,
    got lawyers from every town,
I'm sure we'll hear them speak
    again upon the union ground.
While Vera, she's in prison,
    Manville Jencks in pain,
Come join the Textile Union, and
    show that you are game.

We're going to have a union all over
    the South,
Where we can wear good clothes,
    and live in a better house.
Now we must stand together, and to
    the boss reply:
We'll never, no we'll never let our
    leaders die.

I just happened to think we got about 8 or 9 of the country's best song-writers within the covers of this book.

There's the Kentucky clan, Aunt Molly, Sary, and Jim, and Ella May from North Carolina, Herschel Phillips from Tennessee; there's Joe Hill and John Handcox from Arkansas, Maurice Sugar from Detroit and Earl Robinson from New York.

Up In Old Loray

Here's another that come from the same strike. It was written by a little girl.

By Odel Corley

Up in old Loray, six stories high,
That's where they found us, ready
   to die.

Chorus:
Go put up your aprons,
Come join our strike.
So, goodbye old bosses,
We're going on strike.
(Repeat chorus after each verse)

The bosses will starve you,
They'll tell you more lies
Than crossties on railroads
Or stars in the skies.

The bosses will rob you,
They will take half you make,
And claim that you took it up
In coupon books.

Up in old Loray,
All covered with lint,
That's where our shoulders
Was crippled and bent.

Up in old Loray,
All covered in cotton,
It will carry you to your grave,
And you soon will be rotten.

The Mill Mother's Lament

They sung this one over her grave. 6 union members let her down in the ground...but her songs are gone down in history.

By Ella May Wiggins

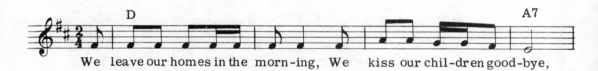

We leave our homes in the morn-ing, We kiss our chil-dren good-bye,

While we slave for the boss-es, Our chil-dren scream and cry.

We leave our homes in the morning,
We kiss our children good bye,
While we slave for the bosses
Our children scream and cry.

And when we draw our money,
Our grocery bills to pay,
Not a cent to spend for clothing,
Not a cent to lay away.

And on that very evening
Our little son will say:
"I need some shoes, mother,
And so does sister May."

How it grieves the heart of a mother,
You everyone must know.
But we can't buy for our children,
Our wages are too low.

It is for our little children,
That seems to us so dear,
But for us nor them, dear workers,
The bosses do not care.

But understand, all workers,
Our union they do fear.
Let's stand together, workers,
And have a union here.

All Around the Jailhouse

Shore do wish the hole world was a-ringin' down songs like this -- beats me why they ain't.

By Ella May Wiggins

Tune: All Around the Watertank, Waiting For A Train.

All a - round the jail-house,— wait - ing for a trial,

One mile from the Un - ion Hall, A - sleep-ing in the jail.

All around the jailhouse,
Waiting for a trial,
One mile from the union hall,
Sleeping in the jail.

I walked up to the policeman,
To show him I had no fear,
He said, "If you've got money,
I'll see that you don't stay here. "

"I haven't got a nickel,
Not a penny can I show. "
"Lock her back up in the cell, " he
    said,
As he slammed the jailhouse door.

He let me out in July,
The month I dearly love,
The wide open spaces all around me,
The moon and the stars above.

Everybody seems to want me,
Everyone but the scabs,
I'm on my way from the jailhouse,
I'm going back to the union hall.

Though my tent now is empty,
My heart is full of joy.
I'm a mile away from the union hall,
Just a-waiting for a strike.

Toiling On Life's Pilgrim Pathway

When Religion turns into hunger, Church songs are changed quick and easy into Fightin' Songs.

By Ella May Wiggins

Verse: Toil - ing on life's pil - grim path - way__ Where - so - ev - er you may be, It__ will help you fel - low work - ers__ If you__ will join the I. L. D.

Toiling on life's pilgrim pathway
Wheresoever you may be,
It will help you fellow workers
If you will join the I. L. D.

Chorus:
Come and join the I. L. D.
Come and join the I. L. D.
It will help to win the victory
If you will join the I. L. D.
(Repeat chorus after each verse)

When the bosses cut your wages
And you toil the labor free
Come and join the textile union
Also join the I. L. D.

Now our leaders are in prison
But I hope they will soon be free
Come and join the textile union
Also join the I. L. D.

Now the South is hedged in darkness
Although they begin to see
Come and join the textile union,
Also join the I. L. D.

VIII – SO YOU HOLLERED FOR A NEW DEAL

The Chiseler's Sorrow

Here's that feller by the name of H. Phillips again. Comes out on a song called The Chiseler's Sorrow. Shows you the faith that folks put in President Roosevelt and the promises he made to help out the workin' folks. Hoover had completely let us down and proved to be a big fizzle. Franklin D. come along like a headlight on a dark night. He was a friendly feller, laughed and talked, and he was a cripple once, maybe he'd understand how it was to be like us.

Anyhow, it'll be songs like this one that shows you who th' Chiselers is, and it'll be songs like this one that ooze them Chiselers right out of their Playhouse.

(H. Phillips)

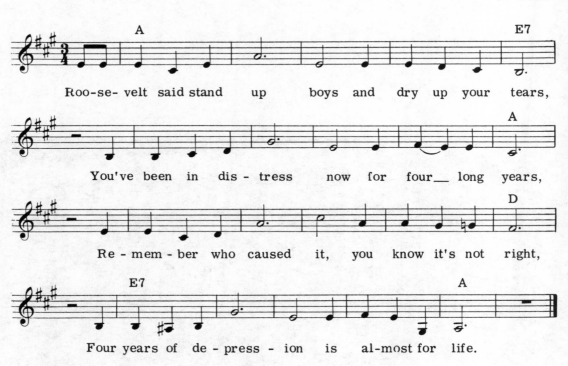

Roo-se-velt said stand up boys and dry up your tears,
You've been in dis-tress now for four__ long years,
Re-mem-ber who caused it, you know it's not right,
Four years of de-press-ion is al-most for life.

Roosevelt said, "Stand up, boys,"
And dry your tears.
You've been in distress now,
For four long years.
Remember who caused it,
You know it's not right,
Four years of depression
Is almost for life.

We've counted on Franklin,
To give us a break.
Our lives and our money
Was all at stake.
Come all you good people
And stand up like men,
And over these chiselers
A victory to win.

The chiselers was worried
When elections drew nigh.
Now aint it a pity
That they did not die.
But when its all over
You know they'll be blue,
When all of our people
Knows they are untrue.

Well, I hate a chiseler,
A chiseler hates me.
If I had the power
Here's where they would be.
They'd all be in prison
And I'd be the judge.
In 99 years
I'd still hold a grudge.

We've counted our money
And counted our time,
We've counted a million
That aint got a dime.
Come all ye good people
Stand up for your rights,
Four years of depression
Is almost for life.

1928-1934

If you ain't read no books on History, you can haul off and sing it.

In twen-ty eight we met our fate When pres-i-dents they run, When Hoo-ver won, he said, it's done, For the pan-ic's now be-gun. We'll have some fun _____ four years to come.

In '28 we met our fate
When presidents they run,
When Hoover won, he said, it's done,
For the panic's now begun.
We'll have some fun
Four years to come.

In '29 he said it's time
That something must be done.
We'll all just hold our money,
Put labor on the bum;
We'll have some fun,
Three years to come.

In '30 they cut our wages,
They said we made too much,
Because we wasn't ragged,
They made us all look tough.
They're having fun,
Two years to come.

In '31 the time had come,
That nothing could be found.
Poor people all a starvin'
And sleepin' on the ground.
They'll have no fun
One year to come.

In '32 we all was blue,
We walked to the polls,
And cast a vote for Franklin D.
And happy now are we,
We yell "Hooray"
For the N. R. A.

In '33 old Franklin D.
Called Congress to the stand,
He asked for power to rule the land,
Said the Union I'll demand.
Now aint that grand
For the working man.

In '34 the Labor Board
Been patient long enough,
The big men all were stubborn
When Wagner he got tough.
They land in jail
Without any bail.

Don't Take Away My PWA

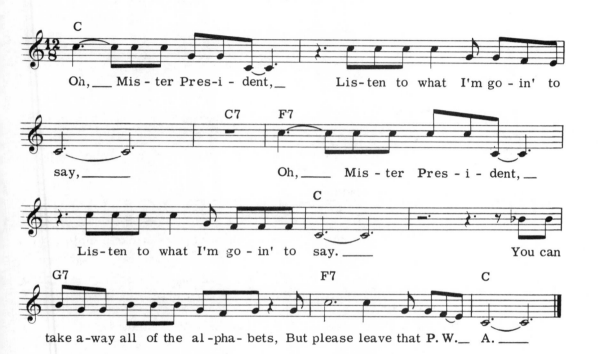

Oh, __ Mis - ter Pres-i - dent, __ Lis-ten to what I'm go - in' to say, _____ Oh, _____ Mis - ter Pres - i - dent, __ Lis-ten to what I'm go - in' to say. _____ You can take a-way all of the al-pha-bets, But please leave that P. W. __ A. _____

Oh, Mister President, listen to
  what I'm going to say.
Oh, Mister President, listen to what
  I'm going to say.
You can take away all of the
  alphabets,
But please leave that PWA.

Now you are in, Mr. President, and
  I hope you's in to stay.
Now you are in, Mr. President, and
  I hope you's in to stay,
But whatever changes that you
  make,
Please keep that PWA.

Now, I don't need no woman an' no
  place to stay,
Now, I don't need no woman an' no
  place to stay,
Because I'm makin' an honest
  livin'
Now on that PWA.

PWA, you the best ol' friend I
  ever seen,
PWA, you the best ol' friend I
  ever seen,
Said, the job aint hard
And the folks aint mean.

I went to the poll and voted, and I
  know I voted the right way.
I went to the poll and voted, and I
  know I voted the right way.
Now, I'm praying to you, Mister
  President,
Please keep the PWA.

NRA Blues

There's something about this one that takes a hold of you. If you don't believe it, try it to the tune of the Crawdad Song (Jailhouse Key). This shows about how all the folks felt about the New Deal and the N.R.A. - back in 19 and 33.

As sung by Bill Cox on Perfect Record 13090-B. (From the collection of Alan Lomax)

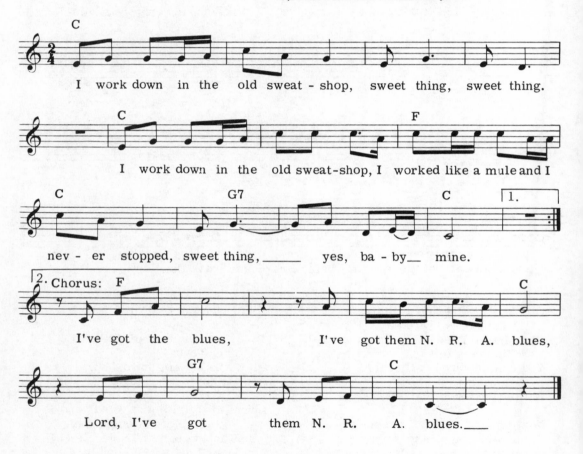

I work down in the old sweat-shop, sweet thing, sweet thing.

I work down in the old sweat-shop, I worked like a mule and I

nev - er stopped, sweet thing, _____ yes, ba - by _ mine.

2. Chorus: I've got the blues, I've got them N. R. A. blues,

Lord, I've got them N. R. A. blues. ___

I work down in the old sweatshop,
Sweet thing, sweet thing.
I work down in the old sweatshop,
I worked like a mule and I never
    stopped,
Sweet thing, yes, baby mine.

When you goin' to join the NRA,
Sweet thing, sweet thing,
When you goin' to join the NRA,
I never had heard the big boss say,
Sweet thing, yes, baby mine.

Chorus:
I've got the blues,
I've got them NRA blues,
   Lord, I've got them NRA blues.

When payday comes and I get my
    check,
Sweet thing, sweet thing.
When payday comes and I get my
    check,
All I get is a little wee speck,
Sweet thing, yes, baby mine.

When you're working for the NRA,
Sweet thing, sweet thing.
When you're working for the NRA,
You'll get shorter hours and get
    th' same pay,
Sweet thing, yes, baby mine.

(Repeat chorus.)

The rich men's all on easy street,
Sweet thing, sweet thing.
The rich men's all on easy street,
And the poor man can't get enough
    to eat,
Sweet thing, yes, baby mine.

When they all join the NRA,
Sweet thing, sweet thing.
When they all join the NRA,
We'll all feel happy and all feel
    gay,
Sweet thing, yes, baby mine.

(Repeat chorus.)

193

CWA Blues

Lots of songs like this sprung loose. Negro and white folks both made 'em up. One about as hungry as th' other'n.

As sung by Walter Roland on Melotone Record 13103-A (15479). (From the collection of Alan Lomax)

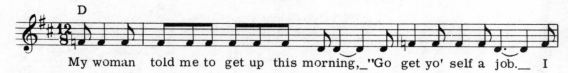

My woman told me to get up this morning,__"Go get yo' self a job.__ I

want you to try to take care of me while the times is hard,"I hol-lered,

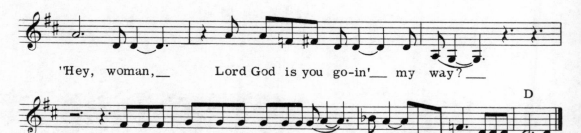

'Hey, woman,__ Lord God is you go-in'__ my way?__

Lord, I be-lieve I'll go get me a job,__Workin' for that C. W. A."__

My woman told me to get up this
    mornin'
"Go get yo'self a job.
I want you to try to take care of
    me,
While the times is hard. "

Chorus:
I hollered, "Hey, woman,
Lawd God, is you goin' my way?
Lawd, I b'lieve I'll go get me a
    job,
Working for that CWA. "

She told me that some folks was
    goin' round here talkin'
'Bout they got jobs for sale,
If you want a good job,
You must go to that old country
    jail,

Chorus:
And holler, "Hey man,
Great God, let me go yo' way,
I just want a job workin'
For that CWA. "

You know that CWA, they payin' you
Nine sixty a week,
You don't have to worry about that
     World's Fair,
Somethin' to eat.

Chorus:
I hollered, "Hey woman,
Lawd, God, is you goin' my way?
Cause I got a job workin'
For the CWA. "

You know I told my woman this
     mornin',
Just about half past three,
Wake up early
And come go with me.

(Repeat chorus)

You know I'm gonna take my
     woman down,
To that world's fair sto'.
I'm gonna carry her this time,
And I wont have to carry her no mo'.

(Repeat chorus)

CCC Blues

What's the matter here? A sour note. This feller seems to of purty well took care of the troubles of the whole world when he said, "She give me a sheet of paper, told me to come back some other day." That kind of sheet of paper would of been better off in the outhouse.

From the singing of Washboard Sam and his Washboard Band on Bluebird Record 7993-B. (From the collection of Alan Lomax)

Chorus:
I'm goin' down, I'm goin' down to
   the CCC,
I'm goin' down, I'm goin' down to
   the CCC,
I know that the WPA won't do a
   thing for me.
(Repeat after each verse)

I told her my name
And the place I stayed,
She said she'd give me a piece of
   paper, -
"Come back some other day. "

I told her I had no people
And the shape I was in.
She said she would help me,
But she didn't say when.

I told her I need a job
And no relief,
And on my rent day
She sent me a can of beef.

She said she'd give me a job. -
Everything was nice and warm -
Takin' care of the dead
In a funeral home.

Ballad of the TVA

'Course you know as well as I do that once in a while some boy and girl will haul off and fall in love in spite of everything the bankers can do about it. I been around this country and seen 'em fall in. So you see you're dealing with an old goes. This here song is a good one. Love song. This ballad spread all through the Mountains of Kentucky and Tennessee and often would change the names of places and people around to fit their own locality. It even spread up to New York City where it was used in a Federal Threatre Project, ''Living Newspaper'' in 1937. Jilson Setters who made it up is an old mountain fiddler.

By Jilson Setters. From ''Ballad Makin' in the Mountains of Kentucky'' by Jean Thomas (Oak Publications).

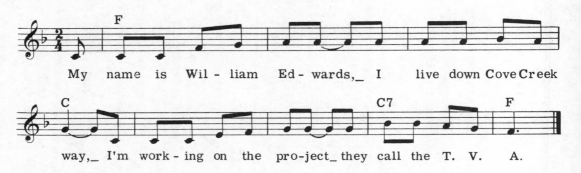

My name is Wil-liam Ed-wards,_ I live down Cove Creek way,_ I'm work-ing on the pro-ject_ they call the T. V. A.

My name is William Edwards,
I live down Cove Creek way.
I'm working on the project
They call the T. V. A.

The Government begun it
When I was but a child,
But now they are in earnest
And Tennessee's gone wild.

Just see them boys a-comin'
Their tool kits on their arm;
They come from Clinch and Holston
And many a valley farm.

From villages and cities,
A French Broad man I see;
For things are up and doing
In sunny Tennessee.

All up and down the valley
They heard the glad alarm,
"The Government means business".
It's working like a charm.

Oh, see them boys a-comin'
Their Government they trust;
Just hear their hammers ringing
They'll build that dam or bust.

I meant to marry Sally
But work I could not find;
The T. V. A. was started
And surely eased my mind.

I'm writing her a letter
These words I'll surely say:
"The Government has surely saved us,
Just name our wedding day. "

We'll build a little cabin
On Cove Creek near her home;
We'll settle down forever
And never care to roam.

For things are surely movin'
Down here in Tennessee;
Good times for all the valley
For Sally and for me.

Oh, things looked blue and lonely
Until this come along;
Now hear the crew a-singin'
And listen to their song:

"The Government employs us
Short and certain pay;
Oh, things are up and comin'
God bless the T. V. A. "

Working for the PWA

Negro blues singers has got the world beat at weaving the story of their whole life, their hard luck and hard times, around the woman they love. You can sing this to about the same tune as the C.W.A. Blues.

From the singing of Dave Alexander, the Black Ivory King, on Decca Record 7307-B(61798), copyright by Alexander. (From the collection of Alan Lomax)

My baby told me this morning, get
    up and go get myself a job.
And I take care of her when times
    get hard.
And I said, hey, woman,
Good gal is you goin' my way?
You know, I believe I'll get me a job
    workin',
Workin' for the PWA.

PWA pays you nine fifty a week.
And don't need to worry about the
    weather, pals, and nothin' to
    eat.
And holler, hey, woman,
Good gal, is you goin' my way?
You know, I b'lieve I'll get me a job
    workin',
Workin' for the PWA.

Well, I woke up this morning, just
    about half past three,
I told my baby to get up early and
    come and go with me.
And holler, hey, woman,
Good gal, is you goin' my way?
You know, I've got me a job workin'
Workin' for that PWA.

I'm goin' to take my woman to the
    welfare store,
I'm gonna carry her this time, aint
    gonna carry her no mo'.
And holler, hey, woman,
Good gal, is you goin' my way?
You know, I got me a job workin',
Workin' on that PWA.

197

Welfare Blues

A hard working man's worst pain and worst accident is when his good gal has got to go out and hit the heavy, heavy to bring him in the bacon. Just aint a man's nature to set at home and have it brung in. It's in his nature to get out and rustle it up and when a woman does it -- well, it's just bassakwards, that's all. But the Negroes have got used to it.

As sung by Speckled Red on Bluebird Record 8069-A.
(From the collection of Alan Lomax)

Now, me an' my ba-by went out And we talked for one hour. She

said, I want you to get out and take the wel-fare flour. An'I said No oo

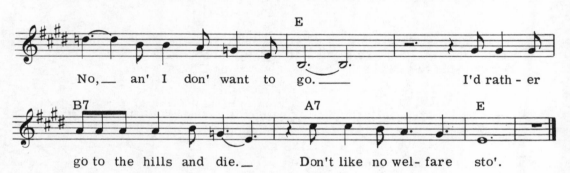

No,— an' I don' want to go.— I'd rath-er

go to the hills and die.— Don't like no wel-fare sto'.

Now, me an' my baby went out
And we talked for one hour.
She said, I want you to get out
And take the welfare flour.

Chorus:
An' I said, No-oo
No, an' I don' want to go.
I'd rather go to the hills and die.
Don't like no welfare sto'.
(Repeat after each verse)

Now you go down in the morning,
Don't ever ask how you feel,
Give you one of them cans of tripe
And some of that molded meal.

Welfare people
Sure gonna treat you mean.
Give you one little can of tripe
Two or three cans of beans.

Now the gov'ment took it in charge,
Said their gonna treat Ev'body
    right.
Give you some peas, beans 'n
    meal,
And then four or five cans of tripe.

Now my baby says she's goin' out
Find herself a li'l ol' job.
Help her care for me, 'cause,
The times has done got hard.

Last Chorus:
And I says, Yeah,
Yeah, then I won't have to go.
Won't have to go to the hills and
    die.
Won't be no Welfare sto'.

Working on the Project

This just goes to show you that you can work on a government project and still not founder yourself on groceries. Bad enough when you got a project to work on. Worse when you get your project cut off. If daddy gits his WPA cut off, what's mama gonna do for Relief?

From the singing of Peatie Wheatstraw. Jordan Master No. 91164, Decca 7311-B. (From the collection of Alan Lomax)

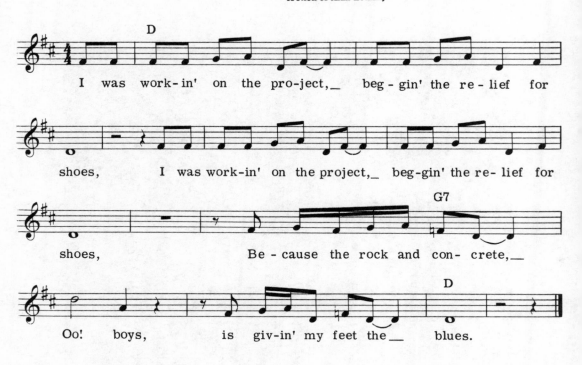

I was work-in' on the pro-ject,__ beg-gin' the re-lief for shoes, I was work-in' on the project,__ beg-gin' the re-lief for shoes, Be-cause the rock and con-crete,__ Oo! boys, is giv-in' my feet the__ blues.

I was workin' on the project, beggin'
    the relief for shoes,
I was workin' on the project, beggin'
    the relief for shoes,
Because the rock and concrete,
    oo boys, is giving my feet the
    blues.

Workin' on the project, with holes
    all in my clothes,
Workin' on the project, with holes
    all in my clothes,
Trying to make me a thin dime,
    oo boys, to keep the rent man
    from the do'.

I'm workin' on the project tryin' to
    make both ends meet,
I'm workin' on the project tryin' to
    make both ends meet,
But the payday is so long, till the
    grocery man won't let me eat.

Workin' on the project, my gal's
    spendin' all my dough,
Workin' on the project, my gal's
    spendin' all my dough,
Now I have waked up on her, well,
    well, and I won't be that weak
    no mo'.

200

Workin' on the project with payday
    three or four weeks away,
Workin' on the project, with payday
    three or four weeks away,
Now how can you live, well, well,
    well, when you can't get no pay.

201

WPA Blues

This old boy must have been stayin' in one of those abandoned buildings you see along the edges of any big town. Lots of folks do this; only a couple of weeks ago up in Harlem the men came to tear a house down and found ten men living in one room on the third floor. Didn't have no electricity or nothin' - but just stayed there because they had a roof over their heads. Sometimes it just seems like everybody was against you, and you're caught up, and bound around by big forces, and rich people and just tossed around like nobody cared. It's when all the people who feel this way get together, and instead of saying "my troubles" say "our troubles." Then's the time the rich folks had better look out.

Everybody's workin' in this town
And it's worryin me night and day,
Everybody's working in this town
And it's worrying me night and day,
That's that mean hard working crew
Says, that work for the WPA.

As sung by Big Bill (Broonzy) on Perfect Record 6-08-61 (C 1380). (From the collection of Alan Lomax)

Says, the landlord come this
        morning
He knocked upon my door,
Asked me was I goin' to
Pay my rent no mo'.
He say, "You have to move
If you can't pay."
Then he turn
And walk slowly 'way.

Well, I started out the next morning,
I put a lock on my do',
So I thought I would move
But I haven't got no place to go.
The real estate people
They done got sore,
They don't rent to no
Relief clients no more.

    Chorus:
    An' I know I'll have to try to
    Find me some place to stay,
    'Cause they're gonna tear my
        house down,
    Is that crew from the WPA.

    Chorus:
    An' I know then
    I have to walk the streets night
        and day,
    'Cause they're gonna tear my
        house down,
    Is that crew from the WPA.

So I went to the relief station
I didn't have a cent.
They say, "Slim, where you stayin',
You don't have to pay no rent."
When I got back home,
They was tackin' a sign on my do',
Sayin', "This ol' house is condemned
An' you can't live here no mo'."

A notion struck me
To stay on a day or two,
But I soon found out
That that wouldn't do.
Early the next morning,
I was laying in my bed,
I heard a mighty rumblin'
An' bricks come tumblin' on my
        head.

    Chorus:
    Then a notion struck me
    I better be on my way.
    'Cause they're tear my house
        down,
    Is that crew from the WPA.

    Chorus:
    I started duckin' and dodgin',
    Tryin' to get out of the way,
    'Cause they're tearin' my house
        down,
    Is that crew from the WPA.

You're On Your Last Go'Round

Every time a guy that's a running for office comes around he kisses your kids, hugs your wife, cranks your car, winds up your cat and puts out your clock. He'll kid you and skid you, he'll pull you and bull you, he'll take you and shake you, he'll scrape you and rape you, he'll kiss you and miss you, he'll smell you and sell you, he'll promise to live with you, marry you, send you money, give you a job, put you up in business, build you a home, plant a garden, ship you some chickens and smuggle you a bottle of whiskey from Old Mexico. He'll promise you everything you need and say the best ain't good enough for you. He'll have you thinking the old world has at last changed and is a heaven on earth – or will be after he's in office the first fifteen minutes. They screek, squeak and speak. They hire guys to write 'em up some mighty purty speeches. But – all of these airy promises, all of the B.S. – whatever becomes of it?

Well, it won't be long til some feller in your town or country will be a combing your wife's hair and a pulling your leg at the same time with a smile on his face that looks like the west end of a heifer a going east. Next time he comes 'round ask him a few things; ask him how he voted on the groceries and job and pension and house and money that you need. Sing him this song: it's just a little old song I sung on the air waves out there on the coast, it might not of coasted back east a tall, I never did find out. Anyhow, it looks better than it sounds. I mean it sounds better when you sing it by yourself than when I sing it by myself and you can use it to kick your congressman's pants when he comes back from his next lying trip to the Capitol. The dirty son of a bitch, anyhow.

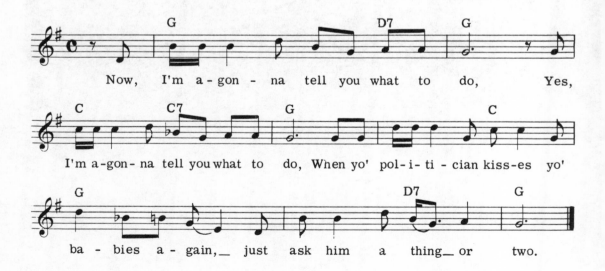

Now, I'm a gonna tell you what to
    do,
Yes, I'm a gonna tell you what to do,
When yo' Politician kisses yo'
    babies again,
Just ask him a thing or two:

How did you vote on Relief?
How did you vote on Relief?
Did you deal me groceries or deal
    me Grief?
Boy, you're on yo' last go 'round.

How'd you vote on my Old Age
    Pension?
How'd you vote on my Old Age
    Pension?
If you voted my Old Age Pension
    down,
Boy, you're on yo' last go 'round.

How'd you vote on Government
    Houses?
How'd you vote on Government
    Houses?
If you took away my roof and left
    me out in the rain,
Man, you're on yo' last go 'round.

How'd you vote on the CCC?
How'd you vote on the CCC?
Are you makin' a Man or a Monkey
    out of me?
Boy, you're on yo' last go 'round.

How'd you vote on this god dam
    war?
How'd you vote on this god dam
    war?
If you sent me to die in machine
    gun fire,
Boy, you're on yo' last go 'round.

How'd you vote on my job here at
    home?
How'd you vote on my job here at
    home?
If you made me a hobo to ramble
    and to roam,
Boy, you're on yo' last go 'round.

I'm Looking for that New Deal Now

You was promised a New Deal and you got a Nude Deal. I guess you done know that. Promised a New Deal and got a War Deal. Some 130,000,000 (hundred and thirty million) folks is a lookin' for that New Deal now. The only New Deal that will ever amount to a dam thing will come from Trade Unions.

I had a friend out there in California that was head foreman of Radio Station KFVD and he was a good Liberal Thinker. I know, 'cause I've heard him think. I use to listen to his speeches and then set down and have a song about 'em. The country's full of Radio Stations, but you aint got much free speech on 'em. This can be sort of a talkin' piece - like the Talkin' Blues. If you can't sing, I know you can talk it off. If you caint, give it to your wife, she can.

All this world is a pok-er game, The way it's played is a dagum shame, I'm

look-in' for___ that New Deal now. All the bank-ers I be-lieve,___

Got a good hand up their sleeve, I'm a-look-in' for_ that New Deal now.

All this World is a Poker Game,
The way it's played is a dad-gum
  shame.
I'm lookin' for that New Deal now.
All the Bankers, I believe,
Got a good hand up their sleeve,
I'm a looking for that New Deal now.

When the Cards was dealt around,
Wall Street drawed the Aces down,
I'm lookin' for that New Deal now.
Then they dealt around the Cards,
The Big Shots up and cleaned the
  Board,
I'm lookin' for that New Deal now.

John D. he filled his Puss,
For th' Workin' folks, times got
    worse,
I'm lookin' for that New Deal now.
When the cards went round the
    Board,
Herbert Hoover marked the cards,
I'm lookin' for that New Deal now.

Very next time the cards was dealt,
They bluffed our Franklin
    Roosevelt,
I'm lookin' for that New Deal now.
Franklin D. , I expect,
Gonna have to look for a brand new
    deck,
I'm lookin' for that New Deal now.

All I asked was enough to eat,
New shoes on th' children's feet,
I'm a lookin' for that New Deal now.
Little bit of work, little bit of fun,
Pocketbook with spendin' money,
I'm a lookin' for that New Deal now.

They raised the pot with the N. R. A.
For honest hours and honest pay,
I'm lookin' for that New Deal now.
But a Turkey Dealer up New York
    Town,
Won the Blue Eagle with his hole
    card down,
I'm a lookin' for that New Deal now.

The Dickman Song

Dickman was a Democratic mayor in St. Louis that cheated his people. They found themselves with no relief. Some was yaller and afraid to do anything about it. But thousands got up and went down to the city hall and stampeded all over the joint. Some of 'em got jailed for it and was throwed in the jug for 6 months. Six months in the hoosegow for hollering out at a chiseling mayor!

Pete says to me tonight, I'll bet those relief officials think that the Hungry People are very crude and certainly very impolite to come marching like nobody's business up to the Relief Office, City Hall or State Capitol asking for Something To Eat.

Maybe so - I bet my socks they think we aint had no bringings up. Think we aint had no raisin's. Raisins, hell. I went with my aunt two weeks in a row out in Glendale, California, and both weeks all she got for her and her old man was a pound of butter and a little sack of raisins. She said to the relief man, "Hey, how about some flour? We want some biscuits with this butter and raisins - raisins - these goddam infernal raisins."

The man looked at her relief card and said, "Sorry, lady, it don't call for anything else for 2 people with no children."

Dickman, O Dickman, O when do
    we eat?
Dickman, O Dickman, O when do
    we eat?
Dickman, O Dickman, O when do
    we eat?
We are so hungry now.
We are so hungry now.

Dickman, O Dickman, O what do
    we wear? (3 times)
We got no clothes no more,
We got no clothes no more.

Dickman, O Dickman, O where do
    we live? (3 times)
We got no home nowhere,
We got no home nowhere.

Dickman, O Dickman, O tax the
    rich. (3 times)
To feed the poor,
To feed the poor.

Waitin' On Roosevelt

You can tell this song was wrote by a feller that knowed what he was a singing about. It's a Love Song of the best kind. It's a man that loves his wife and kids. It's a man that wants to see his wife and kids have plenty to eat, and a good home, and a full cupboard. It's a woman in love with her man. And somebody has run off with their clothes and their groceries and their money, and all they got left is a empty cupboard, and - for a while at least - these folks are a willing to wait.

They got lots of patience, ain't high-tempered, don't want to jump on nobody, don't want to fight nor shoot nobody -- all they want is a good home with 3 square meals a day and a good job at Honest Pay. A empty cigar box might be a dern handy thing to have around the house when a outfit of that kind is needed. But a empty cupboard aint. That's a hoss of a different color.

Words by Langston Hughes. Music adapted by Alan Lomax from "Sitting On Top of the World" by the Mississippi Shieks. © by authors.

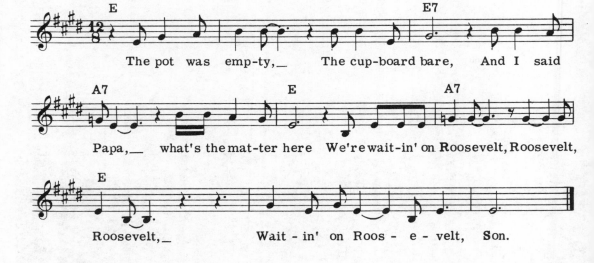

The pot was empty, The cupboard bare, And I said Papa, what's the matter here We're wait-in' on Roosevelt, Roosevelt, Roosevelt, Wait-in' on Roos-e-velt, Son.

The pot was empty,
The cupboard bare,
And I said, "Papa,
What's the matter here?"

Chorus:
"We're waitin' on Roosevelt,
Roosevelt, Roosevelt,
We're waitin' on Roosevelt, son."
(Repeat after each verse)

The rent was due,
The lights was out.
"Oh, tell me, mama,
What's it all about?"

Sister's low sick,
Doctor won't come
'Cause we can't pay him,
The proper sum.

Then one sad day
They put us out,
Mama and Papa,
Meek as a mouse.

Aint got no money,
Aint got no job,
Backbone and navel
Doin' the belly rub.

The pot's still empty
The cupboard bare,
Can't raise no family
On bellies filled with air.

But when they felt those
Cold winds blow
And didn't have no
Good place to go.
Pa said, "I'm tired
Of waitin' on Roosevelt,
Waitin' on Roosevelt, son."

"And when we all get
Hungry and cold,
Gonna stop believin'
Gonna get hard to hold.
Stop waitin' on Roosevelt,
Ol' man Roosevelt,
Waitin' on Roosevelt, son."

.......Pete says a lot of good things. He jots down little notes and leaves them a laying around where he is fairly sure I will come across 'em. He really writes them for his own use, but once in a while I snatch onto one. Here's one here amongst our ten foot pile of waste paper, addresses, blotters, newspapers, diaries, carbon paper, cigarettes, matches, ash trays, letters, rubber balloons, fountain pens, flower vases, calendars, etc. that says, "What ever --".

WHEREVER FOLKS HAVE TALKED ABOUT SOMETHING, OR THOUGHT ABOUT SOMETHING, THEY HAVE ALSO SUNG ABOUT IT.
                                                    Pete

IX- THE OKIE SECTION

Almost everybody is a Okie now days. That means you ain't got no home, or don't know how long you're gonna have the one you are in. Sort of means, too, that you're out of a job. Or owe more than you can rake and scrape.

Okies has come to include all of the folks that the rich folks has et up. I could sleep mighty comfortable with just that one name on my tombstone.

Some politicians throwed mud at John Steinbeck for coining the word, Okie. I want to put my nickel in. He aint the guy that made up that word.

That was made up by people a riding in freight cars and walking down the high ways, and working in the potatoes, and celery, and beets, and apricots, and peaches, and celery, and all of the crops -- they started it. If you was from Texas, they called you Tex. If you was from Missouri, they called you Mizoo. If you was from Alabama they called you Alabam. If you was from Arkansas, you was called Arkie. From Oklahoma, Okie.

I heard that word long time before the Grapes come out. I got a cousin in California right today, his nickname for several years has been Okie, some call him just Oak. He's one of them Oklahoma Yodeling Cowboys. I know a girl called Lefty Lou from Old Mizoo.

These names are all different kinds. They finally got to where they just said, Look at them Okies, that was because they didn't know you personal. And because the folks from Oklahoma literally swamped all of the other states. Iowa might of been ahead, I don't know. But in one case I remember the Iowa people in California had a big picnic, and they had the names of Iowa's towns painted on big signs, and if you was from that town in Iowa, you went over there and chewed the rag with all of the other broke friends. In one case they said, Everybody from a Certain Town in Iowa, stand right over yonder...and by George, so many went over there that there was more in California from that town, than there was left in the town back in Iowa.

It looks like this Okie section ought to be my pet section -- but it ain't. When I first commenced a working on this book, I thought myself it would be. And then I took a looking tour through about 20 of the other

213

states -- and everything was just about as hungry, and in some spots hungrier. Virginia, Tennessee, Pennsylvania, Kentucky, Ohio, New York, New Jersey, Delaware, Maryland, Illinois, and Missouri, and Arkansas, and back to Oklahoma and Texas again. One is about as naked as the other. Roosevelt hit the nail on the head when he said one third of our nation was ill-clothed. So they took our money and bought guns and stuff with it -- for the war -- and then we won't need anything but a white sheet. Same sheet can be used for several of us.

I'm Goin' Down That Road Feeling Bad

First song in this section is the Truth, the living Truth, "I'm Goin' Down That Road Feelin' Bad." Several million of us is doing that very thing. Only since the war scare, feeling worse. When I was out in California they was a shooting 2 of the Steinbeck pictures, "Of Mice and Men," and "The Grapes of Wrath." And they packed me off down there to the studios, I forgot the name of it, and they set me down on a carpet in a directors harum there, and said, Now what we want you to do is to sing a song, just don't even think, and without thinking, just haul off and sing the very first song that hits your mind -- one that if a crowd of 100 pure blood Okies was to hear it, 90 of 'em would know it.

This was the first song that popped to my mind, so without thinking, I sung it. They used the song in the picture, "Grapes of Wrath," which had more thinkin' in it than 99% of the celluloid that we're tangled up in the moving pictures today.

If you're ever down in Oklahoma, or along the 66 Highway to California, and want to get to knowing somebody, some of the working folks, why, just sort of saunter up along side of 'em, or up past their gate, and hum this song -- or whistle it.

They'll come a running out and take you into the house to try to help them scrape up something to eat.

(Dinner is in the middle of the day down in Oklahoma. We go by Grocery Saving Time -- When you can get 'em.)

Words and music by Woody Guthrie
© Copyright 1960 and 1963. Hollis Music, Inc., New York, N.Y. Used by permission.

(Continued on next page)

I'm going down that road feeling bad,
I'm going down that road feeling bad,
I'm going down that road feeling bad,
    Lord, lord,
I ain't gonna be treated this-a-way.

I'm down in that jail on my knees,
I'm down in that jail on my knees,
I'm down in that jail on my knees,
    lord, lord,
I ain't gonna be treated this-a-way.

They feed me on cornbread and
    beans,
They feed me on cornbread and
    beans,
They feed me on cornbread and
    beans, lord, lord,
I ain't gonna be treated this-a-way.

Takes a ten dollar shoe to fit my
    feet,
Takes a ten dollar shoe to fit my
    feet,
Takes a ten dollar shoe to fit my
    feet, lord, lord,
I ain't gonna be treated this-a-way.

'Cause your two dollar shoes hurt
    my feet,
Your two dollar shoes hurt my
    feet,
Your two dollar shoes hurt my feet,
    lord, lord,
I ain't gonna be treated this-a-way.

I'm going where the weather suits
    my clothes,
I'm going where the weather suits
    my clothes,
I'm going where the weather suits
    my clothes, lord, lord,
I ain't gonna be treated this-a-way.

That's why I'm going down the road
    feeling bad,
I'm going down the road feeling bad,
I'm going down the road feeling bad,
    lord, lord,
I ain't gonna be treated this-a-way.

Blowin' Down This Road

I put this song on a Victor record. Don't know if they got 'em in your part of the country or not. The three verses marked with * ain't on the record. I just sing them by heart.

Words and music by Woody Guthrie and Lee Hays. © 1960 (renewed), 1963 (renewed) by Ludlow Music, Inc., New York, NY. Used by permission.

I'm a blowin' down this old dusty
    road,
I'm a blowin' down this old dusty
    road,
I'm a blowin' down this old dusty
    road, Lord, Lord,
And I ain'ta gonna be treated this
    a way.

Lost my farm down in old Oklahoma
Lost my farm down in old Oklahoma
Lost my farm down in old Oklahoma,
    Lord, Lord,
And I ain'ta gonna be treated this
    a way.

I'm a goin' where these dust storms
    never blow
I'm a goin' where these dust storms
    never blow,
I'm a goin' where these dust storms
    never blow, Lord, Lord,
And I ain'ta gonna be treated this
    a way.

They say I'm a dust bowl refugee
They say I'm a dust bowl refugee
They say I'm a dust bowl refugee,
    Lord, Lord,
And I ain'ta gonna be treated this
    a way.

I'm a lookin' for a job at honest pay
I'm a lookin' for a job at honest pay
I'm a lookin' for a job at honest pay,
    Lord, Lord,
And I ain'ta gonna be treated this
    a way.

My children need three square
    meals a day
My children need three square
    meals a day
My children need three square
    meals a day, Lord, Lord,
And I ain'ta gonna be treated this
    a way.

Takes a ten dollar shoe to fit my
    feet,
Takes a ten dollar shoe to fit my
    feet,
Takes a ten dollar shoe to fit my
    feet, Lord, Lord,
And I ain'ta gonna be treated this
    a way.

Your two dollar shoe hurts my feet,
Your two dollar shoe hurts my feet,
Your two dollar shoe hurts my feet,
    Lord, Lord,
And I ain'ta gonna be treated this
    way.

I'm a goin where them grapes and
    peaches grow,
I'm a goin where them grapes and
    peaches grow,
I'm a goin where them grapes and
    peaches grow, Lord, Lord,
And I ain'ta gonna be treated this
    way.

I been living on cold navy beans,
I been living on cold navy beans,
I been living on cold navy beans,
    Lord, Lord,
And I ain'ta gonna be treated this
    way.

* I ain't afraid of no goddam deputy
    sheriff (3 times)
  And I ain'ta gonna be treated this
    way.

* I'll get me a cop if they get me
    (3 times)
  And I ain'ta gonna be treated this
    a way.

* You bastards, you better leave me
    alone (3 times)
  'Cause I ain'ta gonna be treated
    this a way.

217

Dust Storm Disaster

This is a true song. It is about the worst dust storm in anybody's history book. I was in what is give up to be the big middle of it. Right in there north of Amarillo, Texas. I'll never forget how my wife and kinfolks looked. That was before it hit. After it got dark, you couldn't see how nobody looked. You could just reach over and get them by the hand and stand there and wonder how it would all come out. It turned wheat lands into deserts. I've seen hills change locations down there. This song is on one side of another of a Victor record. Purty fair records.

Words and music by Woody Guthrie. © 1960 (renewed), 1963 (renewed) by Ludlow Music, Inc., New York, NY. Used by permission.

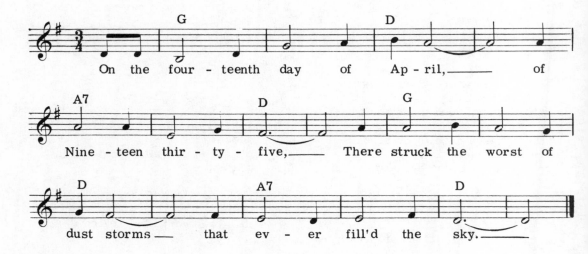

On the four-teenth day of Ap-ril,___ of Nine-teen thir-ty-five,___ There struck the worst of dust storms ___ that ev-er fill'd the sky.___

On the fourteenth day of April in
    nineteen thirty five,
There struck the worst of dust
    storms that ever filled the sky;
You could see that dust storm
    coming, it looked so awful black,
And through our little city, it left a
    dreadful track.

From Oklahoma City to the Arizona
    line,
Dakota and Nebraska to the lazy Rio
    Grande,
It fell across our city like a curtain
    of black rolled down,
We thought it was our judgment, we
    thought it was our doom.

The radio reported, we listened with
    alarm,
The wild and windy actions of this
    great mysterious storm;
From Albuquerque and Clovis, and
    all New Mexico,
They said it was the blackest that
    they had ever saw.

From Old Dodge City, Kansas, the
    dust had rung their knell,
And a few more comrades sleeping
    on top of old Boot Hill.
From Denver, Colorado, they said
    it blew so strong,
They thought that they could hold out,
    but didn't know how long.

Our relatives were huddled into
  their oil boom shacks,
The children they was crying as it
  whistled through the cracks.
The family it was crowded into the
  parlor room,
They thought the Lord was a
  coming, they thought it was
  their doom.

This storm took place at sundown
  and lasted through the night,
When we looked out next morning
  we saw a terrible sight:
We saw outside our windows where
  wheat fields once had grown
Was now a rippling ocean of dust
  the wind had blown.

It covered up our fences, it
  covered up our barns,
It covered up our tractors in this
  wild and windy storm.
We loaded our jalopies and piled
  our families in,
We rattled down the highway to
  never come back again.

Dust Can't Kill Me

Tractors a running your house down reminds me of war tanks. But tractors, dust, tanks, pistols, clubs, gas, or what, can't blow me down, can't kill me -- that's what us Okies think.

Words and music by Woody Guthrie. © 1960 (renewed), 1963 (renewed) by Ludlow Music, Inc., New York, NY. Used by permission.

That old dust storm ___ { Killed my ba - by, ___ / Got my fam - ily, ___ } ___ Can't kill me Lord, ___ can't kill me. ___ / Can't get me Lord, ___ can't get me. ___

That old dust storm killed my baby,
Can't kill me, Lord, can't kill me.
That old dust storm got my family,
Can't get me, Lord, can't get me.

That old Landlord got my
    homestead,
Can't get me, Lord, can't get me.
That old dry spell killed my crops,
    boys,
Can't kill me, no, it can't kill me.

That old tractor got my home,
    boys,
Can't get me, Lord, can't get me.
That old tractor run my house
    down,
Can't run me down, can't get me.

That old pawn shop got my
    furniture,
Can't get me, Lord, can't get me.
That old Highway got my relatives,
Can't get me, Lord, can't get me.

That old dust might kill my wheat,
    boys,
Can't kill me, Lord, can't kill me.
That old dust storm, that old dust
    storm,
Can't kill me, boys, can't kill me.

Can't blow me down, can't blow me
    down,
Can't kill me, Lord, can't kill me.
That old wind might blow this world
    down,
Can't blow me down, can't kill me.

Dust Bowl Blues

It's hard times down in the Dust Country when my Aunt Lottie starts to adding sawdust to her snuff. The real revolution starts down there when she runs clean out of snuff. She calls it her 'nerve tightener'. This song is on a record, too. I heard it after it was made. I didn't think it was any record breaker, but I guess I blowed my flue.

Words and music by Woody Guthrie. © 1964 (renewed), 1977 by
Ludlow Music, Inc., New York, NY. Used by permission.

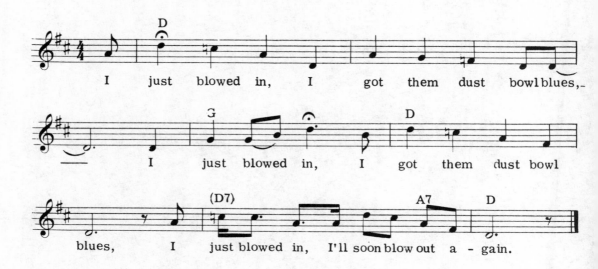

I just blowed in, I got them dust
  bowl blues,
I just blowed in, I got them dust
  bowl blues,
I just blowed in. . . I'll soon blow out
  again.

I guess you've heard about every
  kind of blues,
I guess you've heard about every
  kind of blues,
But you can't sing pretty when the
  dust gets in your flues.

I seen the dust so black that I
  couldn't see a thing,
I seen the dust so black that I
  couldn't see a thing,
And the wind so cold it nearly shut
  your water off.

I seen the wind so high it blowed my
  fences down,
I seen the wind so high it blowed my
  fences down,
It buried my tractor six feet under
  ground.

Well, it turned my farm into a pile
  of sand,
It turned my farm into a pile of
  sand,
I had to hit the road with a bundle
  in my hand.

I spent ten years down in that old
  dust bowl,
I spent ten years down in that old
  dust bowl,
When you get that dust pneumonia,
  boy, it's time to go.

222

I had a gal and she was young and
    sweet,
I had a gal and she was young and
    sweet,
But a dust storm buried her sixteen
    hundred feet.

She was a good gal, long, tall and
    stout,
She was a good gal, long, tall and
    stout,
I had to get a steam shovel just to
    dig my darlin' out.

These dust bowl blues are the
    dustiest blues I know,
These dust bowl blues are the
    dustiest blues I know,
Head over heels in that black old
    dust, had to pack up and go.

Dust Bowl Refugee

This is a song I made up right after my wife and kids and me got out to California. Our last baby was born out there. His name is Bill Rogers Guthrie. Named him over the radio. I mean that the listeners wrote in letters giving names they'd like for him to have. I liked that one a little. My wife liked it a lot. We lived in a little old brown house on the back of a lot behind a family of Chinese folks. They had come to this country to get away from war torn China. We was a trying to get away from the dust and bankers. This song is on a Victor recrod, I think.

Words and music by Woody Guthrie. © 1960 (renewed), 1963 (renewed) by Ludlow Music, Inc., New York, NY. Used by permission.

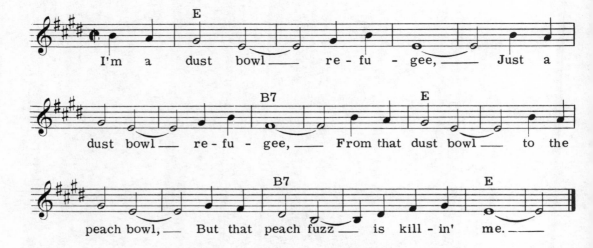

I'm a dust bowl refu-gee,
Just a dust bowl refu-gee,
From that dust bowl to the peach
    bowl,
But that peach fuzz is killin' me.

Cross the mountains to the sea,
Come the wife and kids and me.
It's a hot old dusty highway
For the dust bowl refugees.

Hard, it's always been that way,
Here today and on our way
Down the mountain, cross the
    desert,
Just a dust bowl refugee.

We are ramblers, so they say,
We are only here today,
Then we travel with the seasons,
We're the dust bowl refugees.

From the south land and the drouth
    land,
Come the wife and kids and me,
And this old world is a hard world
For a dust bowl refugee.

Yes, we ramble and we roam
And the highway is our home,
It's a never-ending highway
For the dust bowl refugees.

Yes, we wander and we work
In your fields and in your fruit,
Like the whirlwinds on the desert,
That's the dust bowl refugees.

I'm a dust bowl refugee,
I'm a dust bowl refugee,
And I wonder will I always
Be a dust bowl refugee.

You Okies and Arkies

I made the Arvin Camp lots of times with the old trusty guitar, and listened to the Campers sing in their churches and at their dances, and pie suppers and speakins. I read the paper they put out every week, the "Towsack Tattler", and it was far beyond anything most of the big city papers ever done.

Once I heard a little fourteen year old boy's poem called "I'd Ruther To Die On My Feet Than To Live On My Knees..." Can you beat that? No, you can't. It leapt out of this boy's mind like a young mountain lion, and the road was lined with cops in their big black sedans, laughing, grunting, and talking, and a listening to jazz music on their radios.

You teach kids in school to wash their teeth and brush their hair -- ought to teach 'em to sweep out their city offices, and brush out their state capitals, and keep 'em clean, and also to wear a nice clean mayor all of the time.

You Okies and Arkies get off of the
    row;
You know the C. I. O.
Get out of your trailers if you want
    a raise;
We're not fooling around many
    more days.
Come out of the field, boys, and
    don't go back in,
We've got you out now but about
    fifty men.

I'm telling you, men, times is
    getting hard,
And eighty cent cotton won't buy
    lard.
Tell Mr. John Farmer that we stand
    in a row,
And we're all backed up by the
    C. I. O.
You eat your beefsteak and farm
    with machines,
And us poor cotton pickers live on
    beans.

So Long It's Been Good To Know You

Columbia Broadcasting Company put on a radio program with me in it about the dust and the poor southern sharecroppers, the Okies and the homeless Negroes, and it had sound effects, you know, like a real dust storm and I got letters from Texas that said we was comin' in fine, and a real honest to God duster was blowing at the same time. "You got it Fine," said one letter, "except you ought to throw in a couple of wagon loads of fence posts and a section of wheat land."

This actually happened in Pampa, Gray County, Texas, April 14th, 1935. I was there. The storm was as black as tar and as big as an ocean. It looked like we was done for. Thousands of us packed up and left out. This song is on a Victor record, too, I think. Anybody got four bits?

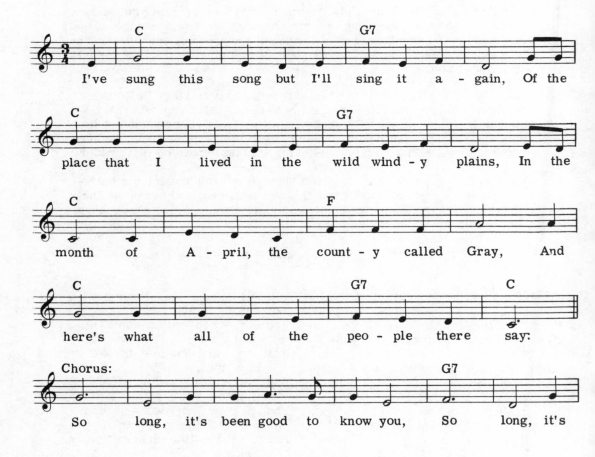

I've sung this song but I'll sing it a-gain, Of the place that I lived in the wild wind-y plains, In the month of A-pril, the count-y called Gray, And here's what all of the peo-ple there say:

Chorus: So long, it's been good to know you, So long, it's

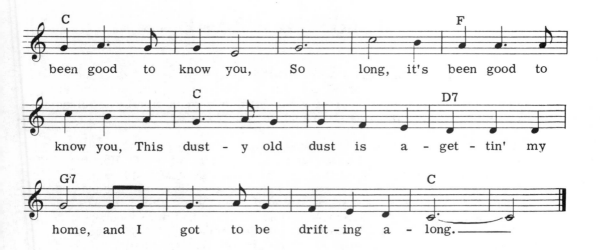

been good to know you, So long, it's been good to
know you, This dust - y old dust is a - get - tin' my
home, and I got to be drift - ing a - long.

I've sung this song but I'll sing it
   again,
Of the place that I lived in the wild
   windy plains,
In the month called April, the County
   called Gray,
And here's what all of the people
   there say:

Chorus:
So long, it's been good to know
   you,
So long, it's been good to know
   you,
So long, it's been good to know
   you,
This dusty old dust is a gettin' my
   home,
I've got to be drifting along.
      (Repeat after each verse)

A dust storm hit and it hit like
   thunder,
It dusted us over, it dusted us
   under,
It blocked out the traffic, it blocked
   out the sun,
And straight for home all the people
   did run singing:

We talked of the end of the world
   and then
We'd sing a song and then sing it
   again,
We'd set for an hour and not say a
   word,
And then these words would be heard:

The sweethearts set in the dark and
   sparked,
They hugged and kissed in that dusty
   old dark,
They sighed and cried, and hugged
   and kissed,
Instead of marriage, they talked like
   this:

The telephone rang and it jumped off
   the wall
And that was the preacher a making
   his call.
He said, "Kind friend, this might be
   the end,
You got your last chance at salvation
   of sin:"

The churches was jammed, the
   churches was packed,
That dusty old dust storm blowed so
   black
That the preacher could not read a
   word of his text,
So he folded his specs, and he took
   up collection, said:

This was the dustiest dust storm
   that ever blowed,
And most everybody they took to the
   road,
They lit down the highway as fast as
   could go,
And sung this song as they blowed:

Talkin' Dust Bowl

Me and my wife has got 3 kids, and this song. This song has brung us more groceries than a dried up farm in Okla. would, especially when you can't make enough out of your work to buy gas or oil - let alone somethin' to go in the kids stomachs, or stuff to wear.

This one hit the Columbia air waves a time or two, once on their School Of The Air, with Alan Lomax, and once on their Pursuit Of Happiness with Norm Corwin a runnin' the tractor, and Burgess Meredith a feedin' th' thrasher. I was the water boy -- water jack -- done been around and half way back. See, I just run in when the others actors' throats got dry, and they wanted to rest, and I swear, they had microbephones up there thicker'n roastin' ears in a green corn field - and kilocycles soaked in Vitaphones, and more fellers in that orchestra than that director could shake a stick at.

You talk this piece off. Pete says it's 4-4 time. If that is out of your calibre, try 38 time, or 16 guage, anything - just play a chord, and talk, and stuff like that -- Pete says he'll hang out a piece of music here to suggest how you talk it...just don't go at it dead, like Hoover reading a speech -- but go at it like a Union Man hollering for a square deal with a flock of Winchester rifles a lookin' you in the face. (With a bastard on the handle of it.)

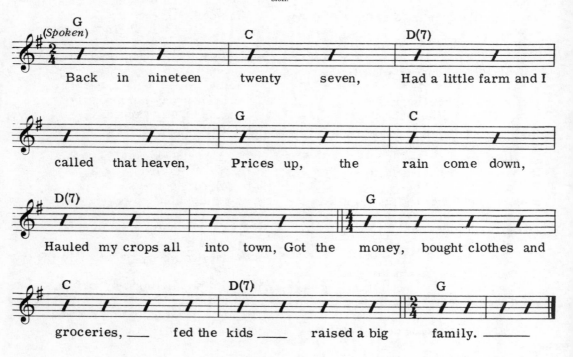

Back in nineteen twenty seven,
Had a little farm and I called that
    Heaven,
Prices up, the rain come down,
Hauled my crops, all in to town,
    Got th' money.... bought clothes
    and groceries,
    Fed the kids.... raised a big
    family.

But the rain quit and th' wind got
    high
Black old dust storm filled th' sky,
I traded my farm for a Ford machine,
Poured it full of this gass-i-lene
    And started.... rockin' and a
    rollin'
    Out to the old California....
    fruit bowl.

Way up yonder on a mountain road
Had a hot motor and a heavy load
Goin' purty fast, wasn't even
    stoppin'
Bouncin' up and down like popcorn
    a poppin'
    Had a breakdown.... nervous bust
    down
    Mechanic feller there said it was
    eng-ine trouble.

Way up yonder on a mountain curve
Way up yonder in the Piney wood,
I give that rollin' Ford a shove,
Gonna coast just far's I could,
    Commenced a rollin'.... pickin'
    up speed
    Come a hair pin turn.... and I
    didn't make it.

Man alive I'm a tellin' you
The fiddles and guitars really flew.
That Ford took off like a flyin'
    squirrel,
Flew half way around the world.
    Scattered wives and children
    All over the side of that
    mountain.

Got to California so dadgum broke,
So dadgum hungry I thought I'd
    choke,
I bummed up a spud or two,
Wife fixed up some 'tater stew.
    Shoved the kids full of it
    Looked like a tribe of thy-
    mometers runnin' around.

Lord, Man, I swear to you
That was shorely mighty thin stew,
So dam thin, I really mean,
You could read a mag-i-zine
    Right through it.... look at
    pictures, too,
    Purty whiskey bottles.... naked
    women.

Always have thought, always have
    figgered,
If that dam stew'd been a little bit
    thinner
    Some of these politicians.... the
    honest ones
    Could of seen through it.

If You Ain't Got The Do Re Mi

Words and music by Woody Guthrie. © 1961 (renewed), 1963 (renewed) by Ludlow Music, Inc., New York, NY. Used by permission.

Lots of folks back east, they say, Leav-in' home ev-ery day,

Beat-in' a hot old dust-y trail to the Cal-i-for-nia line.

Cross the des-ert sands they roll, git-tin' out of the old dust bowl; they

think they're go-in' to a sug-ar bowl,_ here's what they find: The

pol-ice at the port of ent-ry say,_____ "You're

num-ber four-teen thou-sand for to-day": _____ If you

Chorus:

ain't got the Do Re Mi, boys, If you ain't got the

Do Re Mi,_____ Bet-ter go back to beau-ti-ful

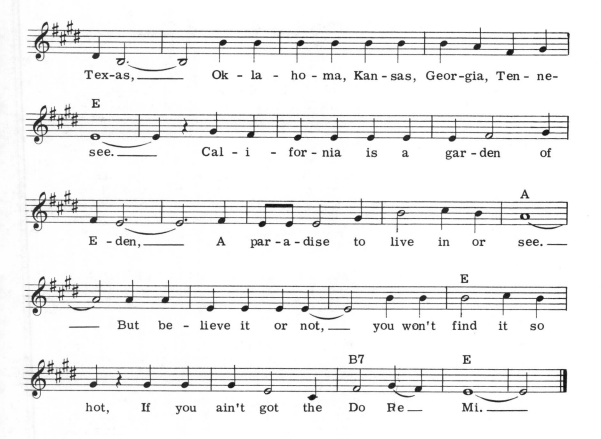

Tex-as,_____ Ok - la - ho - ma, Kan - sas, Geor-gia, Ten - ne-

see._____ Cal - i - for-nia is a gar-den of

E - den,_____ A par - a - dise to live in or see._____

_____ But be - lieve it or not,___ you won't find it so

hot, If you ain't got the Do Re___ Mi._____

Lots of folks back east, they say,
Leavin' home every day,
Beatin' a hot old dusty trail
To the California line.
Cross the desert sands they roll,
Gittin' out of the old dust bowl;
They think they're goin' to a sugar
    bowl,
Here's what they find:

The police at the port of entry say,
"You're number fourteen thousand
    for today:

Chorus:
If you aint got the Do Re Me, boys,
If you aint got the Do Re Me,
Better go back to beautiful Texas,
Oklahoma, Kansas, Georgia,
    Tennessee.

California is a garden of Eden,
A paradise to live in or see.
But believe it or not, you won't
    find it so hot,
If you aint got the Do Re Me.

If you want to buy a home or farm,
That can't do nobody harm,
Or take your vacation
By the mountains or sea.
Don't trade your old cow for a car,
Better stay right where you are,
Better take this little tip
From me:

'Cause the governor on the radio
    today
Jumped up to the microphone and he
    did say:

Repeat Chorus.

When You're Down and Out

I walked the highways of California. I been in every town mentioned in "Grapes Of Wrath" -- every single town the Joads come through. From Salisaw, Oklahoma, and on to California. I been herded around out there like a Hereford steer at cutting time, and been told in many a town that they didn't want me there. Thousands of us Okies was told that. Thousands of us Arkies, too.

All of us that was hit by hard times, dry weather, the banks, the dust, and the tractor. We could of stood the dry weather, even the black dust, and even some more of it, but it was the banks that got us. The politicians wouldn't stick by us. The bankers would not listen to reason. Nobody cared -- except the Union Boys. They was the onliest ones that was on our side through thick and thin.

I wanted to do something about it, but didn't know what. I didn't know whether to sing to 'em or shoot at 'em and I thought about a couple of big pearl handled 44's, and about the money in the banks, and about the hungry people.

But I never did get around to robbing or shooting. I found a better way to beat the rich men and the bankers at their own game, and that's the Union, the C.I.O., or any of it's unions.

Here's a song I scrawled off about the way I felt. It shows how I first thought of robbing and shooting, and then decided the Union was quicker, safer, and better -- because it says, Take Your Money But Don't Run.

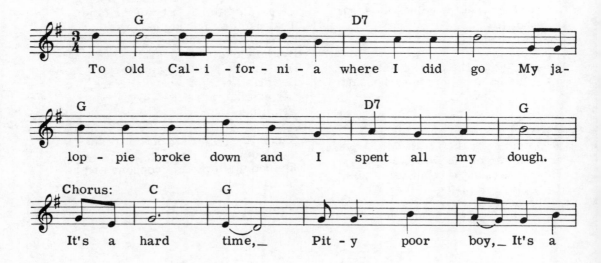

To old Cal-i-for-ni-a where I did go My ja-
lop-pie broke down and I spent all my dough.

Chorus:
It's a hard time,_ Pit-y poor boy,_ It's a

hard time,— when you're down— and out. ———

To old California where I did go
My jalopy broke down and I spent
all my dough.

Chorus:
It's a hard time, Pity Poor Boy,
It's a hard time, when you're
down and out.
(Repeat after each verse)

I rambled around in the cotton
fields,
I worked like the devil but couldn't
make meals,

I dam near to starved in an 80 cent
field,
If you was me, how would you feel?

I rambled and gambled and worked
like a dog,
I slept every night in an old holler
log.

The days they was hot and the nights
they was cold,
The stores full of groceries, the
banks full of gold.

Sometimes I think I will steal a
six-shooter
And turn out to be a Ring Tail
Tooter.

I'll strap my hip with 2 forty-fours
I'll take all their greenback and take
all their gold.

I might not know what it's all about,
I'll join with the Union and soon find
out.

I guess that the Union is better than
guns,
It says get your money, but never to
run.

233

Vigilante Man

For a long time I heard about the Vigilante man, but didn't never know for sure what he was. One night in Tracy, Cal., up close to Frisco, I found out. About 150 of us found out.

It was cold and rainy that night. It was the month of March. A car load of them rounded us up and herded us out into a cow pasture. Some of the boys stayed out there in the rain and some of us went back into town.

They caught us a second time. This time I pulled off a joke on the cops and it made them mad. They took me off alone and made me get out in front of the car in the headlights, and walked me down the road about 2 miles. They left me out in the rain by a big bridge. I crawled down under the bridge and got in a big wool bed roll with a Canadian lumber jack.

I ain't advertising the Canadian army, but them lumber jacks is about as warm a feller as you can sleep with.

Words and music by Woody Guthrie. © 1961 (renewed), 1963 (renewed) by Ludlow Music, Inc., New York, NY. Used by permission.

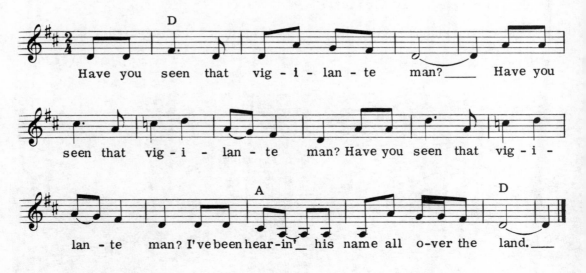

Have you seen that vig - i - lan - te man?____ Have you seen that vig - i - lan - te man? Have you seen that vig - i - lan - te man? I've been hear - in' his name all o-ver the land.____

Have you seen that Vigilante man?
Have you seen that Vigilante man?
Have you seen that Vigilante man?
I've been a hearin' his name all over the land.

Well, what is a Vigilante man?
O, what is a Vigilante man?
Has he got a gun and a club in his hand?
O, what is a Vigilante man?

Rainy night down in the engine
house,
Sleepin' just as still as a mouse,
A man come along and he chased us
out.
Was that a Vigilante man?

Stormy days we passed the time
away,
A sleepin' in some good warm
place.
A cop come along and chased us out
in the rain.
Was that a Vigilante man?

Preacher Casey was just a working
man,
And he said, "Unite the working
man."
He was killed in the river by a
deputy sheriff.
Was that a Vigilante man?

O, why does a vigilante man?
O, why does a vigilante man?
Carry a sawed-off shot-gun in his
hand?
Would he shoot his brother and
sister down?

I rambled around from town to
town,
I rambled around from town to
town,
And they drove us out like a wild
herd of cattle.
Was that the Vigilante man?

Tom Joad

The story of Tom Joad is one that a lot of boys went through. From the Oklahoma penitentiary -- to his home in the dust bowl, and then they had to get away to California -- had to pack up their old car and pull out -- and his mother and his dad, and his sisters and brothers found out about the thugs and the firebugs and the guards and the deputies that guard the fields that the rich man says "are mine" -- "You keep off."

I wonder about them guys, and I wonder what sort of songs they sing when they ain't a black jacking somebody or beating you over the head with a pick handle. This book ain't got no songs in it that was wrote by deputy sheriffs. It ain't got none wrote by company guards, nor cops, nor snitches, nor guys that set fire to the little shacks of the poor folks along the river bottoms. It's just got some songs wrote by some people. Real people. But, a guard or a deputy can always change over on the real people's side.

A long son-of-gun. Take a deep breath and sail into it.

Words and music by Woody Guthrie. © 1960 (renewed), 1963 (renewed) by Ludlow Music, Inc., New York, NY. Used by permission.

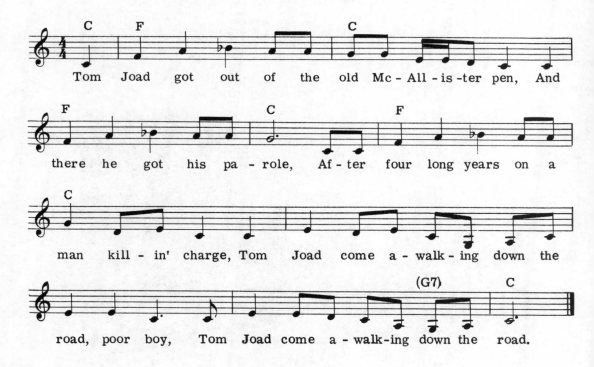

Tom Joad got out of the old Mc-All-is-ter pen, And there he got his pa-role, Af-ter four long years on a man kill-in' charge, Tom Joad come a-walk-ing down the road, poor boy, Tom Joad come a-walk-ing down the road.

Tom Joad got out of the old
McAllister pen,
And there he got his parole,
After four long years on a man-
killin' charge,
Tom Joad come a-walking down the
road, poor boy,
Tom Joad come a-walking down the
road.

It was there he met a truck driving
man
And there he caught him a ride,
Said, I just got out of the old
McAllister pen
Charge called "homicide",
Charge called "homicide."

That truck rolled away in a big
cloud of dust,
Tommy turned his face toward
home,
Met Preacher Casey and they had
a little drink
But he found that his family they was
gone, Tom Joad,
He found that his family they was
gone.

Found his mother's old fashioned
shoe
He found his daddy's hat,
Found little Muley, and little Muley
said,
They been tractored out by the
'cats', Tom,
They been tractored out by the
'cats. '

Tom Joad went down to the
neighboring farm
There he found his family.
They took Preacher Casey and
loaded in a car,
His mother said, we got to get
away, Tom,
His mother said, we got to get
away.

The twelve of the Joads made a
mighty heavy load
Grandpaw Joad did cry.
He took up a handful of land in his
hand,
Said, I'm sticking with the farm till
I die,
I'm a-sticking with the farm till I
die.

They fed him short-ribs, coffee,
and soothing syrup,
And Grandpaw Joad did die.
They buried Grandpaw Joad on the
Oklahoma road,
Grandmaw on the California side,
Grandmaw on the California side.

They stood on a mountain and looked
to the west,
It looked like the promised land,
A bright green valley with a river
runnin' through,
There was work for every single
hand, they thought,
There was work for every single
hand.

The Joads rolled into a jungle
camp
There they cooked a stew,
And the hungry little kids of the
jungle camp,
Said, we'd like to have some, too,
yes,
We'd like to have some, too.

A deputy sheriff cut loose at a man,
He shot a woman in the back,
Before he could take his aim again,
Preacher Casey dropped him in his
tracks, good boy,
Preacher Casey dropped him in his
tracks.

(continued on next page)

They handcuffed Casey and took him
      to jail,
And then he got away,
He met Tom Joad by the old river
      bridge,
And these few words he did say,
      Preacher Casey,
And these few words he did say.

Well, I preached for the Lord for a
      mighty long time,
Preached about the rich and the
      poor,
Us working folks has got to stick
      together,
Or we aint got a chance any more,
      Lord knows,
Or we aint got a chance any more.

The deputies come, and Tom and
      Casey run
To a place where the water run
      down,
A vigilante thug killed Casey with
      a club,
And laid Preacher Casey on the
      ground, poor boy,
And laid Preacher Casey on the
      ground.

Tom Joad, he grabbed that
      vigilante's club
He brought it down on his head,
Tom Joad took flight that dark rainy
      night,
A deputy and a preacher layin' dead,
      two men,
A deputy and a preacher layin' dead.

Tommy run back where his mama was
      asleep
He woke her up out of bed,
He kissed goodbye to the mother that
      he loved,
And he said what Preacher Casey
      said, Tom Joad,
He said what Preacher Casey said.

Everybody might be just One Big
      Soul
It looks that-a-way to me,
Everywhere you look in the day or
      night,
That's where I'm a-gonna be, maw,
That's where I'm a-gonna be.

Wherever little children are
      hungry and cry,
Wherever people aint free,
Wherever men are fighting for their
      rights,
That's where I'm a-gonna be, maw,
That's where I'm a-gonna be.

238

X - DETROIT SETS DOWN

Red Blood showed up in the automobile factories up at Detroit, and the Red Blood people got dam sick and tired of just a being shoved and pushed around. They decided to just haul off and set down til the big boys could have time to think it over.

Thinking, hell. That was something the big boys couldn't do without a hell of a struggle so they bought off their guards and cops and bullies and hell cut loose at Detroit. It was the working folks against the moneyed folks. The folks that come by their money honest and the folks that come by your money dishonest. The honest folks won. The honest ones win every time. Just as sure as the peach trees bloom in the springtime, the folks that are in the right will win out every time.

But it was hard as hell in Detroit. I never was in Detroit, so I caint tell you anything about Detroit, but Detroit is just a fly speck on the wall compared to the Union we got ... and lots of them Rich laughed and said we was drunk on dam fool notions. They thought the sun rose and set up on their ass. They found out the sun and the world is 2 mighty big things, and the Union bigger than that.

SIT DOWN STRIKES IN GENERAL MOTORS' PLANTS

News: March 9, 1937. "Ten thousand are idle. 300 hold three factories of the Hudson Motor Company. Small picket groups headed by a banjo strumming union leader move back and forth between the Hudson plants and the Chrysler factory."

News: March 25, 1937. "Strikers evacuate plants. This is like soldiers returning from the wars. There is a heavy snow fall. The streets are crowded with the wives, children and relatives of the strikers. They carry flags and sing. The line of March (a band leads a "Sit Down Parade") is flanked by the union's flying squadron wearing green over-seas caps. Women wear green berets and armbands. The cheers and the noise of automobile horns sometimes drown out the singing. The men emerge from the buildings. Some are heavily bearded. They carry rolls of blankets, bundles of clothing and suitcases and join the parade. Some of the strikers met at the union hall for a party of singing and hamburgers."

The Fisher Strike

I first thought that this was a gonna be a song about the ocean, but it ain't. It's about some guys that worked in the Fisher Body plant, and shows you what you can do when you get organized. You can show the stud buzzards what's what. You can show a man that 2 men is more important than one man, and that his dam old money ain't worth a fart in a whirlwind – it's the Union that counts. This world belongs to all of th' people. That's the Living Truth. A few rich dudes don't believe it. But Abe Lincoln believed it. Jesus believed it. I believe it, shore as hell, and you'll believe it before it's over with.

The Martins and the Coys had 'em a feud over a liquor still and shot off ten or twelve boys and men on both sides. This is a song that come out of a whole lot better fight. The one where the Union Boys showed the Money Boys what's What.

(same tune as "The Martins and the Coys")

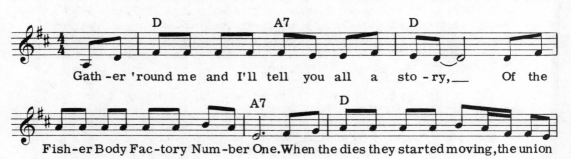

Gath-er 'round me and I'll tell you all a sto-ry,__ Of the

Fish-er Body Fac-tory Num-ber One. When the dies they started moving, the union

men, they had a meet-ing to de-cide right then and there what must be done.

Chorus:

These four thou-sand un-ion boys, they made a lot of noise, They de-

cid-ed then and there to shut down tight. In the of-fice they got snoot-y, so we

start - ed pick -et du - ty. Now the Fish-er Bod - y Shop is Out on strike.

Gather round me and I'll tell you all
    a story
Of the Fisher Body Factory Number
    One,
When the dies they started moving,
The Union men they had a meeting
To decide right then and there what
    must be done.

Chorus:
These four thousand union boys,
They made a lot of noise,
They decided then and there to
    shut down tight.
In the office they got snooty,
So we started picket duty,
Now the Fisher Body Shop is
Out on strike.
(Repeat after each verse)

Now this strike it started one
    bright Wednesday evening,
When they loaded up a boxcar full of
    dies.
When the union boys they stopped
    them
And the railroad workers backed
    them,
The officials in the office were
    surprised.

Now they really started out to
    strike in earnest;
They took possession of the gates
    and building, too.
They placed a guard in either
    clockhouse
Just to keep the non-union men out,
And they took the keys and locked
    the gages up, too.

Bring Me My Robe and Slippers, James

Words and Music by Maurice Sugar

Bring me my robe and slippers,
  James:
Pull up my easy chair.
Bring me my pipe and cushions,
  James,
I'm not going anywhere.

Let me have peace and quiet,
  James,
Free from the noise and din,
And give my regrets to Mister
  Sloan;
Just tell him I'm staying in.

242

Oh, Mister Sloan

Composed March 1937 by Gilliland and Beck, workers
in Chevy No. 4. Mr. Travis is Bob Travis, C.I.O.
organizer for Flint; Mr. Sloan is President of General
Motors.

First time I ever heard the tune "Mr. Gallagher and Mr. Sheen," it
was in 1922 in Oklahoma City. My dad was staying there at the Kingkade
Hotel, and he was a running that year for Corporation Commissioner.
(Longest words I ever see, anyhow, he run for them.) See it has jumped
out again up Flint, Michigan. Well, the song as a whole seems to of got
salvation since the last time I seen it. I like the way it sounds here
better than the way it used to be.

(tune of "Mr. Gallagher and Mr. Sheen")

Oh, Mis-ter Sloan! Oh, Mis-ter Sloan! We have known for a long time you would a-

tone   For the wrongs that you have done, we all know, yes, ev-'ry one. Ab-so-

lute-ly, Mis-ter Trav-is! Pos-i-tive-ly, Mis-ter Sloan!

Oh, Mister Sloan! Oh, Mister
  Sloan!
We have known for a long time you
  would atone
For the wrongs that you have done,
We all know, yes, every one.
Absolutely, Mister Travis!
Positively, Mister Sloan!

Oh, Mister Sloan! Oh, Mister
  Sloan!
Everyone knows your heart was
  made of stone.
But the union is so strong
That we'll always carry on.
Absolutely, Mister Travis!
Positively, Mister Sloan!

Oh, Mister Sloan! Oh, Mister
  Sloan!
We are absolutely sure that you
  would burn
If the salary that you got
Was less than what you earn.
Absolutely, Mister Travis!
Positively, Mister Sloan!

Oh, Mister Sloan! Oh, Mister
  Sloan!
Our homes are what we all now
  wish to own.
But living costs are high,
So we're out to do or die.
Absolutely, Mister Travis!
Positively, Mister Sloan!

Sit Down

If you don't do to suit your boss, why he won't hesitate a dam minute to let you go and he don't care nothin' about how you get by after that. It's root hog or die. Well, the boss ain't th' only pile in the barnyard, if he don't do to suit you, why you can just set down. Boy, that's what gets the big shots, for you to just say; "Well, boys, you go ahead and run your damned old pistol asses factories, and gather in your crops and do the work your own self. Me, I don't have a pot to throw out the window anyhow, if I do work for you at these measly wages. Reckon I'll jest coil up over here with a good Union Book and take it easy." Hot a Mighty, boy, Howdy, Jeeeez, that brings 'em to their milk. (Note: I throwed in the "Jeeeeez" because I didn't want to leave New York completely out.)

Words and Music by Maurice Sugar

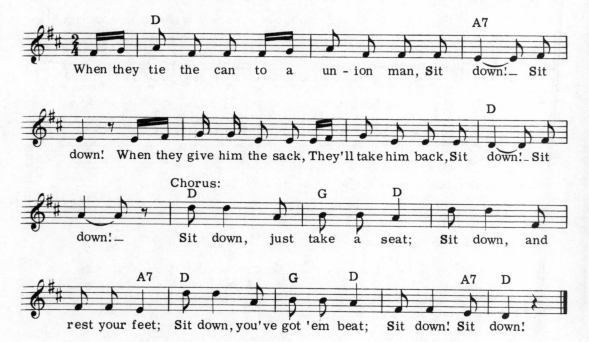

When they tie the can
To a union man,
Sit down! Sit down!
When they give him the sack,
They'll take him back.
Sit down! Sit down!

Chorus:
Sit down, just take a seat,
Sit down, and rest your feet,
Sit down, you've got 'em beat.
Sit down! Sit down!
(Repeat after each verse)

When they smile and say, "No
        raise in pay",
Sit down! Sit down!
When you want the boss to come
        across,
Sit down! Sit down!

When the speed-up comes, just
        twiddle your thumbs,
Sit down! Sit down!
When you want 'em to know, they'd
        better go slow,
Sit down! Sit down!

When the boss won't talk, don't
        take a walk,
Sit down! Sit down!
When the boss sees that, he'll want
        a little chat,
Sit down! Sit down!

We're The Guys

My Dear Rich and Lousy Friend: Thought I would drop you a few lines tonight just to let you know that I think you are sunk.

You remember I promised to sort of do some snitching for you and tell you what was a going on. Well, I have discovered that there are some Working Folks in the world that did not quite fall for the manure that you have been putting out in your newspapers, magazines, shows, radios, and so forth, and they know good and well that you stole everything from them. So it strikes me that they are going to strike out to strike. That means they ain't a gonna do no more work for you til you give them back their property and houses and groceries and whiskey and cars and good looking women and stuff.

Seems only fair that they should feel this a way. I know you ain't enjoyed a good night's sleep in a long time. Your conscience was too screwed up. Then you got sore about something and you tried to raise hell of the folks that worked for you. Then you got 5 more divorces and gambled off a car load of money in a gambling game. Then you had to cut the folks wages down to where you could lose some more next night. Then you lost some more and you got sore and decided to get drunk. Which you did. And when you was drunk you blowed more money in a day than we see in three years.

So you see how it is. Or do you? I doubt it. You got eyes but you cain't see. You got ears but you cain't hear. You ain't got nothing but one long gut that runs right straight through you like a subway tunnel – and you're trying to eat us all up, but some guys are forming a Union to keep you from it. You old Lizard. You old cave full of bats.

Words and music by Maurice Sugar

We're the guys that grow your grub and we're hun-gry all the time.

We're the guys that grow your grub and we're hun-gry all the time.

We're the guys that grow your grub and then you give us the pol-ice-man's club.

Chorus:

So —— we're let-ting you know we're not so slow, We're rar-in' to go, and we're tak-ing the show.

We're the guys that grow your grub
And we're hungry all the time.
We're the guys that grow your grub,
And we're hungry all the time.
We're the guys that grow your grub
And then you give us the policeman's
    club.
So, - we're lettin' you know, we're
    not so slow,
We're rarin' to go and we're takin'
    the show.

We're the guys that make your
    clothes
And we're ragged all the time.
We're the guys that make your
    clothes
And we're ragged all the time.
We're the guys that make your
    clothes
And you give us a poke in the nose.
So, - we're lettin' you know, we're
    not so slow,
We're rarin' to go and we're takin'
    the show.

We're the guys that dig your coal
And we're freezing all the time.
We're the guys that dig your coal
And we're freezing all the time.
We're the guys that dig your coal
And then you give us the lousy dole.
So, - we're lettin' you know, we're
    not so slow,
We're rarin' to go and we're takin'
    the show.

We're the guys that make your cars
And we're walking all the time.
We're the guys that make your cars
And we're walking all the time.
We're the guys that make your cars
And then you stick us behind the
    bars.
So, - we're lettin' you know, we're
    not so slow,
We're rarin' to go and we're not so
    slow.

We're the guys that took your bunk
And you fooled us all the time.
We're the guys that took your bunk
And you fooled us all the time.
We're the guys that took your bunk
And now we are wise -- YOU'RE
    SUNK.
So, - we're lettin' you know, we're
    not so slow,
We're rarin' to go and we're takin'
    the show.

Collective Bargaining In Our Shops

Collective bargaining ain't like arguing with a Collector. It don't mean swapping with a Finance Man. It means when a whole herd of you get together and decide what you're a gonna do. You decide about the work and about the hours and about the money. Not a thing wrong with that that I can see. Now I know it ain't everyday conversation, Collective Bargaining. Too long to carry around in your mouth. But if anybody ever asks you if you believe in it, why you just tell 'em hell yes.

(Vic Bush, Flint, Michigan, 1937)

Col - lect - ive bar-gain-ing in our shops, C – I – C – I – O. ___ And

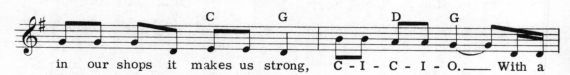

in our shops it makes us strong, C – I – C – I – O. ___ With a

un-ion here, a un-ion there, here a un-ion, there a union everywhere a un-ion, col-

lect - ive bar - gain - ing in our shops, C – I – C – I – O.

Collective bargaining in our shops,
C-I-C-I-O
And in our shops it makes us
    strong
C-I-C-I-O.

With a union here, and a union
    there,
Here a union, there a union
Everywhere a union;
Collective bargaining in our
    shops,
C-I-C-I-O.

When the strike is done and we
    have won,
C-I-C-I-O
We'll hang the scabs all one by
    one,
C-I-C-I-O.

With a scab, scab here, etc.
With a union here, etc.
Collective bargaining in our
    shops,
C-I-C-I-O.

Our boys are sitting in the shops,
C-I-C-I-O
And they won't come out til the
    speed-up stops,
C-I-C-I-O.

    With a sit down here, etc.
    With a scab, scab here, etc.
    With a union here, etc.
    Collective bargaining in our
      shops,
    C-I-C-I-O.

As the years go drifting by,
C-I-C-I-O
The auto union will not die,
C-I-C-I-O.

    With a union here, etc.
    With a sit-down here, etc.
    With a scab, scab here, etc.
    With a union here, etc.
    Collective bargaining in our
      shops,
    C-I-C-I-O.

Knuts to Knudsen

(Just like a college yell)

Knuts to Knudsen,
Slush to Sloan,
Boo's for Boysen,
The Union's our own!

Knudsen was the fireman,
Sloan rang the bell,
Parker started the speed-up,
And G. M. went to hell!

On The Picket Line

The Picket Line is the Working Folks. The thugs and guards and police that throw hand grenades and tear gas bombs are on the side of the Rich Folks. It's the Soup Line that drives you to the Picket Line, and the Picket Line that takes you to Workers' Heaven, plenty of work and fair and square wages. If you stand for that, move over, buddy, and get a wiggle on and come on and show it on the Picket Line.

Tune: "Polly Wolly Doodle"

We win our strike and all our de-mands; Come and picket on the pick-et line. In

one strong un-ion we'll join our hands; Come and picket on the picket line. On the

Chorus:
line, ___ on the line, ___ on the pick - et, pick-et line, ___ The

dir-ty lit-tle scab, we'll use him like a rag, Come and picket on the pick-et line.

To win our strike and all our
  demands;
Come and picket on the picket line.
In one strong union we'll join our
  hands;
Come and picket on the picket line.

Chorus:
On the line, on the line, on the
  picket, picket line,
The dirty little scab, we'll use him
  like a rag,
Come and picket on the picket line.
(Repeat after each verse)

If you've never spent a night in jail,
Come and picket on the picket line.
You will be invited without fail;
Come and picket on the picket line.

If you don't like scabs and thugs and
  stools,
Come and picket on the picket line.
For you show the boss that the
  worker rules,
When you picket on the picket line.

...and here are some extra verses
written by Sark, a worker in Chrysler
Highland Park plant.

Who paid a quarter million bucks
For double-crossing spies,
To crawl like rats into our homes,
'Neath friendship's fair disguise?
If men must lose their souls to
    work,
In such shops we decline,
So now we voice our protest
In a moving picket line.

Chorus:

Our fight is not for us alone,
But for workmen everywhere,
The rights we ask are not unjust
But sensible and fair.
To wear a union button now
Your duty is, and mine.
We'll win this strike when all of us
Get in that picket line.

...Here's another kind of chorus
that some folks sing.

On the line, on the line,
On the pick, pick, picket line,
We'll fight and yell and shout like
    hell,
On the pick, pick, picket line.

There's Something About A Worker

There's some-thing a-bout a work-er, there's some-thing a-bout a work-er, There's some-thing a-bout a work-er that is fine, fine, fine. There's some-thing in his bear-ing, some-thing in what he's wear-ing, Some-thing a-bout his feat-ures all a-shine, shine, shine. He may be a lit-tle in-spec-tor, He may be a big die mak-er, He may be a com-mon work-er on the line, line, line. But the work-er's health-y chest seems to suit the lad-ies best; There's some-thing a-bout a work-er that is fine, fine, fine.

There's something about a worker,
There's something about a worker,
There's something about a worker
That is fine, fine, fine.
There's something in his bearing,
Something in what he's wearing,
Something about his features all a
        shine, shine, shine.
He may be a little inspector,
He may be a big die maker,
He may be a common worker on the
        line, line, line.
But the worker's healthy chest
Seems to suit the ladies best;
There's something about a worker
        that is fine, fine, fine.

There Was a Rich Man
and He Lived in Detroitium

These rich and high hat hogs say that we ain't Christians. They say that we're a trying to do away with all religion. They say we don't believe in a dam thing. They say we are killers, robbers, and a bunch of crazy fools trying to start trouble everywhere we go. Trying to overthrow the United States Government...and other dam lies.

When you say "government", you mean the "people." You mean the folks that are your friends and your neighbors and guys you see every day. They're the United States Government and not them money mad guys that have managed to beat all of us out of our money. They ain't but a few of them. Just about a couple or three thousand, maybe a few more. They say they are the U.S. Government.

Well then, I shore would like to know just who the hell are we? All of the big smart men that ever was or ever will be says we, you and me, are the government -- and when certain louses manage to lie their filthy way into offices of power where they've got to say so, and then try to rob us or starve us or lie to us over and over again - then we ought to all get together and boost the liars and thieves and two faced wind-bags out of our government offices and put in honest, hard-working folks.

That is saving the U.S. Government. That aint throwing it down or destroying it.

To the tune of "Skinnamalinkadoolium" (P. 106)

There was a rich man and he lived
    in Detroitium,
Glory hallelujah, heirojarum.
And all the workers he did
    exploitium,
Glory hallelujah, heirojarum.

Chorus:
Heirojarum, heirojarum,
Skinnamalinkadoolium,
Skinnamalinkadoolium,
Glory hallelujah, heirojarum.
(Repeat after each verse)

The poor man worked til he was
    nearly deadium, etc.
When he got home he fell right
    into bedium, etc.

He asked for a raise but the boss
    only saidium, etc.

"Get out of here, you lousy little
    redium, etc.

The poor man finally came to the
    conclusion, etc.
To get his raise he'd better join the
    union, etc.

He talked to the boss again but not
    alonium, etc.
They said, "Don't forget what the
    union did to Sloanium, etc.

The boss wouldn't talk so they sat
    in the plantium, etc.
All the boss could do was rave and
    rantium, etc.

The moral of this story is that
    unions are no jokium, etc.
A boss who gets smart with the
    union may go brokium, etc.

........*How do you like this book? A postal card or a letter from you would tickle me to death. I don't know for sure just what jail I'll be in* ....

255

Goody Goody

Goody Goody was a love song to start with, but its purty hard to love at a high speed when you're hungry. Real honest to goodness love, though, grows faster and produces a better stalk in a fight for bread and butter than at a dance, or when you're coiled up with a good book. As I recollect, it was a fair tune when it come out first, but it was only a little seed then. Here it is full-grown, full-blossomed and loaded down with real fruit.

(words by members of Women's Auxiliary, U.A.W., Michigan, 1937)

So the un-ion boys have set you back on your heels, goody goody; So they're sit-ting down, and now you know how it feels, good-y goody! So they're down in your plant too; they'll be sure to see it through And the wom-en are be-hind them, now how do you do? So you lie a-wake, a-sing-ing the blues all night, good-y goody, 'Cause this un-ion gang's a bar-rel of dyn-a-mite. Hur-ray and hal-le-lu-jah you

had it com-ing to ya! Good-y good-y for us,_____ good-y

good-y for you,___ And we hope you're sat-is-fied, you ras-cal, you.

So the union boys have set you back
    on your heels,
Goody, Goody.
So they're sitting down and now you
    know how it feels,
Goody, Goody.
So they're down in your plant, too,
They'll be sure to see it through,
And the women are behind them,
Now how do you do?
So you lie awake just singing the
    blues all night,
Goody, Goody.
Cause this union gang's a barrel
    of dynamite,
Hurray and hallelujah,
You had it coming to ya,
Goody, goody for you,
Goody, goody for us,
And we hope you're satisfied,
You rascal, you.

*...and here's a Goody Goody that
was born in a strike in Lebanon,
Pennsylvania. It was given to us by
a organizer in LaFollette. I use to
sing this song in Texas honky tonks
and saloons and at the country
dances and I like it ten times better
the Union way. Give me mine Union
Maid.*

When we walked out on you we set
    you back on your heels,
Goody, goody.
You can't make money so now you
    know how it feels,
Goody, goody.
You gave the lawyer your money,
    too,
Just as we gave ours to you.
Now you're broken in little pieces,
Oh, how do you do.
You lie awake nights just rubbing
    your hands,
Goody, goody.
And you found out that the union is
    a barrel of dynamite.
Hooray and hallelujah.
You had it coming to you,
Goody, goody for you,
Goody, goody for us,
We hope you're satisfied,
You rascal, you.

Rock-A-Bye-Baby

I heard this song all my life. Mama used to put me to sleep with it. Now
here it comes out in Union Form and wakes me up.

Rock-a-bye baby, on the tree top;
When you grow up, you'll work in a
    shop.
When you are married, your wife
    will work, too,
So that the rich will have nothing to
    do.

Hush-a-bye baby, on the tree top;
When you grow old, your wages
    will stop.
When you have spent the little
    you've made,
First to the poorhouse, then to the
    grave.

XI - THE FARMERS GET TOGETHER

There Is Mean Things Happening In This Land

"When the planters in East Arkansas saw that the people were joining the union, they told them to git off the land. They didn't wait for some of them to git – they threw them off. It was a cold winter. The hungry people had no place to go. When they held union meetings the laws clubbed them til they lay like dead. It didn't make no difference if they was men or women. They killed some union members and threw others in jail. That was in the winter, in 1936.

"In the spring, at cotton chopping time, it didn't make much difference if we was working or not – our young ones was still hungry. So we began to talk about a strike. Most of us was workin' from sun up to sun down for less than 70 cents a day. We wanted $1.50 a day for ten hours work. We made handbills and posters and signs telling what we wanted and plastered them up all over the place. There was about four thousand altogether who said they would go on strike.

"The planters got scared. The laws arrested every man they could git hold of and took them back to work at the point of guns. They beat up men and women and they shot some and tried to scare us. They ran a lot of folks out. But they couldn't break the strike. We had marches. We all lined up, sometimes more than a hundred of us on a line, and marched through the plantations and cross country. In lots of places where we marched the choppers stopped work and went on strike with us. At one plantation the scabs they had brought from other places dropped their hoes and run like rabbits for cover when they saw us comin'.

"As we were marching, we were asking, like somebody asked in the Bible: 'What you mean that you crush my people and grind the faces of the poor'." – John Handcox

...if you want to leave out the chanting part and just make a song out of the choruses, it goes mighty well that way, too.

There is mean things hap-pen-ing in this land, There is mean things hap-pen-ing in this land But the un-ion's go-ing on, And the un-ion's go-ing strong, There is mean things hap-pen-ing in this land.

Chant:

On the eighteenth day of May
The Union called a strike,
But the planters and the bosses
Throwed the people out of their
    shacks.

Chorus:
There is mean things happening
    in this land,
There is mean things happening
    in this land,
But the union's going on and the
    union's going strong,
There is mean things happening
    in this land.
(Repeat after each verse)

The planters throwed the people off
    the land,
Where many years they'd spent,
And in the hard cold winter,
They had to live in tents.

The planters throwed the people out,
Without a bite to eat,
They cursed them and kicked them,
And some with axe handles beat.

The people got tired of working for
    nothing,
And that from sun to sun,
But the planters forced some to work
At the point of guns.

There is mean things happening in
    this land,
There is mean things happening in
    this land,
Oh, the rich man boasts and brags
    while the poor man goes in
    rags,
There is mean things happening in
    this land.

There is mean things happening in
    this land, (2 times)
Oh, the farmer cannot eat, 'cause
    he's raised too much wheat,
There is mean things happening in
    this land.

There is mean things happening in
    this land, (2 times)
Too much cotton in our sacks so we
    have none on our backs,
There is mean things happening in
    this land.

There is mean things happening in
    this land, (2 times)
Lots of groceries on the shelves,
    but we have none for ourselves,
There is mean things happening in
    this land.

There is mean things happening in
    this land, (2 times)
Oh, we'll have even less to eat when
    the drums commence to beat,
There is mean things happening in
    this land.

There is mean things happening in
    this land (2 times)
But when the working men refuse to
    put on their old war shoes,
There'll be GOOD THINGS
    happening in this land.

There'll be GOOD THINGS happening
    in this land, (2 times)
When the workers take a stand and
    unite in a solid band,
There'll be GOOD THINGS happening
    in this land.

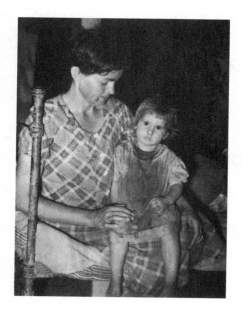

No More Mournin'

"I'm just a broken-down cowboy from Texas. I represent about 50 white people in my local. We are going to try and do our best to have a good representation at the next convention and we are going to have Negro folks coming with us, too. The Mexican and the Negroes are okay and they are organizing with us.

"I am glad that I had the opportunity to come down here because I learned a whole lot. We been in the ditch, on the ditch and everywhere but in the well to get here, but I'm glad we came. We may get our heads knocked off, but I think we've learned how to protect ourselves." - W. Jeff Fleming, cowboy from Texas, at the 3rd Annual Convention of the S.T.F.U., 1937

This old, old Negro spiritual was sung by John Handcox in sharecroppers' union meetings all over the south, and by now it's spread through the whole country.

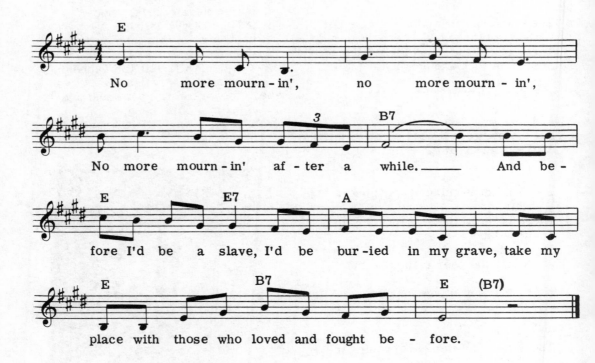

No more mourn-in', no more mourn-in',
No more mourn-in' af-ter a while.___ And before I'd be a slave, I'd be bur-ied in my grave, take my
place with those who loved and fought be - fore.

No more mournin', no more
  mournin',
No more mournin' after while,
And before I'll be a slave,
I'll be buried in my grave,
Take my place with those who
  loved and fought before.

No more cryin', no more cryin',
No more cryin' after while,
And before I'll be a slave,
I'll be buried in my grave,
Take my place with those who
  loved and fought before.

No more weepin', no more weepin',
No more weepin' after while,
And before I'll be a slave,
I'll be buried in my grave,
Take my place with those who
  loved and fought before.

No more sorrows, no more
  sorrows,
No more sorrows after while,
And before I'll be a slave,
I'll be buried in my grave,
Take my place with those who
  loved and fought before.

Oh, freedom, oh, freedom,
Oh, freedom after while,
And before I'll be a slave,
I'll be buried in my grave,
Take my place with those who
  loved and fought before.

No more misery, no more misery,
No more misery after while,
And before I'll be a slave,
I'll be buried in my grave,
Take my place with those who
  loved and fought before.

No more slavery, no more slavery,
No more slavery after while,
And before I'll be a slave,
I'll be buried in my grave,
Take my place with those who
  loved and fought before.

Ten Little Farmer Men

by John M. Henry
from Sharecroppers Voice, Vol. III, Number 4,
September, 1937.

Ten little farmer men, all sitting
fine;
The money lender got one and then
there were nine.

Nine little farmer men toiling long
and late;
The tax collector got one and then
there were eight.

Eight little farmer men working
like eleven;
The long drought got one and then
there were seven.

Seven little farmer men working
double tricks;
The big flood got one and then there
were six.

Six little farmer men struggling to
survive;
The insects got one and then there
were five.

Five little farmer men raising
crops galore;
"Over production" got one and then
there were four.

Four little farmer men working fast
and free;
Soil erosion got one and then there
were three.

Three little farmer men, all a'fret
and stew;
The dust storms got one and then
there were two.

Two little farmer men working in
the sun;
Competition got one and then there
was one.

One little farmer man, couldn't be
outdone;
Satan took the hindmost and then
there was none.

Ten little farmer men, all down and
out,
Met to try to find out what it was all
about.

Organized a Union right there on the
spot;
Each took out his card and signed it
on the spot.

Enemies now can't get one without
getting all;
The enemy therefore never gets any
one at all.

In Union bonds they now take up
their stand;
All for one and one for all - to a
man.

United, one by one their foes they
subdue;
What Union did for them it can do
for you.

*** Ladeez an' gentul-men... 'nuff
sed.

Raggedy Raggedy Are We

"We can't get any flour, snuff, shoes, sugar, coffee, thread or anything from the landlord but meat and meal. We have a divil of a time. No soap, soda or salt. Can't borrow a dime, not a damn cent. If this ain't hell, I'll eat you. We work our damn heads off and git nothing. The harder we work, the deeper in debt we gits." - From "The Collapse of Cotton Tenancy" by Johnson, Embree and Alexander.

Words by Lee Hays and John Handcox. Music: Traditional. © 1967 (renewed) by Sanga Music, Inc. All rights reserved. Used by permission.

Ragg - 'dy, Ragg - 'dy are we, Just as rag-ged as rag - ged can be. We don't get noth -ing for our la - bor, so ragg -'dy ragg - 'dy are we.

Raggedy, raggedy are we, (oh lawdy),
Just as raggedy as raggedy can be,
We don't get nothing for our labor,
So raggedy, raggedy are we.

So hungry, hungry are we,
Just as hungry, as hungry can be,
We don't get nothing for our labor,
So hungry, hungry are we.

So homeless, homeless, are we,
Just as homeless, as homeless can be,
We don't get nothing for our labor,
So homeless, homeless are we.

So landless, landless are we,
Just as landless as landless can be,
We don't get nothing for our labor,
So landless, landless are we.

So cowless, cowless are we,
Just as cowless, as cowless can be,
The planters don't 'low us to raise 'em,
So cowless, cowless are we.

So hogless, hogless are we,
Just as hogless, as hogless can be,
The planters don't 'low us to raise 'em,
So hogless, hogless are we.

So cornless, cornless are we,
Just as cornless as cornless can be,
The planters don't 'low us to raise it,
So cornless, cornless are we.

So pitiful, pitiful are we,
Just as pitiful as pitiful can be,
We don't get nothing for our labor,
So pitiful, pitiful are we.

265

The Planter and the Sharecropper

"I hear people always talkin' about the hard times they have been havin' since the depression. But most of us farmers and sharecroppers and tenants here in the south have always had depression. In 1929, before the trouble on Wall Street and in the banks, everybody was supposed to be prosperous. But we farmers in the south didn't make more than an average of a hundred and eighty-six dollars that year, all told, and a lot of us made a lot less. We had to buy tools and seed and fertilizer and pay taxes and interest on our debts out of that money. That didn't leave much for eating and buying a pair of overalls and paying a doctor when somebody was sick. And there was plenty sickness. Our young ones sickened and died of Pellagra and Consumption.

"In 1937 and '38 most of the sharecroppers around here were lucky if they made ten or fifteen cents a day. It's always been hard times for the farmer. It's always been like that Negro sharecropper, Handcox, said in that song of his about the sharecropper and the planter:

> Makes no difference how much the sharecropper raise,
> The planter he gets all the praise.

"Seems like that's the way it's always been with us."

This was composed by John Handcox, who lived in Brinkley, Arkansas, until circumstances constrained him to leave Arkansas. He now lives in Charleston, Missouri. He is a young Negro, perhaps 25 years old. This poem was composed in 1935. He recorded it in Washington, D.C. in March, 1937.

The planter lives upon the sweat of
    the sharecropper's brow;
Just how the sharecropper lives,
    the planter cares not how.
The sharecropper raises all the
    planter can eat,
And then gets tramped down under
    his feet.

The sharecropper raises all the
    planter can wear,
Whilst he and his family have to go
    bare.
The sharecropper works and toils
    and sweats,
The planter brings him out in debt.

The planters has good and wholesome
    food to eat;
The sharecropper has cornbread,
    molasses and fatback meat.

A lot of good things the planters has
    to waste,
But the sharecropper knows not how
    it taste.

The sharecropper's wife goes to the
    kitchen washtub and field,
Whilst the planter's wife enjoys
    herself in an automobile.
The planter's children dresses up
    and goes to school,
Whilst the sharecropper's puts on
    rags and follows a mule.

If you asks the planters for your
    rights
You might as well to spit in his face
    and ask for a fight.
The planter says he inherits his
    wealth from birth,
But it all comes from the poor man
    who tills the earth.

The planters gets together and they
    plots and plans -
You can bet your life its all against
    the poor man.
The planter takes the sharecroppers
    mule, wagon and plough,
Don't allow them to have a home nor
    a cow.

When the sharecropper dies he has
    to be buried in a box,
Without any necktie or any socks.
Makes no difference how much the
    sharecropper raise,
The planter he gets all of the
    praise.

The planter lives in a house as fine
    as the best,
Wears good clothes and gets all of
    the rest.
The sharecropper works hard and
    wears cotton sacks,
And lives in the filthy, raggedy,
    broken down shacks.

The poor man has fought all the rich
    man's wars,
And now he is punished without any
    cause.
The sharecropper labors the
    planter's pockets to swell,
But the planter's unjust deeds are
    sending him straight to hell.

No rich planter to be do ever I
    crave,
But I want to be something more
    than a planter's slave.
And now if anyone thinks this aint
    the truth,
He can go to the South and get
    proof!

———————————————

Landlord, what in the hell is the
    matter with you?
What has your labor ever done to
    you?
Upon their backs you ride,
Don't you think your labor never git
    tired.

- from another poem by John Handcox

267

Roll The Union On

"I am asking you, farmers, if you ever made a bale of cotton or a stalk of corn to organize. I am a union man to start with. I have been in 48 states of the union and I know we must organize. You want black and white men to come together. And that is right. That is the way it should be." - J.W. Bushea, member of the American Farmers' Association before the 3rd Annual Convention of the S.T.F.U.

It takes all kinds of colors to make a picture...................................

Chorus:

We're gon - na roll, ___ We're gon - na roll, ___ We're gon - na roll ___ the un - ion on, ___ We're gon - na roll, ___ we're gon - na roll, ___ ___ We're gon - na roll ___ the un - ion on. If the plant - er's in the way we're gon - na roll it o - ver him, Gon - na roll it o - ver him, Gon - na roll it o - ver him, If the plant-er's in the way we're gon - na

roll it o - ver him, Gon - na roll __ the un - ion on.

Chorus:
We're gonna roll, we're gonna
   roll,
We're gonna roll the union on.
We're gonna roll, we're gonna
   roll,
We're gonna roll the union on.
(Repeat after each verse)

If the planter's in the way,
We're gonna roll it over him,
Gonna roll it over him,
Gonna roll it over him,
If the planter's in the way,
We're gonna roll it over him,
Gonna roll the union on.

If the boss is in the way, etc.

If the merchant's in the way, etc.

If the banker's in the way, etc.

If the preacher's in the way, etc.

If Futrell's in the way, etc.

If Wall Street's in the way, etc.

Down In Old Henderson

Guy who made this up was an organizer for the old Southern Tenant Farmers' Union, the Union of the sharecroppers. They stuck him in jail, but he said as soon as he got out he'd start organizing again. So this is a jailhouse song that is more than just a jailhouse song.

Down in old Henderson, down on my
    knees,
Asking the captain to stop feeding
    peas.
Stop feeding peas, yes, stop feeding
    peas,
Asking the captain to stop feeding
    peas.

Judge Cowper sentenced me to six
    months on the gang,
Thinking he would break me and I'd
    join his gang.
But he has failed, yes, boys, he has
    failed,
I'll fight the harder for my ideals.

They carried me to the chain gang
    and, oh, what a sight!
Working young boys from morning
    to night,
Working young boys at the age of
    sixteen
Who had innocent faces and were
    not mean.

I woke the next morning, looking
    once around,
All I could hear was rock quarry
    bound.
Rock quarry bound, yes, rock
    quarry bound,
All I could hear was rock quarry
    bound.

They awoke you each morning at
    four o'clock,
Said: "Get to hell out of here.
    Start busting rock."
Start bustin' rock, yes, start
    bustin' rock,
Get the hell out and start bustin'
    rock.

They'll give you rock hammers and
    throw you in line,
Then they will chain you and take
    your good time.
Take your good time, yes, take
    your good time,
Then they will chain you and take
    your good time.

I thought about running while the
    fog was so low,
But something whispered, "Larry,
    don't go. "
Larry, don't go, no, Larry, don't
    go.
But something whispered, "Larry,
    don't go. "

I'll take my punishment, act like a
    man,
Obey the rules and do all I can.
Do all I can, yes, do all I can,
But if they try to whip me I'll get me
    a man.

I'll fight for my liberty, I'll get it
    someday,
Go back to the firing line and there
    I'll stay,
Telling the workers the conditions
    they're in,
Organize forces and fight til we win.

It's Me, O Lord

New words to an old spiritual

It's me, it's me, it's me, O Lord, Stand-ing in the need of land._ It's me, it's me, it's me, O Lord, Stand-ing in the need of land._ Tain't the bank-er, tain't the plant-er, but it's me, O Lord, Stand-ing in the need of land,_ Tain't the bank-er, tain't the plant-er, but it's me, O Lord, Stand-ing in the need of land.

It's me, it's me, it's me, O Lord,
Standing in the need of land.
It's me, it's me, it's me, O Lord,
Standing in the need of land.
Taint the banker, taint the planter,
But it's me, O Lord,
Standing in the need of land.
Taint the banker, taint the planter,
But it's me, O Lord,
Standing in the need of land.

It's me, it's me, it's me, O Lord,
Standing in the need of a home.
It's me, it's me, it's me, O Lord,
Standing in the need of a home.
Taint the lawyer, taint the
        merchant,
But it's me, O Lord,
Standing in the need of a home.
Taint the lawyer, taint the
        merchant,
But it's me, O Lord,
Standing in the need of a home.

It's me, it's me, it's me, O Lord,
Standing in the need of bread.
It's me, it's me, it's me, O Lord,
Standing in the need of bread.
Taint the grocer, taint the baker,

But it's me, O Lord,
Standing in the need of bread.
Taint the grocer, taint the baker,
But it's me, O Lord,
Standing in the need of bread.

Song of the Evicted Tenant

Words: Icie Jewel Lawrence - 11 year old daughter of
an Arkansas sharecropper.
Tune: House of the Rising Sun

(*Best sung unaccompanied*)

It was way down in old St. — Franc-is bot-toms Where they call it — the dev-il's — den, And man-y a poor ten-ant has lost their — home — And me, — O God — I'm one.

It was way down in old St. Francis
     bottoms
Where they call it the devil's den
And many a poor tenant has lost
     their home
And me, O God, I'm one.

About the twentieth of January
When God sent a great big flood
It run the planters from their
     beautiful homes
And now they live in tents.

The planters said to the tenants one
     morning
"O boys, how do you like this?
"O boss, it ain't a-hurting me."
The tenant answered him.

"If you will stay in refugee camps
Or stay in the tenant's home
You will learn not to be a-feared of
     ice
Or fear the shining sun.

"O boss, don't you see where you
     done wrong
When you throwed me out of my
     shack?
I had to build me a tent
Out of my old picksacks. "

273

Mister Farmer

This song was sung during the '39 milk strike in New York State.

Pete plays the old time 5 string banjo like a shore nuff old timer. But he ain't old enough to be of any age. One of the youngest dadburn men I believe I ever run into. Wrote the music out to all of the songs in this here book, and will coast through 3 or 4 more if he aint careful.

Pete rears back like a hound dog howling at a fire whistle, and gets that banjo to going and blowing, and this is one song that he really goes to town on. Take 'er, Pete, and don't mention my name.

tune: Pretty Polly

Mis - ter Farm-er, Mis-ter Farm - er, come go a - long with me, Mis - ter Farm-er, Mis - ter Farm - er, Come go a - long with me. —— Come hitch up with the milk trust and we'll keep the sys - tem free. ——

Mister Farmer, Mister Farmer,
   come go along with me,
Mister Farmer, Mister Farmer,
   come go along with me.
Come hitch up with the milk trust
   and we'll keep the system free.

Mister Farmer, Mister Farmer,
   you know it's election year,
Mister Farmer, Mister Farmer,
   you know it's election year.
You'll get baseball and sandwiches
   and pickles and beer.

So they followed the milk trust
   stooges and what did they find,
So they followed the milk trust
   stooges and what did they find,
Nothing in their pockets and a knife
   from behind.

Classification, classification, you'll
   be the death of me,
Classification, classification, you'll
   be the death of me.
I never can figger what my milk
   check's gonna be.

Mr. Borden, Mr. Sheffield, you've
    treated us unfair,
Mr. Borden, Mr. Sheffield, you've
    treated us unfair,
Now our barns are unpainted and our
    cupboards are bare.

Well, some began to grumble and
    some began to moan,
Some began to grumble, and some
    began to moan,
Up come the mortgage man and took
    away their homes.

Come all ye dairy farmers and
    listen unto me,
Come all ye dairy farmers and
    listen unto me.
Don't trust the milk trust or you'll
    stay in poverty.

. . . . *and how about this?* . . . .

Here it is nineteen forty and I aint
    got a dime,
Here it is nineteen forty and I aint
    got a dime.
I guess I just voted for the wrong
    man last time.

The Man Frank Weems

"On the 8th day of June we had another march. Jim Reese was leadin' it and Frank Weems, one of the Negro farm hands was walkin' along next to him. We was singin' union songs when a fellow comes up an' says the planters was comin'. Frank Weems and Jim Reese said; 'Keep marchin', boys. You aint breakin' the law.'

Pretty soon a bunch of planters and riders an' town bums ride up to us in their automobiles. We stay in line, lookin' at 'em, wonderin' what they're a-goin' to do. When they git out of their automobiles we see they all got guns and baseball bats. We don't say anything.

'Where you goin'?' one of them asks.

'Down the road,' says Jim.

Then they begin sluggin' us with those guns an' bats. A lot of men run for their lives. A lot of us fall down and can't git up again. Then pretty soon they git back in their automobiles and ride away.

Jim Reese, he lays there on the road for maybe four hours. Then he looks around an' he seen Frank Weems layin' there beside him. He looks bad. 'Are you all right, Frank?' he asks.

But Frank Weems doesn't answer him. Then Jim gits worried and gits up to go for help. When he comes back Frank Weems is gone. No man in Earle ever saw Frank Weems again. We keep askin' where is Frank Weems? We keep askin' is he in the swamp or in Blackfish lake or rottin' in a ditch somewhere. We keep askin' it. Where is Frank Weems?"

In April, 1937, Frank Weems appeared. He went to the Workers Defense League and told his story; When he had regained consciousness he had dragged himself into a ditch and rested. He then spent a week in a hobo jungle and from there made his way to the north.

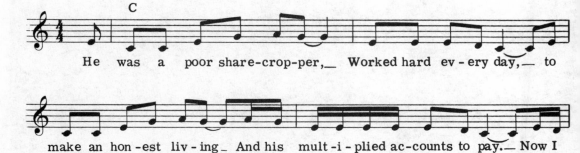

He was a poor share-crop-per,_ Worked hard ev-ery day,_ to make an hon-est liv-ing_ And his mult-i-plied ac-counts to pay._ Now I

Chorus:

want some-one to tell me, to tell me, And tell me right, Yes, I

want some-bod - y to tell me, — Where is the man Frank Weems?

He was a poor sharecropper,
Worked hard every day,
To make an honest living
And his multiplied accounts to pay.

Chorus:
Now I want someone to tell me,
    to tell me,
And tell me right,
Yes, I want somebody to tell me,
Where is the man Frank Weems?
(Repeat after each verse)

He was a farmer in Crittendon
    County,
A county just east of Cross,
Where they call them out with farm
    bells,
And work under a riding boss.

Frank heard about the union,
Then he sought to know its aims,
And when he had well understood,
He sure did sign his name.

I'm sure he told his companions
What a grand thing the union would
    be,
And if we gave it our brave support,
Some day it will make us free.

It was in nineteen hundred and
    thirty six,
And in the month of June,
When the S. T. F. Union pulled a
    strike,
That troubled the planters on their
    thrones.

The planters they all became
    troubled,
Not knowing what 'twas all about,
But they said, "One thing I'm sure
    we can do,
That's scare them niggers out."

Frank Weems was one among many
That stood out true and brave,
Although he was taken by cruel
    hands,
Now he do sleep in an unknown
    grave.

Sleep on, Frank, if you are
    sleeping,
Rest in your unknown grave.
Ten thousand union brothers to
    mourn your loss
And to give your children bread.

277

We Ain't Down Yet

Been held down, nailed down, beat down, shot down, shut down, set down, drove down, shoved down, pushed down, talked down, chained down, blowed down, showed down, chopped down, hoed down, plowed under, held under, ducked under, dusted under, tractored under, shot at and missed, spit at and hit, called for and couldn't come, called to war and wouldn't go, called to work and couldn't eat, called to fight for something we ain't got, bulldozed, lied to, knocked up, held up, hijacked, raped, skint, lent, broke, bent, pistol whipped, gassed, bombed, machine gunned, struck, log chained, lied about, gossiped on, cussed out, seduced, screwed up, misled, stripped naked, left ragged, hungry, broke, disgusted, busted, not to be trusted, but in spite of all this and many more things, We Aint Down Yet.

Tune: Turkey in the Straw.
Words from a bulletin of the Farmers' Union Educational Service.

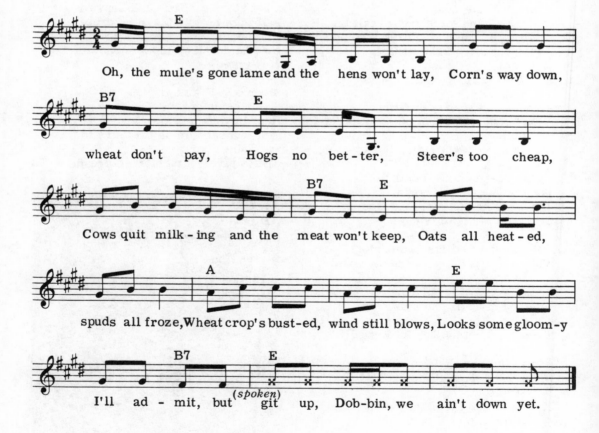

Oh, the mule's gone lame and the hens won't lay, Corn's way down, wheat don't pay, Hogs no bet-ter, Steer's too cheap, Cows quit milk-ing and the meat won't keep, Oats all heat-ed, spuds all froze, Wheat crop's bust-ed, wind still blows, Looks some gloom-y I'll ad-mit, but *(spoken)* git up, Dob-bin, we ain't down yet.

Oh, the mule's gone lame and the
    hens won't lay,
Corn's way down, wheat don't pay,
Hogs no better, steer's too cheap,
Cows quit milking and the meat
    won't keep.
Oats all heated, spuds all froze,
Wheat crop's busted, wind still
    blows,
Looks some gloomy, I'll admit, but
Git up, dobbin, we ain't down yet.

Oh, the coal's too high and the
    crop's too low,
Freight rate's doubled, got no show,
Money's tighter, morals loose,
Bound to get us, what's the use?
Sun's not shining like it should,
Moon aint beaming like it could,
No use stopping to debate,
Git up, dobbin, we'll co-operate.

Oh, the wheels all wobble, the
    axle's bent,
Dashboard's broken, top's all rent,
One shaft splintered, t'other sags,
Seat's all busted, end gate lags.
May hang together, believe it will,
Careful driving make it still,
Roads smoothed out til it won't
    seem true,
Join the Union. We'll all pull
    through.

Feller asked me before this book was printed, says, what kinda songs you got in this book? Well, I says, it's songs made up by poor folks, and that just about covers it.

We sing about the hard times we're having; we sing about the hard times everybody like us is having.

We just take a step further and point the finger at the boss, who's to blame. We take another step and blame his class, and his system.

We make up songs about our heroes and our leaders, and our martyrs. And we also make up songs about the bosses, the murderers, and the ones who don't care if we starve to death.

We're singing of the fight we're making, and the strikes, the accidents, the trials, that stand up like big sign posts pointing the way. We sing of how we're sticking together, and of the people that's helping us, and we're singing of the time when our fight's gonna be won.

XII–ONE BIG UNION

Most Folks believe in Union. They believe in One Big Union. Preachers preach it, screechers screech it, Talkers talk it, Singers sing it. One Big Union has got to come. You believe in it. I know you do. You believe in it because the bible says You'll all be One in the Father. That is as High as Religion goes. Then on over there somewhere it says, God is Love. So you see that the Reason you got Religion is so's everybody can All be One in Love.

Bible says God Owns Everything. That means that a Man is wrong when he jumps up and says, I own This Land, I own this House, I Own this Factory, YOU KEEP OUT!

But, when you get together and go to forming One Big Union, so Everybody can divide up the good things equal, or as you need 'em, why th' Rich Man dishes out some money to a lot of Killers, and they come a running down and pour your guts full of lead. They say they are "religious," say they're "Christians," say they're "good." They say we're so lowdown and mean that we ought to be shot down like a beef steer. We ain't got no money. We're broke. Ain't got nothin'. We're on th' Poor Folks Side -- and th' Working Folks Side.

Th' very first thing you got to do to be a Christian is to sell all your goods and give it to the Poor. These big greedy Rich Men ain't no more Christians than the Man in the Moon -- they're liars and thieves and killers and the Truth ain't in 'em. They ain't got sense enough to run the United States, and tell us what to do.

I studied religion 6 years ... and prayed some days for hours, and talked to lots of folks every day about living and loving and giving. That's religion. That's Real Religion. Living, Loving and Giving.

The Rich War Lords believe in Killing, Hating, and Taking. They hire people to do it for them. They hire your brother to grab up a badge and a gun and mow you down in front of a shop, or a mine, or a mill, or a factory. They even spend wagon loads of money on picture shows, magazines, newspapers, radios, and for phonograph records, and everything in the world, even preachers, to make you think they are Right, and us poor folks are Wrong.

They don't believe in the One Big Union. They tell us to hate each other, to fight each other, and to kill each other. As long as you let them run your country, it will be hell on earth, and a bloody mess.

There are some Murderers and cold hearted Killers in the American Legion that lead the boys to beat up the workers and to shoot them full of holes. Not all of the Legion Boys are like this. You might be one of them that is 'against it. For God's Sake, man, get on the side of the Poor Folks.

The Hooded Legion and the Klu Klux Klan are legions of the Devil and nothing but a wild tribe of Superstitious Killers. They're against the C.I.O. They're against everything good, because they work for the Rich Hogs, and they ain't got nerve enough to come out with their bare face a hanging out, because they're Cowards and Rats, and there ain't one spark of Truth in their whole Legion. They won't fight unless ten or a hundred of them can jump on one man, and they won't show their face. I hate 'em worse than I hate rattlesnakes, and hope that they someday wake up to the Truth and come out from under their silly masks, and commence a fighting over on the poor folks side.

Song of the West Virginia Miners

There's Silver On The Sage Tonight, Out On The Rancho Grande,
There's Boots and Saddles Hangin' On The Wall, and the Moon's Comin'
Over The Mountain ... and Cigarettes Are All Lit Up In The Dark,
and the Rio Grande is skipping through The Dew and the Sidewalks of
New York are littered, as usual, with kids a playing baseball, and auto-
mobiles a tryin' to wedge around some way or another ... and So What?

Is there anything in all of this to write a song about? I reckon they is.
That's all you hear. But about real honest to God, hard working, low-
paid People that live and die in a dam fool hole in the ground, there's
material to write 1,000 church books plumb full of songs ... but I just
set here and cuss and spit and fume and fuss and wonder why in Tarna-
tion you don't ever hear these real Redblood Songs of the Real American
Workers sung on the silly, foolish, blabbering, gossiping, god-damned
Radios?

Tune: "We Are Climbing Jacob's Ladder"

We have worked in dark and danger,
We have worked in dark and danger,
We have worked in dark and danger,
    Workers in the mine.

Though we work hard we are
    starving (3)
    Workers in the mine.

Company holds us all in slavery (3)
    Workers in the mine.

But we'll rise and gain our freedom (3)
    Workers in the mine.

We are building up the union (3)
    Workers in the mine.

Every new man makes us stronger (3)
    Workers in the mine.

Powder Mill Jail Blues

Here's one you can warble to th' tune of "Birmingham Jail" or "Down In The Valley" -- or whatever you call it. In order to be at your best as you yodel it, I'd suggest that you go hungry for a couple of days, and then go down to the Picket Line and miss another day or two, and then when your stomach gets to a thinkin' your mouth is on a Set Down Strike, why, you'll be in the proper Spirit to sing this song.

No, I was just a Teethin'. I don't believe in you a going hungry. That's all right if you like it, but groceries was put here to eat, and I believe, by dam, in eatin' 'em. So you can sing it either way, drunk or sober, I mean full or empty. But try it.

Another one of them bean songs. Tell you what. If you got a neighbor that don't know what it's all about, you know, you can hang your head out your window, and sing it to where they'll get wind of it -- and then you'll be a doing more than the feller that went to school 15 years and didn't do a dam thing.

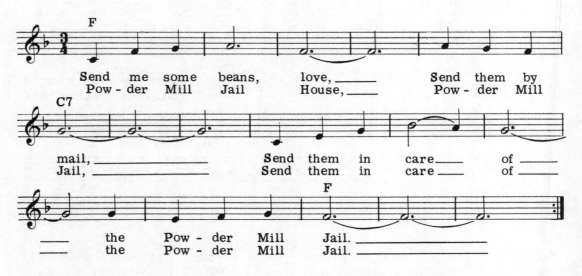

Send me some beans, love, send
  them by mail,
Send them in care of the Powder
  Mill Jail.

Chorus:
Powder Mill Jail House, Powder
  Mill Jail;
Send them in care of Powder Mill
  Jail.
(Repeat chorus after each verse.)

Roses love sunshine, violets love
  dew,
Only men in this jail know what we've
  been through.

The Postmaster has worked both
  faithful and true,
To get those jailbirds some pork and
  beans through.

The inspector has come and said it
  was OK,
If they get any beans, they will get
  them that way.

Powder Mill Jail House, down on
  your knees,
Praying to Luttrell to give our hearts
  ease.

They didn't have razors there in the
  jail,
Until they were sent some by U. S.
  mail.

But if someone will come and make
  us a bail,
We'll never come back to this Powder
  Mill Jail.

Little David Blues

This song comes from a strike in Alcoa, Tennessee. The scabs who stayed inside the mill were so besieged by the strikers that they couldn't get anything to eat, until someone hit on the idea of having food sent in through the mails, which the strikers could not stop. The strikers made up the song to make fun of the position of the scabs inside.

Little Cowell ain't so popular amongst the real red bloods down there around Davidson, Tenn. He's drawed down the same reputation that the dirty little coward in the Jesse James song. His name was Little Robert Ford. You can be a bastard if you want to, but somebody'll jump up and write a song about you sure as the sky above, and the song will outlast the money you get, it'll even outlast the whiskey you drink and the gals you blow it on.

Scabbin's called "spizwinking" down there in Tennessee. Well, there's a new cuss word. A scab ain't nothin' but a low down, spizwinkin' son of a so and so, and the miners can tell you what that so and so is.

They say the Sheriff's dues and doctor bill are only two of th' many things they take out of your pay down there. They issue script, I hear.

I reckon them Sheriff Dues and Doctor's Bills comes out of your pay to pay for the blackjack he broke over your head last week. And the Doctors charge you to fix your head back, so's th' high sheriff can take another crack at it next week.

Wouldn't you hate to go down in history as a "little stubbed up Runt?" I ruther go down as a Union Man.

by Tom Lowery, Davidson, Tenn.
Tune: "All Night Long"

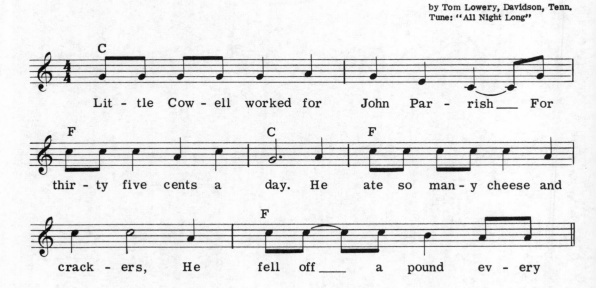

Lit - tle Cow - ell worked for John Par - rish___ For
thir - ty five cents a day. He ate so man - y cheese and
crack - ers, He fell off ___ a pound ev - ery

day. It's all night long, from mid-night on.

Little Cowell worked for John Parish
For thirty five cents a day.
He ate so many cheese and crackers,
He fell off a pound a day.

Refrain:
It's all night long, from the mid-
night on.
(Repeat after each verse)

Then he came to Davidson a-working
For Mr. Hubert and E.W. too,
And Cowell knows just exactly, boy,
How to deny you.

You go in the mines and find water,
It's right up to your knees,
You surely don't like to work in it,
But you don't do as you please.

They'll take you by the collar,
They'll mall you in the face,
They'll put you in the water hole,
If it's up to your waist.

You come out of the office.
After working hard all day,
Your sheriff dues and your doctor
bill,
You surely got to pay.

Men go through the office,
They go through one by one,
They'll ask for two dollars in script,
And oh, Gee, make it one.

You get your handful of script,
And you go right in the store,
You find a fellow with a black
mustache,
Writing it down on the floor.

You ask for a bucket of lard,
And--"What's meat worth a pound?"
"We sell it to you at any price,
'Cause we're spizwinkin' now."

You ask for a sack of flour,
And then you'll ask the cost.
It's a dollar and a quarter a sack,
And fifty cents a yard for cloth.

I went into the store one day,
Mr. Cowell was frying some steak,
I warned it would give him,
Scab colic and the bellyache.

Little Cowell took another man's job
At twenty dollars a month,
He's one little sawed off spizwink
scab,
And a little stubbed up runt.

287

Davidson-Wilder Blues

This song comes from the same strike, down in Davidson, Tennessee.

Words by Ed Davis, a Wilder Striker

C
Mis- ter Shiv-ers said if we'd block our __ coal He'd

G7 **F**
run four days a week, And there's no rea- son we

C **F** **C**
should-n't run six __ we're load-ing it so damned cheap, It's the worst old

G7 **C** **Chorus:**
blues that I ev - er had. I've got the

G7 **C**
blues, I shore God got 'em __ bad. I've got the

F **C**
blues, the worst I've ev - er had. It must be the

G7 **C**
blues of the Da - vid - son Wild - er scabs.

Mr. Shivers said if we'd block our
    coal
He'd run four days a week,
And there's no reason we shouldn't
    run six
We're loading it so darned cheap.
It's the worst old blues that I ever
    had.

Chorus:
I've got the blues,
I shore God got 'em bad.
I've got the blues,
The worst I've ever had.
It must be the blues
Of the Davidson-Wilder scabs.

He discharged Horace Hood
And told him he had no job.
Then he couldn't let Thomas Shepherd
    couple
'Cause he wouldn't take the other
    fellows job.
It's the worst old blues that I ever had.

Mr. Shivers told Mr. Boyer,
He said, I know just what we'll do.
We'll get the names of the union men
And fire the whole dern crew.
It's the worst old blues that I ever had.

We paid no attention to his firing,
And went on just the same,
And organized the holler
In L. L. Shivers name.
It's the worst old blues that I ever had.

Mr. Shivers told the committeemen,
He said, Boys, I'll treat you right.
He said, I know you're all good union
    men
And first class Campbellites.
It's the worst old blues that I ever had.

I feel just like a crossbreed
Between a devil and a hog,
And that's about all I could call
    myself
If I sign that yaller dog.
It's the worst old blues that I ever had.

There's a few things right here in
    town
I never did think was right,
For a man to be a yaller dog scab
And a first class Campbellite.
It's the worst old blues that I ever had.

There's a few officers here in town
That never let a lawbreaker slip.
They carried their guns when scabb-
    ing begun,
Till the hide came off of their hips.
It's the worst old blues that I ever had.

Flem Boles organized the holler
About a hundred strong,
And stopped L. L. Shivers
From putting the third cut on.
It's the worst old blues that I ever had.

Mr. Shivers got rid of his Negro,
And a white man took his place.
And if you want me to tell you what I
    think about that,
It's a shame and a darned disgrace.
It's the worst old blues that I ever had.

Dick Stultz is for the union men,
And Bully Garret against us all.
Dick kicked Bully in the stomach,
And you oughta heard Bully squall.
It's the worst old blues that I ever had.

Paw Evans has got a tater patch
Away out on the farm.
Aleck Selis guards that tater patch
With a gun as long as your arm.
It's the worst old blues that I ever had.

I'd ruther be a yaller dog scab
In a union man's backyard,
Than to tote a gun for L. L. Shivers
And to be a National Guard.
It's the worst old blues that I ever had.

The Ballad of Barney Graham

Barney was killed by company guards early in May, 1933. He was a Union Man 100%. Now he's a Union Man 1000%. The governor and the State Secretary of Labor knowed of the plans to kill Barney more'n a week before th' killin', but they didn't try to stop it.

"Red Cross doctored up the scabs and the guards and their families, but they wouldn't doctor us strikers."

"We was a holdin' out because they wasn't a payin' us but 28-1/2 cents a ton for diggin' coal...."

A man would starve plum total to death on that.

A man would raise up out of them chains.

But, a scab would be a coward, and afraid to raise up an' tell th' boss what's what.

This song was wrote down by Barney's Daughter, Della Mae. A time will come when Barney and Della Mae will be famous.

by Della Mae Graham

On April the thirtieth
In nineteen thirty-three
Upon the streets of Wilder
They shot him brave and free.

They shot my darling father,
He fell upon the ground,
'Twas in the back they shot him,
The blood came streaming down.

They took the pistol handles
And beat him on the head,
The hired gunmen beat him
'Til he was cold and dead.

When he left home that morning,
I thought he'd never return,
But for my darlin' father,
My heart shall ever yearn.

We carried him to the grave-yard,
And there we lay him down,
To sleep in death for many a year,
In the cold and sodden ground.

Although he left the union
He tried so hard to build,
His blood was spilled for justice,
And justice guides us still.

Union Train

This song is like a person you meet that don't pretend to be anything on a stick, nor anything fancy, or done up with ribbons. But you'll keep on a coming back to it, because it's so easy to sing, and so much good rhythm in it, and it just seems to hit the spot like a good bitter bottle of beer on a hot summer day.

There's a Un - ion Train a - com-in', ___ A - com- in' through the night,

Get your tick - et read-y, boy, To make this Un - ion ride.

There's a Union Train a comin'
A comin' through the night,
Get your ticket ready, boy,
To make this union ride.

There's a Union Train a comin'
Comin' down the line --
Your Union Card's your ticket
When you ride this Union line.

There's a Union Train a comin'.
Comin' round the bend,
Whistlin' and a blowin'
Full of Union men.

There's a Union Train a comin'
Pullin' mighty hard,
Stoppin' at the station
In the good old Union yard.

There's a Union Train a comin'
Down that Union track --
Aint no scabs ride this train
Or hold that Union back.

Go to the big rich gambler
Dressed in silk so fine --
Take off, take off, them silken duds,
Better ride that Union line.

O go to the silken ladies
Dressed in silk so fine --
Better tell all your cops and guards
To clear that Union line.

Go tell that big rich banker
That stole your money and mine --
You got to give your money to the
    poor
To ride this Union line.

291

My Children Are Seven In Number

I lived a couple of years down in Okemah, Oklahoma, with Sam White and his family. Eleven of us lived in a 2 room house. We slept four in a bed, with everybody's feet in everybody's face. I could wake up any time of the night and tell you who was at home and who wasn't.

Eleanor Kellogg has covered the subject pretty well in this song. (I don't think she's the Kellogg that makes the millions out of breakfast food. She's one of the millions that get up of a morning with a flock of kids and cain't afford a drop of skimmed milk, nor a spoonful of sugar, nor any kind of store bought breakfast food for her kids.)

I see Barney Graham comes up again in this song, like a big searchlight that's a gonna break through a lot of places, and show you just who is stealing you blind.

Tune: "My Bonnie Lies Over The Ocean"
Words: Eleanor Kellogg

I'm get-ting my meals from the Red Cross, __ I'm sweat-ing my time on the road, ____ I'm liv-ing on corn-bread and grav-y, ____ My trou-bles they are like a load, ____ Lard, ____ Lard, ____ we're strik-ing for buck-ets of lard, ____ lard, ____ lard, ____ We're strik-ing for buck-ets of lard. ____

I'm getting my meals from the
  Red-Cross,
I'm sweating my time on the road,
I'm living on cornbread and gravy,
My troubles they are like a load.
Lard, Lard, we're striking for
  buckets of lard, (Repeat)

My children are seven in number,
We have to sleep four in a bed,
I'm striking with my fellow workers,
To get them some more clothes and
  bread.
Shoes, shoes, we're striking for
  pairs of shoes. (Repeat)

Pellagra is cramping my stomach,
My wife is sick with T. B.,
My babies are starving for sweet
  milk,
Oh, there's so much sickness for
  me.
Milk, milk, we're striking for
  gallons of milk (Repeat)

I'm needing a shave and a haircut,
The barbers I cannot afford,
My wife cannot wash without soap-
  suds,
And she has to borrow a board.
Soap, soap, we're striking for bars
  of soap. (Repeat)

My house is a shack on the hillside,
It's floors are unpainted and bare,
I haven't a screen to my windows,
And carbide cans do for a chair.
Homes, homes, we're striking for
  better homes.

O, Aid-Truck go over the mountain,
O, Aid-Truck come back with a load,
For we are just getting a dollar,
A few days a month on the road.
Gas, gas, we're bumming a gallon
  a gas. (Repeat)

They shot Barney Graham our leader,
His spirit abides with us still,
The spirit of struggle for justice,
No bullets have the power to kill.
Barney, Barney, we're thinking of
  you today. (Repeat)

Oh miners, go on with the union,
Oh miners, go on with the fight,
For we're in the struggle for justice,
And we're in the struggle for right.
Justice, justice, we're striking for
  justice for all. (Repeat)

Bonny of the Union

And here's another good one, with a good chorus.

Tune: "My Bonnie Lies Over The Ocean"
Words: Ruby Cox and Myrtle Baxter

Our Blue Bell has cut all our wages,
And raised our production rate, too;
Now workers we must have some
  action,
So what are you going to do?

Chorus:
Sign up, sign up,
Sign up a member each day, each
  day,
Sign up, sign up,
Let's sign up a member each day.

The Soup Song

Here's another'n to th' same tune. This was in the heads of several jillion folks in Hoover's last days. But lots of 'em was too scairt to bust loose and sing it. Then, when Hoover got heaved, and we got the grease, and Wall Street got the thigh, well, Union songs got loose like a wild herd of folks that was dead right.

You're hungry. I'm hungry. Both work hard. Either work hard or work harder a tryin' to find work. He's got our groceries that you and me raised and made. So, what're we gonna do?

Gonna get together and ask him for our share of them eats. Nice way of course. Ain't a gonna hurt him. Don't like to bounce nothing off from his head. Then, we go and ask him. We "get together" and we go and ask him how about a little stuff to eat and wear and some spare change to tote around in your pocket? And if he don't give it to us, we'll jest natural have to take it th' hard way. Dam shore cain't go ragged and hungry.

Tune: "My Bonny Lies Over The Ocean"
Words: Maurice Sugar

I'm spending my nights at the flop-
house,
I'm spending my days on the street,
I'm looking for work and I find none.
I wish I had something to eat.

Chorus:
Soo-oup, soo-oup,
They give me a bowl of soo-oup.
Soo-oup, soo-oup,
They give me a bowl of soup.
(Repeat after each verse.)

I spent twenty years in the factory,
I did everything I was told,
They said I was loyal and faithful,
Now, even before I get old:

I saved fifteen bucks with my banker,
To buy me a car and a yacht.
I went down to draw out my fortune,
And this is the answer I got:

I fought the war for my country
I went out to bleed and to die
I thought that my country would help
me
But this was my country's reply:

I went on my knees to my Maker
I prayed every night to the Lord
I vowed I'd be meek and submissive
And now I've received my reward:

Down the Street We Hold Our Demonstration

Circle 8, promenade, grab yo' partner, demonstrate!

Tune: "Round Her Neck She Wears A Yellow Ribbon"

Down_ the street_ we hold our dem-on-stra-tion,_ We
hold 'em in Nov-em-ber, and on the first of May; And if_ they ask_ us
What the hell we're do-ing, We're fight-ing for our free-dom and it's
not far a-way. Not far a - way,_ Not far a - way, We're_
fight-ing for our free-dom and it's not far a -way.

Down the street we hold our
demonstration,
We hold 'em in November, and on
the first of May;
And if they ask us what the hell
we're doing,
We're fighting for our freedom and
it's not far away.
Not far away,
Not far away,
We're fighting for our freedom and
it's not far away.

Ballad of the Blue Bell Jail

"Blue Bell Jail" is really a Garment Factory. Reason why you call it a Jail is because when the time comes, you got to go right to your place and go to work, and you cain't visit nor talk at any time. (Fraid you might wake up and get wise to what's a goin' on. You might get together and make th' boss give you better pay or shorter hours, and let you visit and laugh and talk to your friend while you're workin'.)

Tune to this song is one you know, "Hand Me Down My Walking Cane."

Blanche Kinett was a gal to think. She thought pretty near every day. She thought every minute. She set down during the noon hour on Feb. 28, 1939, and wrote this Union Song. Wrote it way down there in Greensboro, North Carolina. You write one.

Tune: "Hand Me Down My Walking Cane"
Words: Blanche Kinett

O, come on un - ion, go my bail,__ O, come on un - ion, go my bail, O, come on un - ion, go my bail; Get me out of this Blue Bell Jail, All my free-dom's tak - en a - way, tak-en a - way.

O, come on union, go my bail,
O, come on union, go my bail,
O, come on union, go my bail,
Get me out of this Blue Bell Jail,
All my Freedom's taken away, taken
   away.

If we had the sense of a fool (3 times)
We wouldn't set here like a fool.
All our freedom's taken away, taken
   away.

For we know that a mule will balk
   (3 times),

Let's get busy with this union talk.
All our freedom's taken away, taken
   away.

We are worn and the place is tough
   (3 times),
O, my Lord, we've had enough.
All our freedom's taken away, taken
   away.

This union sure will do the trick
   (3 times)
It will make the bosses sick.
All our freedom's taken away, taken
   away.

Write Me Out My Union Card

Here's another'n to the tune of "Walkin' Cane." That shot got me: Time
To Fight Those Hungry Blues Away.

O, write me out my union card
   (3 times)
Organize, we'll all fight hard,
Time to fight those hunger blues
   away.

We gotta re-arm, is what they say,
   (3 times)
It's another excuse to cut our pay.
Time to fight those hunger blues
   away.

So come with me on the picket line
   (3 times),
We'll stay there til the bosses sign.
Time to fight those hunger blues
   away.

In the bosses' war the worker gets
   (3 times),
A bellyful of bayonets,
Time to turn those hunger blues
   away.

So write us out our union card
   (3 times),
Organize, we'll all fight hard.
Time to fight those hunger blues
   away.

Roane County

"I wrote this song during the hosiery strike at Harriman, Tennessee. That was early in 1934. I had just gotten out of jail and thinking about how happy I was to be home again but I knew I would have to leave home to find work somewhere else if your strike was broken."--Hershel Phillips, who wrote this song.

by Hershel Phillips

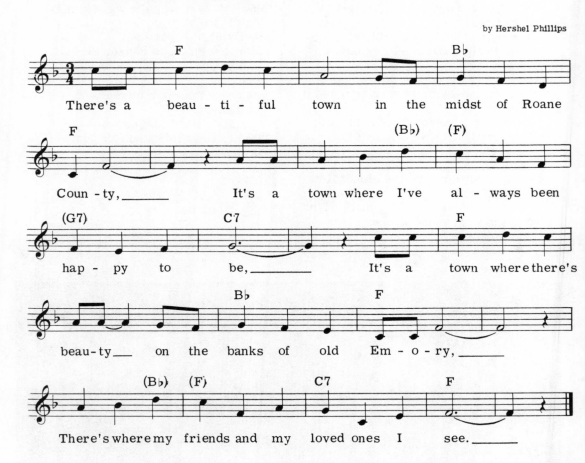

There's a beautiful town in the midst of Roane County,
It's a town where I've always been happy to be,
It's a town where there's beauty on the banks of old Emory,
There's where my friends and my loved ones I see.

For many long years in the mill we've been toiling,
Our work and our labor, it all seemed in vain,
But we organized for some well known reason,
And just three months later was called out on strike.

298

The firm got in touch with the law
  of Roane County,
The sheriff and his men were all on
  the scene.
When the people came out for the
  oath they had taken,
To stay with the Union and never
  betray.

Some went to the Mill and there they
  betrayed us,
Some's gone to their grave I'm sorry
  to say,
But some is still out to wait that
  decision,
They seem determined to go all the
  way.

They went to the Judge and got an
  injunction,
The sheriff and his men would not
  speak one good word.
We was captured and placed in the
  jail of Roane County,
And locked in the cell for the crime
  we had done.

In Roane County jail our friends
  came to see us,
Seemed to think we would be there
  till June,
But to their surprise our bonds were
  accepted,
And now with our friends we are
  happy again.

If I go away to hunt re-employment,
I'll go to the north, to the east, or
  the west.
But I'll always remember my home
  in Roane County,
In the beautiful hills of old Tennessee.

Shirt Factory Blues

Would you think that the shirt on your back had give somebody the low down blues? Wouldn't be that a way if the folks that makes the shirts got good money for their work. But they don't. Sometimes they ain't even got a decent shirt to wear their self. Just like a mechanic ain't got a decent car to drive around in, just like a farmer ain't got enough to eat, just like a fruit picker ain't got enough to feed a good, husky blow fly. Open up your shirt collar and sing this to the tune of the Brown Ferry Blues.

Tune: "Browns Ferry Blues"
Words: Cleda Helton and James Pyle
of LaFollette, Tennessee

I wan-na go home but there ain't no use, The un-ion gals won't turn me loose,_ Lawd, Lawd,_ got them shirt_ fact-'ry blues._____ Lit-off wants to work but it ain't no use, flays his wings like an old gray goose, Lawd, Lawd, got them shirt fact-'ry blues.____

I wanna go home but there aint no
  use,
The union gals won't turn me loose,
Lawd, Lawd, got them shirt factory
  blues.
Litoff wants to work but there aint
  no ues,
Flaps his wings like an old grey
  goose,
Lawd, Lawd, got them shirt factory
  blues.

They called a strike and we came out,
We walked the streets and we kept
  them out,
Lawd, Lawd, got them shirt factory
  blues.
We were down and just about out,
When Charley Handy helped us out,
Lawd, Lawd, got them shirt factory
  blues.

We went down and we walked about,
The scabbing girls wouldn't come
  out,
Lawd, Lawd, got them shirt factory
  blues.
Sherman knocked Chelo on the head,
Chelo thought that he was dead,
Lawd, Lawd, got them shirt factory
  blues.

Sorokin got his picture took,
Came out in the paper and God how
  it looked,
Lawd, Lawd, got them shirt factory
  blues.
They went down to haul the shirts out,
The girls went down and bawled them
  out,
Lawd, Lawd, got them shirt factory
  blues.

We don't want no bully bosses,
Want shorter hours and union bosses,
Lawd, lawd, got them shirt factory
  blues.
Do-nuts and coffee are so fine,
Stay out of the factory all the time,
Lawd, lawd, got them shirt factory
  blues.

Got A Union in the Country

The Union of the people is the best thing about them. You ain't a full fledged human till you know about the Union. You ain't a full grown man or woman till you get with the Union. You're as wrong as hell if you are against the Union. We are the real, raw, redblooded people of this wicked old world, and we aim to make it a better one to live in. Gonna see to it that everybody gets what they need. That's all we ask, is that too much? Is that wrong? Hell, no. Get with us. All over the country. Here's the good old Union Echo ringing like a cathedral bell down through the hills and hollers of good old North Caroliner. Caroline!

"I'm Ann West, from Greensboro, North Carolina. I belong to the Workers Alliance there. I wrote this song because of the Stretch-out Plan they were instituting in the Highland Shop. I wrote it here in the summer school for the workers."

Tune: "I'm jealous"
Words: Ann West, Aug., 1939

Got a un-ion in the coun-try, Got a un-ion in the town, Takes good old mem-bers to bring the new ones down, We're grow-ing, Oh, don't you see? I said we're grow-ing, and we're hap-py as we can be.

302

Got a union in the country,
Got a union in the town,
Takes good old members to bring
    the new ones down.
We're growing, oh, don't you see?
I said, we're growing, and we're
    happy as we can be.

You took my labor,
You took my home,
But God's sake, Boss, leave my
    union alone.
I'm starving, oh, they're starving
    me,
I said, I'm hungry, just as hungry
    as I can be.

Takes a rubber band to stretch,
Takes a cannon ball to roll,
Takes an organized group to knock
    the stretch-out cold.
We're organized, it's a damn good
    thing,
I said, we're organized, we'll get
    things done, you'll see.

Oh, the union is our leader,
And it's pretty damn strong.
So come on, fellow workers, help
    us right our wrongs.
We're winning, oh, don't you see,
I said, we're winning, and soon
    we'll all be free.

Oh, the Highland workers,
Lord, they didn't go in,
That damned old stretch-out was a
    mighty bad sin.
We're fighting, we're fighting now,
And we'll be fighting til the work-
    load's gone somehow.

Oh, won't it be wonderful,
Oh, won't it be grand,
To see the working-class people
    own all the land.
March forward, you'll soon possess
A little of it and, in time, we'll get
    the rest.

The Ballad of John Catchins

What governor of what state will have his people a singin' songs like this about him when he's dead and gone?

This is written as we heard it sung by Mr. and Mrs. Joe Gelders down there in Brimingham, Alabama. The tune is one that gets in your head and plays around like a tree full of young squirrels. I heard the same tune sung out in California, about their troubles in the cotton picking. It is an old tune with a real old country whang to it, that you're gonna be a singin' a mighty long time.

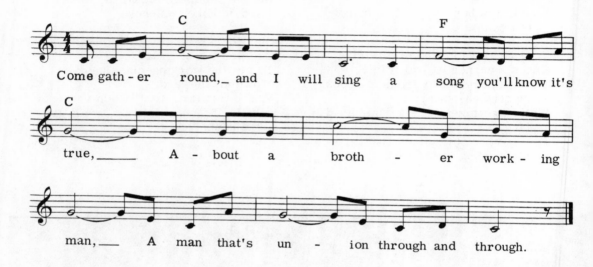

Come gather round and I will sing
A song, you'll know it's true,
About a brother working-man,
A man that's union through and
    through.

John Catchins is a union man,
He joined on charter day,
He did not like a company town,
Where they used clacker 'stead o'
    pay.

Tne furnace where he made his
    time,
Is Thomas mill in Birmingham,
Republic Steel they owned that
    plant,
And they're the roughest in the
    land.

In '33 the Eagle came
And brought the N. R. A.
John Catchins said, "Our time has
    come,
We'll organize this very day."

And then they had election day
To vote the Union straight,
And when the vote was counted up
Republic got a measly eight.

Those rich men's hearts are
    harder still
Than steel made in their mill,
Republic would not be content
To obey the laws of the government.

John Girdler called his Board
    around,
A frame-up for to plan,
"We're goin' to drive that Union
    out
And we will use what means we
    can. "

They sent for Thomas Carpenter,
The superintendent scratched his
    head,
They gave him a drink from a
    silver cup,
Then this is what the Super said:

"That man's that's Union through
    and through,
John Catchins is his name,
He leads the men on the picket
    line,
And he's the one we've got to
    frame. "

"When we reduce the wages down
Or double up a job or two,
Or when the price of the rent goes
    up,
He criticizes me and you. "

"He's taught his family union ways,
His wife and children all,
He tells them they must organize,
Because divided they will fall. "

"So he's the one we've got to frame
No matter what it will entail,
We'll put him safely underneath,
The sheriff's big and rocky jail. "

"We'll call in that detective guy,
The one named Milt MacDuff,
We'll tell him what we're paying
    for,
And make him do his dirty stuff. "

They put John Catchins in the jail,
The lies that they did tell,
"We'll close the roads to heaven
    up,
And send their lousy souls to
    Hell. "

Come gather round us, brothers
    all,
Together let us shout,
"If we must take that jail-house
    down,
We're goin' to get John Catchins
    out. "

When Brother John is free again,
He'll have a big surprise,
We'll all be in the C. I. O.
Republic Steel we'll organize.

The Marion Massacre

"During the 1929 Textile strikes in North Carolina the workers at the Marion Manufacturing Co. held out against evictions and hunger and disease for nine weeks. They went back to their jobs at the end of nine weeks when the company promised to grant most of their demands. These promises were never kept, and the company officials, fearing another strike, began to bully and threaten the workers.

The foreman on the night shift was worse than most. One night he began to threaten and goad one of the boys. When the boy could stand it no longer he ran to the lever which controls the power of the plant and pulled it. The machines stopped. The men walked out. That was Oct. 2, the first day of the second strike at the Marion Manufacturing Co., the same day that Sheriff Adkins and his deputies shot and killed six men and wounded twelve others, most of whom were shot in the back while trying to escape the fumes of tear gas.

On Oct. 4, the people of Marion held a funeral for four of their dead. They brought flowers from the hills and decorated the caskets. A ribbon, their union colors, linked the coffins.

No minister of the town of Marion or of the neighboring towns had come near the dead or their families. A stranger from another State had come to perform last rites. But during the service an old mountain preacher, Cicero Queens, who stood among the people, dropped to his knees before the coffins, spread out his arms and this is what he said:

'O, Lord Jesus Christ, here are men in their coffins, blood of my blood, bone of my bone. I trust, O God, that these friends will go to a better place than this mill village or any other place in Carolina. O God, we know we are not in high society, but we know Jesus Christ loves us. The poor people have their rights, too. For the work we do in this world, is this what we get when we demand our rights? Jesus Christ, Your Son, O Lord, was a working man. If He were to pass under these trees today, He would see these cold bodies lying here before us. O God, mend the broken hearts of these loved ones left behind. Dear God, do feed their children. Drive selfishness and cruelty out of your world. May these weeping wives and little children have a strong arm to lean on. Dear God, what would Jesus do if He were to come to Carolina?'

When the funeral passed the cotton mill where soldiers were on guard, a young militiaman, in violation of regulations, took off his hat and rested his rifle."

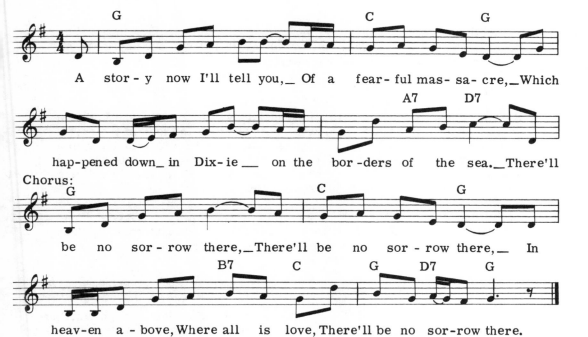

A stor-y now I'll tell you,_ Of a fear-ful mas-sa-cre,_Which

hap-pened down_ in Dix-ie _ on the bor-ders of the sea._There'll

Chorus:

be no sor-row there,_There'll be no sor-row there,_ In

heav-en a-bove, Where all is love, There'll be no sor-row there.

A story now I'll tell you,
Of a fearful massacre,
Which happened down in Dixie
On the borders of the sea.

Chorus:
There'll be no sorrow there,
There'll be no sorrow there,
In heaven above,
Where all is love,
There'll be no sorrow there.

'Twas in Marion, North Carolina,
In a little mountain town,
Six workers of the textile mills
In cold blood were shot down.

"Tis ever the same old story
With the laborers of our land,
They're ruled by mighty powers,
And riches they command.

Why is it over money,
These men from their friends
    must part,
A leaving home and loved ones
With a bleeding, broken heart?

But some day they'll meet them
On that bright shore so fair,
And live in peace forever,
There'll be no sorrow there.

It started over money,
The world's most vain desire,
Yet we realize the laborer
Is worthy of his hire.

These men were only asking
Their rights and nothing more,
That their families would not suffer
With a wolf at every door.

The Marion Strike

Worst dam thing in this world is being a slave. Best thing is to all be free. Some guys got the idea you and me ought to work our daylights out while they set around and take it easy.

If they are right, I am wrong.

Here's where they fired down on six hungry working folks, and laid 'em in the ground. Just like you wasn't fit to be on the face of the earth. If that's democracy, I'm a horse's ass. If that's Christianity, I'm a mangy hound. Democracy is where you're free to go and do and say what you please. Christianity is, by George, to like folks, not to rob 'em and starve 'em and shoot 'em and kill 'em.

High time the government done something about this kind of crap. Folks will get to where they ain't got no more faith in the government, 'less the government works for 'em instead of against 'em.

Tune: "Wreck Of Altoona"   Words: J. G., Greenville, S. C.

Then they had the strike in North
   Carolina,
Up there at the Marion Mill,
Somebody called for the sheriff
To come down there on the hill.

The sheriff came down there to
   the factory,
And brought all of his men along,
And he says to the mill strikers,
"Now boys, you all know this is
   wrong. "

"But sheriff, we just can't work
   for nothing,
For we've got a family to feed,
And they've got to pay us more
   money
To buy food and clothes that we
   need.

"You've heard of the stretch-out
   system,
A-going through the country today,
They put us on two men's jobs,
And just give us half the pay.

"You know we helped give you your
   office,
And we helped to give you your pay,
And you want us to work for nothing,
That's why we're down here today. "

So one word just brought another,
And the bullets they started flying,
And after the battle was over,
Six men lay on the ground a-dying.

Now people, labor needs protection,
We need it badly today.
If we will just get together,
Then they can't do us that way.

Now I hear the whistle blowing,
I guess I'd better run along.
I work in the factory,
That's why I wrote this little song.

"I'll go join the union, then"
Those were the words you said,
And I knew they'd bring you to me
A-lyin' cold and dead,
A-lyin' cold and dead.

Go tell that sheriff
And his gunmen, too,
That the reason my life is broken
Is 'cause they murdered you,
Is 'cause they murdered you.

Our Children They Were Sickly

The other day down in Oklahoma City I went out there to the edge of town to the garbage dump, and to the dry sandy bed of the Canadian River, to a Shack Town, called Community Camp. A house there cost you the whole sum of seven dollars. Rent is a dollar a month. Mosquitoes are so big they sound like army planes a flyin' over. So thick you could stir 'em with a stick. The kids are out there, puny and hungry and ragged - and Oklahoma City is one of the richest Oil Fields in the world -- and these people had done the hard and heavy work of a making it that way. Six thousand people are scattered through the filthy, dingy camp.

I met a preacher and he said he wanted to go with Pete and me around to preach at the little towns and have us sing for him and take up collection, and tell folks about the War.

We said, who do you reckon is causin' all of these Wars? He says: "Why, it's the old Devil". We said, "Yes, but who is workin' FOR the Devil?" and he scratched his chin for a minute and says, "Why, it's these Rich Folks, that tries to pile up all of the Treasures on Earth, of course." And we said, "What are we a gonna do about that?" And he said, "Well, us - us poor folks that's all so fired down and out has just got to - just GOT to show the Rich Ones What's What."

You did-n't do no wrong no,__ You did-n't do no crime;__ You gave a-way your young years__ to slave-ry in the mine,_____ To slave-ry in the mine.

Our children they were sickly,
They had no clothes to wear;
Our little ones were sickly,
And no one seemed to care,
And no one seemed to care.

The CIO Is Bigger Than It Used To Be

Tune: "Old Gray Mare Ain't What It Used To Be"

The CIO is bigger than it used to
  be,
Bigger than it used to be,
Bigger than it used to be.
The CIO is bigger than it used to
  be,
Many long years ago.

Chorus:
Many long years ago,
Many long years ago,
The CIO is bigger than it used to
  be,
Many long years ago.

The CIO is stronger than it used to
  be,
Stronger than it used to be,
Stronger than it used to be,
The CIO is stronger than it used to
  be,
Many long years ago.

O, The Monkeys Have No Tails in Zamboanga

Some new verses to an old song ... also comes from Alabama, as you see.

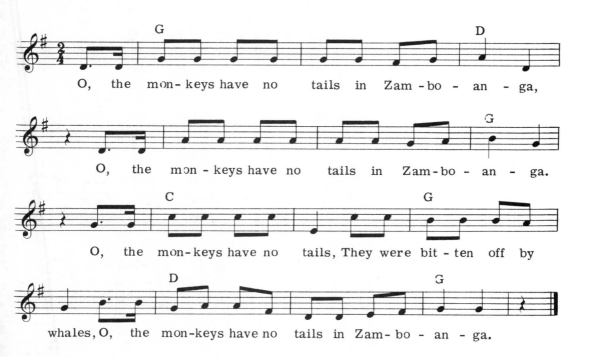

O, the mon-keys have no tails in Zam-bo-an-ga,
O, the mon-keys have no tails in Zam-bo-an-ga.
O, the mon-keys have no tails, They were bit-ten off by whales, O, the mon-keys have no tails in Zam-bo-an-ga.

O, the workers have no vote in
Alabama,
O, the workers have no vote in
Alabama,
O, the workers have no vote,
No shirt, no pants, no coat,
O, the workers have no vote in
Alabama.

O, the workers pay high tolls in
Alabama,
O, the workers pay high tolls in
Alabama,
O, the workers pay high tolls,
And the money all has holes,
O, the workers pay high tolls in
Alabama.

O, the workers have no schools
in Alabama,
O, the workers have no schools
in Alabama,
O, the workers have no schools,
But the bosses are the fools,
O, the workers have no schools
in Alabama.

Goodbye Semaria

Well, I'm a monkey's uncle. Anything is liable to run out of a zoo if you leave the cages open. Friend, have pity on a poor hobo. Enough of anything's enough. I agreed to sort of ramble through this book of songs and do a little plain and fancy raving about hungry folks and rich folks but after all, enough of anything's enough. Now there comes out from under a rock, this guy. This guy called his girls that worked for him, "sisters, his jewels." But the varmint wouldn't give the girls decent salaries, so just to see them around over the town you might think they was diamonds in th' rough. They hit it plenty rough. This is to the tune of "Camptown Races" or "Doo Da Day," anyhow, low pay. Sometimes a skunk wins. Not this time.

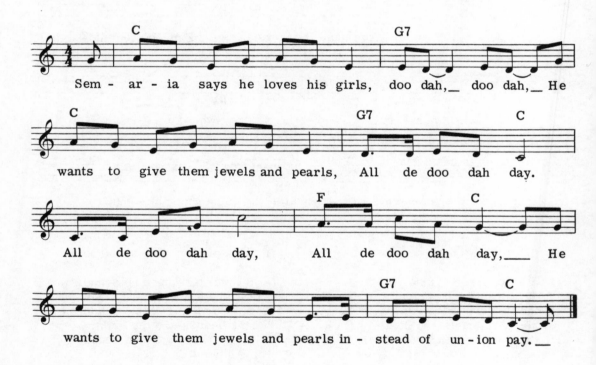

Semaria says he loves his girls,
  doo da, doo da,
He wants to give them jewels and
  pearls, all de doo da day.
    All de doo da day,
    All de doo da day,
He wants to give them jewels and
  pearls,
Instead of union pay.

Drop your needle and sing this song,
  doo da, doo da,
For the union's here ten thousand
  strong, all de doo da day
    All de doo da day,
    All de doo da day,
For the union's here ten thousand
  strong
To bring a better day.

For sweatshop pay we've stitched
and sewed, doo da, doo da,
But now we're travelling on a union
road, all de doo da day,
    All de doo da day,
    All de doo da day,
But now we're travelling on a union
road,
Goodbye, Semaria.

The Union Fights the Battle of Freedom

The South Side Negro Chorus of Local 76 of the I.L.G.W.U. sang this.
It was first made up to support the Newspaper Guild Strike of Chicago
in 1938.

Tune: "Joshua Fought The Battle of Jericho"

The un-ion fights the bat-tle of free-dom, free-dom, free-dom, The

un-ion fights the bat-tle of free-dom, and the boss comes tum-bling

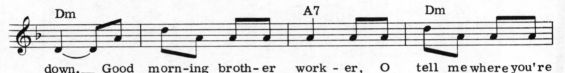

down.__ Good morn-ing broth-er work-er, O tell me where you're

bound,_O tell me what you're strik ing for, and tell me what you've found.

Chorus:
The union fights the battle of
   freedom, freedom, freedom.
The union fights the battle of
   freedom,
And the bosses come tumbling
   down.

Good morning brother worker,
O tell me where you're bound.
O tell me what you're striking for
And tell me what you've found.

We're fighting for a contract,
For recognition, too.
We know we'll win that contract
With the proper help from you.

We find the public's with us,
We find they're on our side.
We hear a mighty chorus
That fills our hearts with pride.

We've told you all our story,
We've told you where we stand.
You can help us win the glory
For our striking union band.

We'll Be Wearing Union Buttons

All of the old songs are gettin' remodeled every year. Just like the new model cars. And you know I believe to my soul they run better than the old ones. This one operates to the tune of "Coming Around The Mountain." And we're a comin, boy, Howdy.

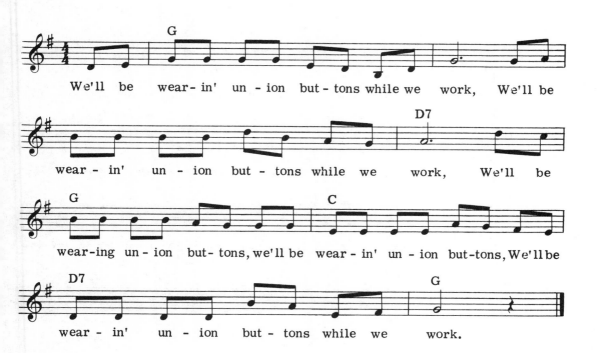

We'll be wearin' union buttons
  while we work,
We'll be wearin' union buttons
  while we work,
We'll be wearin' union buttons,
We'll be wearin' union buttons,
We'll be wearin' union buttons
  while we work.

We'll all be union members when
  we work,
We'll all be union members when
  we work,
We'll all be union members,
We'll all be union members,
We'll all be union members when
  we work.

We'll be gettin' living wages when
  we work,
We'll be gettin' union wages when
  we work,
We'll be gettin' union wages,
We'll be gettin' union wages,
We'll be gettin' union wages when
  we work.

We'll be building up the union
  while we work,
We'll be building up the union
  while we work,
We'll be building up the union,
We'll be building up the union,
We'll be building up the union
  while we work.

The Boss Is Having a Terrible Time, Parlez-Vous

Parley-Vous used to be a war song. Now it's broke loose in the union. The union ain't a-foolin', it's taking all of the old songs, and the war songs and the funeral songs, and the church songs, and the love and sweetheart songs. And it's a-puttin' some sense to 'em.

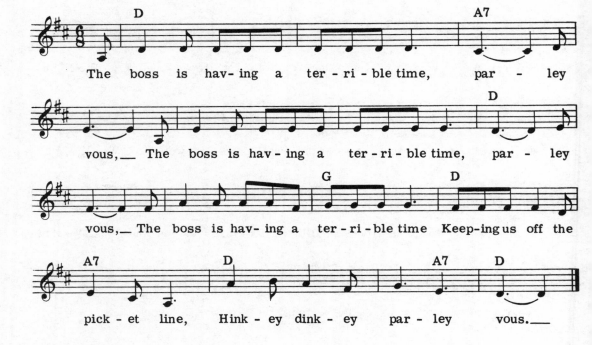

The boss is having a terrible time, parley-vous, The boss is having a ter-ri-ble time, par-ley vous,__ The boss is hav-ing a ter-ri-ble time, par-ley vous,__ The boss is hav-ing a ter-ri-ble time Keep-ing us off the pick-et line, Hink-ey dink-ey par-ley vous.__

The boss is having a terrible time,
    parley-vous,
The boss is having a terrible time,
    parley-vous,
The boss is having a terrible time,
Keeping us off the picket line,
Hinky dinky, parley-vous

The scabs are having a terrible
    time, parley-vous,
The scabs are having a terrible
    time, parley-vous,
The scabs are having a terrible
    time,
Getting through the picket line,
Hinky dinky, parley-vous.

The workers picket every day,
    parley-vous,
The workers picket every day,
    parley-vous,
The workers picket every day,
For shorter hours and higher pay,
Hinky dinky, parley-vous.

Oh, we are going to win this strike,
    parley-vous,
Oh, we are going to win this strike,
    parley-vous,
Oh, we are going to win this strike,
We'll picket all day and we'll picket
    all night,
Hinky dinky, parley-vous.

When a scab dies he goes to hell,
  parley-vous,
When a scab dies he goes to hell,
  parley-vous,
When a scab dies he goes to hell,
The rats and skunks all ring the
  bell,
Hinky dinky, parley-vous.

The boss is shaking at the knees,
  parley-vous,
The boss is shaking at the knees,
  parley-vous,
The boss is shaking at the knees,
In his silken B. V. D. 's,
Hinky dinky, parley-vous.

They say it is a terrible war,
  parley-vous,
They say it is a terrible war,
  parley-vous,
They say it is a terrible war, so
What the hell are they fighting it for,
Hinky dinky, parley-vous.

We Pity Our Bosses Five

This was made up by Murray Nathan during a strike of workers of the
Metropolitan News Company in New York City. A boss once drove up
unnoticed in his car; the policeman on duty started humming it softly as
a hint to the pickets who took it right up.

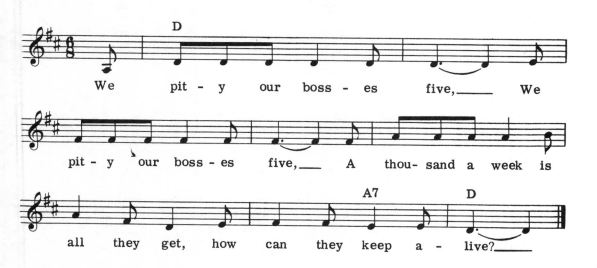

We pit-y our boss-es five,___ We
pit-y our boss-es five,___ A thou-sand a week is
all they get, how can they keep a - live?___

We pity our bosses five,
We pity our bosses five;
A thousand a week is all they get,
How can they keep alive?

O, we pity our boss's son,
We pity the boss's son,
Fifty a week is all he gets,
The lousy son of a gun.

It Ain't Gonna Work No More

"You can fool some of the people all of the time and all of the people
some of the time, but you can't fool all of the people all of the time."
Abe Lincoln said something like that. Strikes me about right.

Tune: "Ain't Gonna Rain No More"

There was a man in our town who thought him-self quite wise; He

tried to push our wag - es down and pull wool o - ver our eyes. But it

ain't gon-na work no more no more, It ain't gon-na work no more. The

boss has found that we are bound that it ain't gon-na work no more.

There was a man in our town
Who thought himself quite wise.
He tried to push our wages down
And pull wool over our eyes.

Chorus:
But it aint gonna work no more,
  no more,
It aint gonna work no more.
The boss has found that we have
  found
That it aint gonna work no more.

Our union he must recognize,
And give us union pay.
Or we'll stay out till earth and
  skies
And moon have passed away.

Chorus:
O, we'll make his clothes no
  more, no more,
We'll make his clothes no more.
Til he's on the square and treats
  us fair,
We'll make his clothes no more.

The bosses tried to cheat us,
They robbed us left and right,
But now we know our power,
We'll organize and fight.

Chorus:
O, we aint gonna slave no more,
    no more,
We aint gonna slave no more,
We're fighting for a living wage,
We aint gonna slave no more.

O, join a fighting union,
It is the only way,
You'll ever get a living wage.
Come on and join today!

Ma and Pa (A Unionization Plan)

Words by an Organizer in the Huntville, Ala. hosiery mills. No tune.

Ma and Pa have been at outs
Ma would quarrel, and Pa, he
    pouts,
Bud and I get lots of spanks
When we play our little pranks.

Ma'd call Pa a yellow scab
And Pa'd yell out, "Cut that gab"
And Sis'd sit and look so sad
'Cause she had a yellow dad.

Ma at once flew in the air
And grabbed Pa right by the hair
A rolling pin in the other hand,
"If you stay here, you'll be a man!"

"All you do is growl and brawl
About what's done at the labor hall
And if I could do it over again
I'd marry a man that had a brain. "

Then on his bean she took a whack
And gave him a kick below his
    back
"Unless you get a union card
You'll have to sleep in my back-
    yard. "

"I've taken an oath today
Just before I kneeled to pray
And if my bread I have to grab
I will NOT sleep with a yellow
    scab. "

And then Pa said, "Dear wife of
    mine
Be considerate, just give me time
I'll join the church and the union
    too
If it takes them both to sleep with
    you.

"I'll go to the local and pay my
    dues
And I'll buy you a pair of high
    heeled shoes
I'll get us all a union card
Before I'll sleep in your backyard. "

Pa lit out and he jumped the gate
Split his pants but he couldn't wait
To the union hall he struck a line,
And Ma said, dear hubby mine!

When he returned, Ma hugged his
    neck,
Did you get a card? I got a deck!
Ma then said, "You've saved the
    day, "
So Bud and I went out to play.

Calls for an Honest Square Dance

If you don't know this dance already, look it over a couple of times and you'll catch on. Many's the night I didn't bat an eye at square dances all over the country. Many a blister I wore on my fingers a takin' my turn on the fiddle, guitar, and mandolin. I've hollered loud enough to scare half the bankers plumb out of the country, and heard folks laugh so much the sheriff couldn't stop 'em.

I ain't a gettin' a divorce from them good times, either. And I ain't forgettin' the good, honest, natural fun that folks can have when you give 'em half a chance -- I mean when they're workin' and a prosperin' and a gettin' by.

People is the gladdest, saddest, and sometimes the maddest things you ever seen. But in their square dances, they're at their gladdest and when you get it into your head, big boy, that you can take everything away from us, and all of our good honest fun, and laughin' and music and dancing -- you just naturally got another thought a comin'.

These here honest square dance calls was figured out by a mighty pretty Oklahoma girl, call her Agnes Cunningham -- with Oklahoma's pride and joy, the RED DUST PLAYERS.

Calls:

First couple, balance and swing,
Down the center and divide the
   ring.
Down the center and cast off six,
The tenant farmer's in an awful
   fix.

Swing at the head and the foot
   couples too,
Side four go right and left through.
Beans all gone, there aint no more,
Down the center and cast off four.

Swing at the head and the foot
   couples too,
Side four go right and left through.
Down the center and cut off two,
What the heck can a poor man do?

Home you are and everybody swing,
Alemande left, go around the ring.
Eight millions acres of company
   land,
Partner by the right, and right and
   left grand.

Meet your partner, promenade!
Join the union, don't be afraid!

2nd couple balance and swing,
Down the center and divide the
   ring.
Gent to the left and lady to the
   right,
The tenant union's gonna put up a
   fight.

Swing at the head and the foot
   couples too.
Side four go right and left through.
Down the center as you done before
Down the center and cut off four.

Swing at the head and the foot
   couples too,
Side four go right and left through.
Better join the union too,
Down the center and cast off two.

Home you are and everybody swing,
Alemande left and go round the
   ring.
Half the land is all dried out,
Ant the rest is up the landhog's
   snout.

Meet your partner, promenade!
Join the union, don't be afraid!

3rd couple balance and do the same,
We aint playin' til they change the
    game.
Down the center and cast off six,
The union's gonna see that they
    change it quick.

Swing your honey right off the floor,
Recruiting officer, git away from
    my door.
You dont' catch me in the rich
    man's war.
Down the center and cast off four.

Swing at the head and the foot
    couple too,
Side four right and left go through.
Cast off two and before we're
    through,
We're gonna cast off the landhog,
    too.

Home you are and everybody swing,
Alemande left and go round the ring.
Billions of dollars the oil man's
    making.
While the Tax is added to the price
    of bacon.

This sorta thing has got to stop.
Grab your partner and hippity hop.
Grab your partner and promenade,
Everybody here is a union made.

You Guys Got To Organize

Words and music by David Robinson. © 1938 by David Robinson.

I bummed my way from Ten - nes - see caught a freight two mile and a pus-sy foot three, got a roar-in' blis-ter un-der my toe, and it hurts like Ho - ly Moe. You guys ___ got-ta or-gan-ize, yes sir, ___ start to - day, ___ You guys ___ got- ta or - gan-ize there ain't no oth - er way.

I've bummed my way from
   Tennessee,
Caught a freight two mile and a
   pussyfoot three,
Got a roarin' blister under my toe,
And it hurts like Holy Moe.

Left the nicest bunch of fellers back
   home,
Left my maw and paw 'cause I had to
   roam,
And talk to every one of you guys,
And tell you how to get wise.

   Chorus:
   You guys got to organize,
   Yes, sir, start today,
   You guys got to organize,
   There aint no other way.

"Now this song is mostly about my
pappy, so I'm going to tell you about
him now. He was a very thin man, and
he was a miner. He worked down in the
mines all his life, since he was 10
years old. In fact, he had a red nose,
but it wasn't from sunburn ... and this
is about my pappy."

My pappy was as thin as a rail,
And his face was always terrible
   pale.
So oneday, "Paw, how come?" says
   I,
"You don't weigh more than a fly."

"So paw, he looks at me kinda funny
   and says like this:"

"Now, son," says paw, "When I was nine,
My own paw sent me down in the mine.
When you work down there nigh forty-five year,
You aint no goddam steer. "

Chorus:
Way down, way down in the mines,
You can't see the sun,
Way, down way down in the mines,
It aint no goddam fun.

"No, sir, it wasn't much fun, and my pappy stood it as long as he could. Long hours and low wages. So one day he got up on his hind legs and this is what happened."

One day last spring up spoke my paw,
"This place begins to stick in my craw.
Go out and fetch in all of the guys,
We've got to organize. "

(Repeat first chorus)

"So I went out just like he said and brought in Mike and Smoky and George and Joe and the rest of the bunch. And pappy started talking to 'em. And what I mean, he really gave it to 'em like this:

"Now, listen, Mike and Smoky, " he said,
"All those with more than bone in their head,
If we don't speak up what's on our minds,
We'll all be left behind.

(Chorus)

"And he gave the feller a swell speech, you know. Talked to 'em and got 'em all het up about the whole thing. But my pappy was one of them anarchists, you know, he couldn't wait. He had to go in and talk to the boss all by himself. So this is what happened."

The next day my pappy says to the boss.
"The boys are sick of your applesauce.
If you don't talk turkey mighty soon,
We'll blow your mine to the moon. "

"You see, one of them anarchists, like I said. But the boss ain't never been spoken to like this in his life before, so he answered back":

"Now, the boss was one tough son of a gun,
And he grabbed a hick'ry stick and swung for fun.
"To see you git the hell from here. "
And he claps my paw on the ear.

"HEY, MAC, SMOKY, GEORGE, JOE, MAC, he knocked my paw cold. Git the boys!"

"When pappy woke the followin' day
The first words that he managed to say.
"It's a dam good thing my head is so hard,
He's got my union card. "

(Chorus)

323

Union Maid

Peter and me was fagged out when we got to Oklahoma City from New York, but not too fagged out to plow up a Union Song. Pete flopped out acrost a bed, and I set over at a writing machine, and he could think of one line and me another'n until we woke up an hour or two later with a great big 15 pound, blue-eyed Union Song, I mean Union – named the Union Maid. Whim, wham, and the mule throwed the governor.

Here's another one comin' out of chute #7, Rider #19. This is an older one made up by the I.W.W.'s to the same tune – an old Indian song. But I don't think the Indians will mind. Fact is they're in the Union same as the rest of us. (What are you guards and deputies gonna sing? Let's hear you sing!)

Words and music by Woody Guthrie. © 1961 (renewed), 1963 (renewed) by Ludlow Music, Inc., New York, NY. Used by permission.

There once was a Un - ion Maid, She nev - er was a-

fraid Of guards and ginks and com - pa - ny finks Or

dep - u - ty sher-iffs that made the raid. She went to the Un - ion

Hall, When a meet - in' it was called, And

when the Leg - ion boys came 'round she al - ways stood her

ground. Oh you cain't scare me, I'm stick - in' by th'

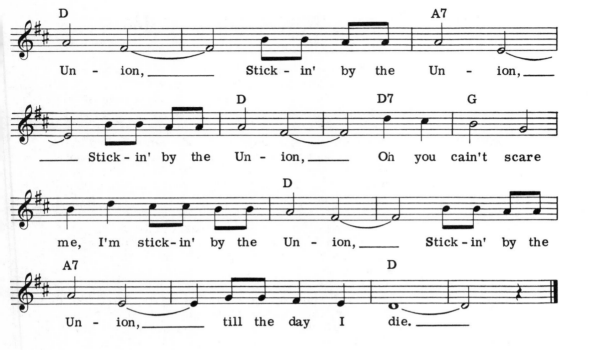

Un - ion, _____ Stick - in' by the Un - ion, _____ _____ Stick - in' by the Un - ion, _____ Oh you cain't scare me, I'm stick-in' by the Un - ion, _____ Stick - in' by the Un - ion, _____ till the day I die. _____

There once was a Union Maid,
She never was afraid
Of guards and ginks and Company
    finks
Or deputy sheriffs
That made the raid. . .
She went to the Union Hall
When a meetin' it was called,
And when the Legion boys come
    'round
She always stood her ground.

Chorus:
Oh, you cain't scare me, I'm
    sticking by th' Union,
Sticking by the Union, sticking by
    the Union,
Oh, you can't scare me I'm
    sticking by the Union,
Sticking by the Union till the day
    I die.
(Repeat after each verse)

She went to the Picket Line
One morning just at nine,
And the guard and ginks and Company
    finks,
Come a skipping through
The morning dew.
They had their clubs and guns
They had their knives and bombs,
They stood as still as if they's dead,
When she jumped up and said:

When the Union boys they seen
This pretty little Union queen
Stand up and sing in the deputies'
    face,
They laughed and yelled
All over the place
And you know what they done?
These two-gun Company thugs,
Then they heard this Union Song,
They tucked their tails and run.

325

Better Go Down and Jine the Union

It was one hot day on the desert between Phoenix, Ariz., and Needles, California, that this song was borned. I ain't a stretchin' the truth when I tell you that my feet was so full of blisters that I had to take off my shoes and carry them down the road.

Been stranded out there for several days and had been a having hard luck at catching rides. The highway was paved. It was so hot out there you couldn't walk barefooted, and you could not wear your shoes with about 6 big water blisters on each foot. What in the hell was you gonna do?

Well, I drug over to one side of the road, and set myself down on a gallon oil can and set my feet in the shade of a little weed there, and got to thinking about them big cars a humming up and down the road, and some of 'em with just one little feller in 'em.

Well, I don't know, I just got to thinking about the Union trouble I'd heard about around over the country, and had never thought about Unions much before -- but it was a setting right there on that desert in the hot sun that I got to humming this tune - and took my old guitar down from off my back and sung her just like you find her here.

Words and new music adaptation by Woody Guthrie. © 1963 (renewed) by Ludlow Music, Inc., New York, NY. Used by permission.

Uncle Sam started him a Union,
Uncle Sam started him a Union,
Uncle Sam started him a Union,
Called it the U. S. A.

Forty eight states jined the Union,
　(3 times)
Called 'em the U. S. A.

They all made the one big Union,
　(3 times)
Called it the U. S. A.

The Banking Men started 'em a
　Union (3 times)
Most of the Robbers jined it.

The Finance Men started 'em a
　Union, (3 times)
Most of the crooks they jined it.

The Landlords started 'em a Union,
　(3 times)
Most of the Lords they jined it.

The Store Men started 'em a Union,
　(3 times)
Most of the _____ jined it. (fill in
　to suit yourself)

The Rich Guys started 'em a Union,
　(3 times)
Most of the Hogs they jined it.

John L. Lewis started him a Union,
　(3 times)
Called it the C. I. O.

The Workin' Folks jined the Union,
　(3 times)
Called it the C. I. O.

The Cotton Pickers jined the Union,
　(3 times)
Called it the C. I. O.

You better go down and jine the
　Union, (3 times)
Everybody else is jinin'.

It's one little, two little, three little
    Unions,
Four little, five little, six little
    Unions,
Seven little, eight little, nine little
    Unions,
Call 'em the U. S. A.

Harry Bridges

The trouble Harry Bridges had on the west coast took place while I was
making various noises on the radio there in Los Angeles and, well, I just
sort of thought they ought to be some kind of a little song wrote up about
old Harry and the tough old human race for which he stands.

I'll sing you the tale of Harry Bridges,
He left his family and his home,
He sailed across that rolling ocean
And into Frisco he did roam.

Now Harry Bridges seen starvation
A creepin' along that ocean shore
"Gonna get good wages for the long-
    shoremen",
That's what Harry Bridges swore.

Now the big ship owners they shook
    their timbers,
Moaned and groaned and hung their
    head.
They flapped their fins and said,
    "We'll get him. "
'Cause they figured that he was a red.

Now Harry joined with the C. I. O.
    boys,
He told the sailors to unite,
And most of the seamen followed
    Harry,
'Cause they figured that he was right.

Well, they carried him away to
    Angel's Island,
It was there they had his trial,
They wept and sighed and lied and
    cried,
But Harry licked 'em with a smile.

This is a song about Harry Bridges,
And the Union battle he did fight.
Said, "Unionism is Americanism. "
Well, I figure he's just about right.

327

Scabs in the Factory

Here's Skip To My Lou, the old play party tune, skipping to a new set of words. Scabs in the factory just naturally throw a wrench in the machinery and a kink in your meal ticket.

Words: Dorothy Howard,
Lafollette, Tenn.

Scabs in the fac-to-ry, that won't do, Scabs in the fac-to-ry, that won't do,

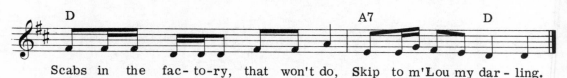

Scabs in the fac-to-ry, that won't do, Skip to m'Lou my dar - ling.

Scabs in the factory, that won't do,
Scabs in the factory, that won't do,
Scabs in the factory, that won't do,
Skip to m' Lou, my darling.

Three cents a dozen, that won't do,
Three cents a dozen, that won't do,
Three cents a dozen, that won't do
Skip to m' Lou, my darling.

Twelve hours a day, that won't do,
Twelve hours a day, that won't do,
Twelve hours a day, that won't do,
Skip to m' Lou, my darling.

Bully bosses, that won't do,
Bully bosses, that won't do,
Bully bosses, that won't do,
Skip to m' Lou, my darling.

Fifty cents a day, that won't do,
Fifty cents a day, that won't do,
Fifty cents a day, that won't do,
Skip to m' Lou, my darling.

Two and a half a week, that won't do,
Two and a half a week, that won't do,
Two and a half a week, that won't do,
Skip to m' Lou, my darling.

Seven and a half an hour, that won't
  do,
Seven and a half an hour, that won't
  do,
Seven and a half an hour, that won't
  do,
Skip to m' Lou, my darling.

XIII - MULLIGAN STEW

Now this here section is just sort of a section.

I mean we couldn't throw it in no certain heap and say that's where it belonged. So you might say here is a section of songs that you don't know where they belong. After all, the world is full of money that shore as hell ain't where it belongs. But again I've got off onto the subject of money.

Some New and some Old, that means some of 'em have been here longer than others.

How do you get out of here to the United States?

You know, I'm just a settin' here a wonderin' if this book of songs will ever get printed up in some foreign languages. Might.

At least, you dadgum money folks cain't say that this book was smuggled in from some furrin country. It's been a hangin' right smack in your face for fifty years.

Worried Man Blues

Rich fellers are worried nowadays. 'Fraid us poor folks are gonna get sore and take our groceries back. 'Fraid we might set down at the side of the road and refuse to go to the war. 'Fraid the real people like you and me will take a notion to run our own business and -- 'fraid we'll get together and go to work on something.

I know of little 3 year old kids all over the country that can do better than most of these politicians. They at least wouldn't stand around and let you starve, or your house get rotten and fall down on your family, or send your kids off to some war 7 or 8,000 miles across the dadgum ocean.

Old Abe Lincoln said this country and everything in it belongs to everybody, and when some little bunch of fellers passes a law of some kind and says it's theirs, and kicks everybody out down the road to ramble around like a lost herd of whiteface cattle, why, we ought to walk up, all together, and say, "Howdy, boys, just come over to eat and sleep and stay with you, seein' as to how you got all of our eats, and houses, and stuff."

You been singing the Worried Blues too long.

From the singing of the Carter Family.

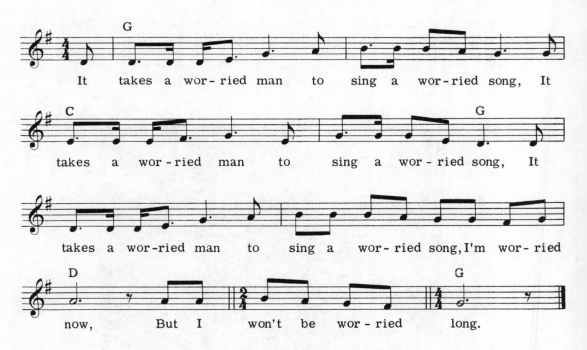

It takes a wor-ried man to sing a wor-ried song, It takes a wor-ried man to sing a wor-ried song, It takes a wor-ried man to sing a wor-ried song, I'm wor-ried now, But I won't be wor-ried long.

Chorus:
It takes a worried man to sing a
  worried song,
It takes a worried man to sing a
  worried song,
It takes a worried man to sing a
  worried song,
I'm worried now, but I won't be
  worried long.

I went across the river, and I lay
  down to sleep,
I went across the river, and I lay
  down to sleep,
I went across the river, and I lay
  down to sleep,
When I woke up, I had shackles on
  my feet.

Twenty nine links of chain around
  my leg,
Twenty nine links of chain around
  my leg,
Twenty nine links of chain around
  my leg,
And on each link, was a 'nitial of
  my name.

I asked that judge, what's gonna be
  my fine,
I asked that judge, what's gonna be
  my fine,
I asked that judge, what's gonna be
  my fine,
Twenty one years on the Rocky
  Mountain Line.

The train arrived, sixteen coaches
  long,
The train arrived, sixteen coaches
  long,
The train arrived, sixteen coaches
  long,
The gal I love is on that train and
  gone.

If any one should ask you who made
  up this song,
If any one should ask you who made
  up this song,
If any one should ask you who made
  up this song,
Tell 'em it was I and I'll sing it all
  night long.

Ludlow Massacre

"In September, 1913, in Southern Colorado, several thousand coal miners went on strike. They wanted better hours. They did not want to trade in the company stores where the price of food was high, but in any stores they pleased. They wanted recognition of their union.

"John D. Rockefeller, Jr., who controlled most of the mines in that region would not have minded some of the demands, but he said it was "against his principles" to recognize the union.

"The strike straggled on. Rockefeller filled the mines with scab labor. He filled the towns with gunmen and militiamen until the homes of the strikers were no longer safe and they had to leave them and live in a colony of tents near Ludlow. Even in these tents the strikers and their families were not safe. The men dug trenches around each tent and made holes in the tents so that women and children could slip out easily and hide in the earth when the tents were being shot full of bullets.

"On April 20, 1914, an accident occurred. It is not known quite what happened, whether a striker shot a scab or a soldier shot at a striker. But a battle began and spread over an area of three miles. The two hundred soldiers and deputies, many of whom were recently sworn in gunmen, equipped with revolvers, machine guns and tear gas marched on the tent colony. They riddled the tents with bullets. The camp caught on fire. In the trenches which had been dug to protect women and children from gun fire, 'they died like trapped rats when the flames swept over them'. Thirty three, more than half of whom were women and children were either shot or burned to death. Over a hundred were wounded, burned, or otherwise injured. The battle lasted 14 hours. Then the camp was evacuated. The women and children and the dead and wounded were taken to Trinidad. The men began to organize themselves on a military basis, taking positions on the surrounding hills. There were more battles."

Words: Alfred Hayes; Music: Earl Robinson © 1966 by the authors.

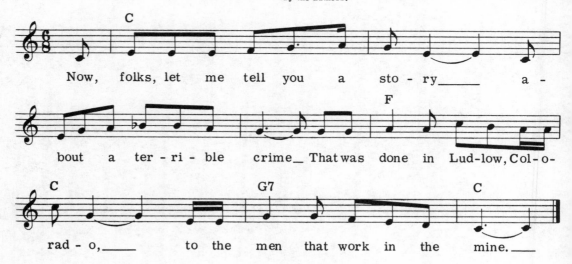

Now, folks, let me tell you a sto - ry_____ a - bout a ter - ri - ble crime_ That was done in Lud-low, Col-o-rad - o,_____ to the men that work in the mine._____

Now folks, let me tell you a story
About a terrible crime
That was done in Ludlow, Colorado,
To men that work in the mine.

Our children they were so hungry,
Our wives were thin and worn.
We were striking 'gainst a rich man,
Meanest ever was born.

John D., he'd stacks of money,
John D., he'd silver and gold.
John D., he was warm in winter
While mining folks went cold.

He sent down his hired gunmen,
They'd orders to shoot on sight.
He sent down troops with helmets
To break the miner's fight.

John D., he was a Christian,
John D., the psalms he sung.
But he'd no mercy in his heart,
He shot down old and young.

One night when all were sleeping,
All wrapped up in their dreams,
We heard a loud explosion,
We heard most terrible screams.

"Oh, save us from the burning
    flames,"
We heard our children cry.
But John D. laughed and shot them
    down
Right there before our eyes.

Folks the country over
And mining camps around,
Their hearts got sick with pity
At what happened in our town.

It was a terrible crime to do,
It was an awful thing.
And mining men like me made up
This little song to sing,

To sing it to the people,
Poor folks that work and sweat.
What John D. did in Ludlow
They never should forget.

It was just a downright murder,
I aint afraid to say.
It was done by a man with money,
And they always get away.

So, folks, you heard my story
About the Ludlow crime
That was done in Colorado
To the men that work in the mine.

Don't Kill My Baby and My Son

For a year or so my dad was undersheriff of Okemah, Oklahoma, and he used to tell me many a sad tale about that old black jailhouse. I remember one night when I was about eight or nine years old that I was caught out after dark and had to walk through the old dark town after curfew hour - and I was barefooted on the sidewalk - so there wasn't a sound to be heard - except a wild and blood curdling moan that filled the whole town, and it kept getting louder as I walked down the street to the old rock jailhouse. And I heard a Negro lady sticking her head through the jailhouse bars and moaning at the top of her voice.

That was lonesomer than all of the animals of the wild places that I've run onto, and I've slept many a night on the desert alone, and in the hills and mountains, and can listen to a panther or a coyote and tell you what's on his mind by the tone of his yell.

This Negro lady had a right new baby, and a son that was doomed to hang by her dead body with the rise of the morning wind, and my dad told me the whole story.

Several years has gone by and I wrote this song down, because that lady's wail went further, went higher, and went deeper than any sermon or radio broadcast I ever heard.

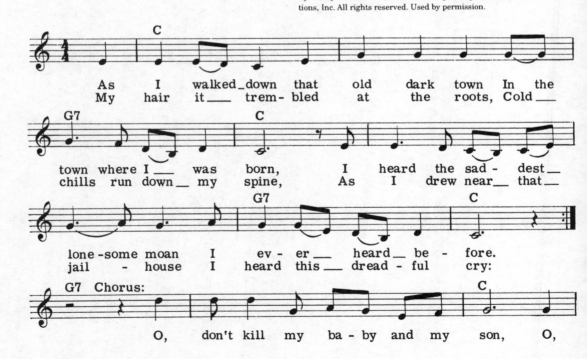

don't kill my ba - by and my son, You can stretch my neck on that

old ri - ver bridge, But don't kill my ba - by and my son.

As I walked down that old dark
   town
In the town where I was born,
I heard the saddest lonesome moan
I ever heard before.
My hair it trembled at the roots
Cold chills run down my spine,
As I drew near that jail house
I heard this deathly cry:

   Chorus:
   O, don't kill my baby and my son,
   O, don't kill my baby and my son.
   You can stretch my neck on that
      old river bridge,
   But don't kill my baby and my
      son.

Now, I've heard the cries of a
   panther,
Now, I've heard the coyotes yell,
But that long, lonesome cry shook
   the whole wide world
And it come from the cell of the
   jail.

Yes, I've heard the screech owls
   screeching,
And the hoot owls that hoot in the
   night,
But the graveyard itself is happy
   compared
To the voice in that jailhouse that
   night.

Then I saw a picture on a postcard
It showed the Canadian River Bridge,
Three bodies hanging to swing in the
   wind,
A mother and two sons they'd
   lunched.
There's a wild wind blows down the
   river,
There's a wild wind blows through
   the trees,
There's a wild wind that blows
   'round this wide wide world,
And here's what the wild winds say:

Jesus Christ Was a Man

I wrote this song looking out of a rooming house window in New York City in the winter of 1940. I saw how the poor folks lived, and then I saw how the rich folks lived, and the poor folks down and out and cold and hungry, and the rich ones out drinking good whiskey and celebrating and wasting handfulls of money at gambling and women, and I got to thinking about what Jesus said, and what if He was to walk into New York City and preach like He used to. They'd lock Him back in jail as sure as you're reading this. "Even as you've done it unto the least of these little ones, you have done it unto me."

Words and music by Woody Guthrie. © 1961 (renewed), 1963 (renewed) by Ludlow Music, Inc., New York, NY. Used by permission.

Je - sus Christ was a man that trav - eled through the land, A car - pen - ter true and brave; He said to the rich, "Give your goods_ to the poor," So they laid Je - sus Christ in his grave. Yes

Chorus:

Je - sus was a man, a car - pen - ter by hand, a car - pen - ter true and brave And a dir - ty lit - tle coward named Ju - das Is - car - iot, he laid Je - sus Christ in his grave.

Jesus Christ was a man that
traveled through the land,
A Carpenter true and brave;
He said to the rich, "Give your
goods to the poor",
So they laid Jesus Christ in his
grave.

Chorus:
Yes, Jesus was a man, a
Carpenter by Hand,
A Carpenter true and brave.
And a dirty little coward called
Judas Iscariot,
He laid Jesus Christ in His grave.

The people of the land took Jesus
by the Hand,
They followed Him far and wide;
"I come not to bring you Peace, but
a Sword."
So they killed Jesus Christ on the
sly.

He went to the sick and He went to
the poor,
He went to the hungry and the lame;
He said that the poor would win this
world,
So they laid Jesus Christ in His
grave.

One day Jesus stopped at a rich
man's door,
"What must I do to be saved?"
"You must sell your goods and
give it to the poor",
So they laid Jesus Christ in His
grave.

They nailed Him there to die on a
cross in the sky,
In the lightning and thunder and
rain;
And Judas Iscariot he committed
suicide,
When they laid poor Jesus in his
grave.

This wide wicked world of soldiers
and slaves,
Rich man, poor man and thief;
If Jesus was to preach what He
preached in Galilee,
They would lay Jesus Christ in His
grave.

When the love of the poor shall
turn into hate,
When the patience of the workers
gives away;
"Twould be better for you rich if
you'd never been born"
For you laid Jesus Christ in His
grave.

Mama Don't 'Low No Bush-Wahs Hangin' Around

This song was born in Washington, D.C. at a Union meeting. We filled the hall up twice that night. At the end of the program they called out all of the entertainers, the big Boogie-Woogie piano players, Leadbelly, and me. We had a big jam session, played this tune, and all at once I hollered the chorus out. Reckon it must have been my Union raisins. Mighty hot song.

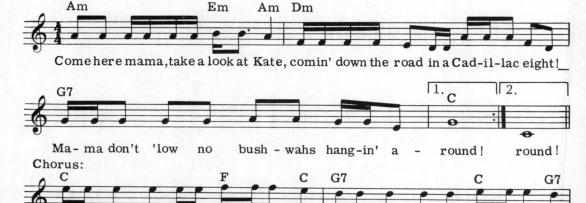

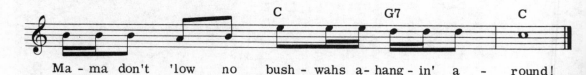

Come here, Mama, take a look at Kate,	Big fat man with a pocket full of money
Comin' down the road in a Cadillac 8,	Took my likker and he took my honey,
Mama don't 'low no bush-wahs hangin' around!	Mama don't 'low no bush-wahs hangin' round.
	Banker come to take my farm
Chorus:	He took my gal off under his arm,
Mama don't 'low 'em a hangin' around,	Mama don't 'low no bush-wahs hangin' 'round!
Mama don't 'low 'em hangin' around,	
Mama don't 'low no bush-wahs a hangin' around!	Finance man he took my tractor,
(Repeat after each verse)	He grabbed my gal and really smacked 'er,
	Mama don't 'low no bush-wahs hangin' 'round.

All these politicians men
Got a good hot gal and a bottle of
  gin,
Mama don't 'low no bush-wahs
  hangin' around.

Two bush-wah women a playin' in
  the sand,
Both of 'em wishin' the other was a
  man,
Mama don't 'low no bush-wahs hangin'
  aroun'!
I'm just an old hard working man,
I ride 'em like I find 'em do the best
  I can,
Mama don't 'low no bush-wahs hangin'
  'round!

I got me a gal at the Union hall,
Then Union gals is the best of all,
Mama don't 'low no bush-wah
  hangin' aroun'!
These bush-wah widders aint got
  no man,
They ought to do their lovin' on the
  Union plan,
Mama don't 'low no bush-wahs
  hangin' aroun'!

Last Chorus:
Hangin' aroun', hangin' aroun',
Mama don't 'low no hangin'
  aroun'!
Mama don't 'low no bush-wahs
  hangin' aroun'!

Hallelujah, I'm a Ku Klux

The Ku Klux, or the Klip Joints or whatever you call 'em are to my notion the wrongest tribe of folks I ever seen. There's the Outlaws that took money from the rich and give it to the poor, but the Ku Klux, some strange way, always side in with the Rich Guys. If they beat up a Rich Man it's because a Richer one told them to.

They say the Ku Klux are against the C.I.O. That's enough to make me join the C.I.O. tomorrow. When you got to hide your face to do it, boy, you're going against your own self, and when you try to go around horse-whipping people or smearing hot tar and loose feathers on 'em - that's just as mean and low as you can fall. No. C.I.O. Union has ever treated folks this a way.

The Ku Klux better look out. They're just a digging their own grave. Just because some big rich man told you to do it. Who tells the Grand Lizzard what to do? You ask him.

Tune: "Hallelujah, I'm A Bum"

When my old man said I was hun-dred per - cent, I sought out a klea - gle and to him I went, Hal-le-lu - ja, I'm a Ku Klux, Hal-le-lu - ja, a - men, Hal-le-lu - ja, I'm a Ku Klux, I be - long to the Klan.

You Low Life Son of a Bitch

I've known hundreds of my best friends that cussed every other breath. Few sentences got by without being salted down with good sweaty cuss words lashing the Truth at somebody or something. Truck drivers, cotton pickers, fruit workers, miners, steel hands, longshoremen, sailors, factory hands, store clerks, even the shy and innocent little girls, the daisies that blossom in the dark, the angels that fly out the old brick doors of the Schools For Girls, and the department store girls, and the chorus girls and the High School girls - don't kid yourself, the minute they get off to theirself, to where they can cut loose and be natural, their manner of speech turns from ink into lightning and thunder.

Thank God, they ain't lost in the caves of Fear and Put On - we got a redblood race of people here. And their hard working words are sharper than a Rich Man's bayonet. That's why we always win. Our words are real.
They tell me down in Oklahoma that the Indian language ain't got no cuss words in it. Well, wait til they get a little raggedier and hungrier. They'll work up some.

Meanwhile, the American lingo seems to be flavored with 'em. It's a flavor that we come by plumb natural. It's the words of honest to goodness, hard working, hard hitting, hard luck people that don't ever pretend to be something on a stick. They're just what they are and that's all they are.

There's folks in America that are up in some sort of silly society where they seldom ever get to do or say a single thing they'd really like to, so they've got it figured out to where you hadn't to rear back and cuss. If they do, they lose their false reputation, or their silly standing, or their empty foothold or something. Anyway, they have been born in a life of greed and put on and they have got there by pretending they're something they ain't, so they never for a minute can be human, natural or down to earth.

This book is populated with some mighty good cuss words which ought to be preserved for future generations. These are not vulgar. When you see a thief stealing and you call him a god damned lowdown thief, that's not vulgar, for it's true. However, thieves don't like to be called thieves so they kick you out of church if you make a habit of it.

But this book didn't come from the pews of a church. It jumped out of the dry and hungry throats of thirty million people that have been cheated for 10,000 years. I think their honest cussing is the power and dynamite of their language and of their songs as the Bible is a book with cussing on every side: the honest and hungry prophets raving and snorting and ripping into the bellies of the Rich and Powerful Rulers and Lying Priests who beat their people into slavery and dope them with superstitions and false ceremonies and dictate to them what to do, where to go, what to read, who to love, what to eat, what to drink, what to wear, when to work, when to rest and where to bring your money. The prophets cussed and they raved plenty. Because they was out there in the hills and hollers yelling and echoing the Real Voice of the Real People, the poor working class and the farmers and the down and out.

You low life trifling bastard,
You low life son of a bitch,
You selfish, greedy, low down
   thief,
You goddam thieving snitch.
You yaller-back, piss-complected
   skunk,
You scheming, conniving
That's what I call a greedy rich
   thief,
Now what do you think about that?

You money changing, mangy hound,
You profit worshipping dog,
You home-wrecking, baby killing
   pimp,
You swine, you filthy hog.
You sissy, prissy cowardly snake,
You whole-hog loafer worf,
You gambling, framing, cheating
   cheat,
No wait, that aint enough.

You mother-killing, baby starving,
Grocery taking, profit making,
Haywired, insane, organizer of
   death,
You worshipper of greed and the
   devil.
Who are you and where are you?
You stool pigeon for the greedy
   side,
You bodyguard of the bigshot lord,
You worshipper of riches and greed
You know who you are.

Bourgeois Blues

Don't run off. That just means "bushwa." Bushwa means moneyed folks with a lot of high falooting notions. Think they're just a shade better than you and me, or that they got a perfect right to twist us a loose from our money any old way they can, or that Negroes are "niggers" and are to be looked down on, or that colored people are all right so long as they "stay in their place."

Bushwa folks are just a little tangled up in the head, that's all, you know, just sorta uppity or sissy or think they're smart. Leadbelly is a Negro Blues singer and "King of the Twelve String Guitar," and you can't fool him.

Here's a song he wrote after some business men and landlords in Washington, D.C., had insulted him, his wife and a carload of friends, some white, some Negro. They refused to let them eat at the same cafe or stay in the same house. They tried several and was turned down. Leadbelly said, "What kind of town is this, anyhow?" and his friends said, "This is a bushwa town." So in a few minutes, Leadbelly exploded with this song and fired it into the faces of the stuck-up Bushwas at several of their very most elegant parties.

I've lived with Leadbelly and his wife Martha many weeks and they're 2 of as good a friends as I ever had. Lots of books have already been written about his prison life and his story and full page pictures has appeared in magazines. Leadbelly, to my notion, and his wife are Real Folks.

Words and music by Huddie Ledbetter. Edited with new additional material by Alan Lomax. © 1959 (renewed) by Folkways Music Publishers, Inc., New York, NY. Used by permission.

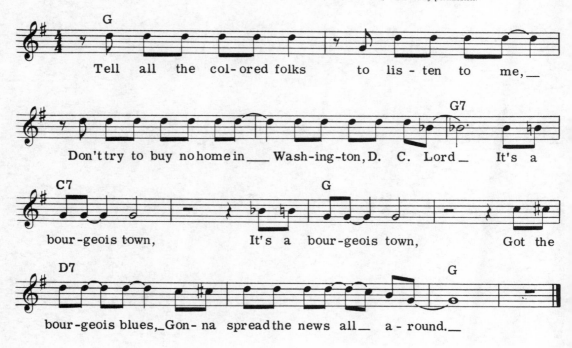

Sung by Leadbelly in Musicraft
album "Negro Sinful Songs. "

Tell all the colored folks to listen
  to me,
Don't try to buy no home in
  Washington, D. C.

  Chorus:
  (Lord) It's a bourgeois town, it's
    a bourgeois town,
  Got the bourgeois blues, gonna
    spread the news all around.

Me an' my wife run all over town,
Everywhere we'd go, the people
  turn us down.

Me an' Marthy, we was standing
  upstair,
I heard the white man say, "I don't
  want no niggers up there. "

  Chorus:
  He was a bourgeois man living
    in a bourgeois town,
  Got the bourgeois blues, gonna
    spread the blues all around.

The white folks in Washington,
  they know how
Chuck a colored man a nickel just
  to see him bow.

The D. A. R. wouldn't let Marion
  Anderson in,
But Mrs. Roosevelt was her best
  friend.

In the home of the brave, land of
  the free,
I don't want to be mistreated by no
  bourgeoisie.

345

How About You?

This song was composed and sung by Jim Garland, a Kentucky coal miner, in 1932. The reason for this song was that after working in the mines for six months he hadn't been able to buy his wife a pair of slippers. He went on strike with the miners and has got an injunction signed by the President, headed by the President of the United States against Jim Garland and others, saying that he would have to face the Federal Courts and probably have his furniture thrown onto the highway. Jim says that this was the reason he composed this song from his own feelings.

How well do I re-mem-ber_ how class struggle brought me through,_ I went out ____ on strike in thir-ty-two. ____ They brought the thugs a-gainst me,_ and the state mi-li-tia too._ And they kicked me in the gut-ter,_ How _ a-bout you?

Chorus:
How ___ a-bout you? Can't you see this sys-tem's rot-ten through and through?_ It gives mil-lions to the

boss-es,___ the Cap- i - tal - ist - ic few,___ But en-

slaves the toil - ing mass-es,_ like me___ and you.

How well do I remember how class
   struggle brought me through,
I went out on strike in 1932.
They brought the thugs against me
   and the State militia, too,
And they kicked me in the gutter,
How about you?

  Chorus:
  How about you, how about you?
  Can't you see this system's
    rotten through and through?
  It gives millions to the bosses,
    the capitalistic few,
  But enslaves the toiling masses,
  Like me and you.
  (Repeat after each verse)

We need a brand new system, that's
   one thing that is true,
The boss will have to work like me
   and you.
We'll all have homes to live in, and
   a job to work at, too,
But there'll be no boss to rob us,
Me and you.

We know the boss won't like it, to
   work like me and you,
But there's one thing he can always
   do,
He can jump in the lake if he wants
   to and break himself in two,
But he cannot rob us workers,
Me and you.

347

We Shall Not Be Moved

This is an old pre-Civil War spiritual, used to be sung by Negro slaves. Has lasted to be sung in Union halls all over this country. The words here were made up by strikers at the Rockwood, Tennessee, hosiery plant in 1938, but you can make up your own verses to it and you ought to as most folk do.

"They shot up my house with machine guns, and they made me run away from where I lived at, but they couldn't make me run away from my union which is this union here. And until the end of my life, as I climb up to the highest hill of elevations, I will always be singing my union song, that we shall not be moved." - A.B. Brookins, at the 3rd Annual Convention of the S.T.F.U. in 1937.

We shall not be,
we shall not be moved,
We shall not be,
we shall not be moved, Just like a
tree that's plant - ed by the wa - ter,
We shall not be moved.

We shall not be	Their orders are being canceled,
We shall not be moved,	We shall not be moved,
We shall not be	Their orders are being canceled,
We shall not be moved,	We shall not be moved,
Just like a tree that's planted by the water,	Just like a tree that's planted by the water,
We shall not be moved.	We shall not be moved.

They kidnap organizers;
We shall not be moved.
They kidnap organizers;
We shall not be moved.
Etc.

They black-jacked Daniels,
We shall not be moved.
They black-jacked Daniels,
We shall not be moved.
Etc.

We're not afraid of tear gas,
We shall not be moved.
We're not afraid of tear gas,
We shall not be moved.
Etc.

We're not afraid of gun thugs,
We shall not be moved.
We're not afraid of gun thugs,
We shall not be moved.
Etc.

Ain't Gonna Study War No More

Dadgone shore somebody is a studying war. Wonder who? Ever hear of
the little girl who was watching a big parade and said, "Mama, I think
sometime they're going to call a war and no one's going to come."
If you don't know this old spiritual, you sure ought to.

Gon - na lay down my sword and shield,

down by the riv - er - side, down by the riv - er - side,

down by the riv - er - side. Gon-na lay down my sword and shield,

down by the riv - er - side, gon - na stud - y_____ war no

Chorus:

more. Ain't gon - na stud - y war no more, ain't gon - na

stud - y war no more, ain't gon - na stud - y war no

more. Ain't gon - na stud - y war no more, ain't gon - na

stud-y war no more, ain't gon-na stud-y ____ war no more.

Gonna lay down my sword and
    shield,
Down by the riverside,
Down by the riverside,
Down by the riverside,
Gonna lay down my sword and
    shield,
Down by the riverside,
Aint gonna study war no more.

Chorus:
Aint gonna study war no more,
Aint gonna study war no more,
Aint gonna study war no more.
Aint gonna study war no more,
Aint gonna study war no more,
Aint gonna study war no more.

Gonna lay down my burden,
Down by the riverside,
Down by the riverside,
Down by the riverside,
Gonna lay down my burden,
Down by the riverside,
Aint gonna study war no more.

Gonna try on my long white robe,
Down by the riverside,
Down by the riverside,
Down by the riverside,
Gonna try on my long white robe,
Down by the riverside,
Aint gonna study war no more.

Gonna try on my starry gown,
Down by the riverside,
Down by the riverside,
Down by the riverside,
Gonna try on my starry gown,
Down by the riverside,
Aint gonna study war no more.

Wartime Blues

This is a verse from a blues sung by the one and only Blind Lemon Jefferson, about the first and the greatest blues singer there was. It was made up, as you can see, about 1917 when they were drafting everybody to fight over in France. The poor folks and the Negroes, as a class, are about the poorest in this country, were wonderin' just what the hell they were goin' over to fight for.

What you gon - na do,___ when they send your man to war?

What you gon - na do___ when they send your man to war?

What you gon - na do___ when they send your man to war?

Gon-na drink mud-dy wa-ter and sleep in a hol-ler log.___

What you gonna do when they send
  your man to war?
What you gonna do when they send
  your man to war?
What you gonna do when they send
  your man to war?
Gonna drink muddy water and sleep
  in a holler log.

Some verses we made up after
readin' this over....

What you gonna do when they send
  your man to war?
What you gonna do when they send
  your man to war?
What you gonna do when they send
  your man to war?
Aint you gonna wonder what he's
  fightin' for?

Twenty years ago they sent us once
  before.
Twenty years ago they sent us once
  before.
Twenty years ago they sent us once
  before.
They made a peace and they said
  we wouldn't fight no more.

Don't own no factories and no
  munitions plant,
Don't own no factories and no
  munitions plant,
Don't own no factories and no
  munitions plant,
I don't grow rich by killing in some
  far off land.

I'm singin' to you poor folks,
  ever'body old and young,
I'm singin' to you poor folks,
  ever'body old and young,
I'm singin' to you poor folks,
  ever'body old and young,
I'm against this war 'cause I know
  that killing's wrong.

Listen young gal, listen sonny boy
  to me,
Listen young gal, listen sonny boy
  to me,
Listen young gal, listen sonny boy
  to me,
Wall Street wants to send you 3000
  miles across the sea.

Gonna sing this song, though they
  lock me up in jail,
Gonna sing this song, though they
  lock me up in jail,
Gonna sing this song, though they
  lock me up in jail,
Boy, if they try to draft you, turn
  those guns the other way.

Red Cross Store

Sometimes known as the Recruitin' Store, and other names. This is another blues made up around the time of the first world war. This version here we got from Huddie Ledbetter, better known as Leadbelly, King of the Twelve String Guitar Players Of The World. Guess it speaks pretty well for itself. Wonder what would happen if we all just got up and told 'em NO-O?

New words and new music arranged by Huddie Ledbetter. Edited with new additional material by John A. Lomax and Alan Lomax. © 1936 (renewed) by Folkways Music Publishers, Inc., New York, NY. Used by permission.

Chorus:
I told her no - o
Baby, you know I don't want to go.
Yes, and I ain' goin
Down to dat Red Cross Sto'.
(Repeat after each verse.)

She says, papa, I come here to let you know,
They want you down at that Red Cross Sto'.

She says, papa, I come here to set down on yo' knee;
Ain' you gonna fight for you and me?

Says, daddy, I jus' come here 'cause I'm your wife,
Ain' you gonna fight for you an' your wife?

She come here and she shook my
    han',
Ain' you goin' down and fight like
    a man.

She says, I come here because
    they's feeding you might fine,
Mixing everything up with whiskey
    and wine.

She says, daddy, they's feeding
    better than I ever seen,
Feeding everybody offa pork and
    beans.

She come back here an' says,
    they's feedin' offa ham,
Say, get away from here gal, I
    don't give a damn.

Listen, I'll tell you somep'n,
    somep'n mighty funny,
The rich mens they has got all
    the money.

She says, don't you know they need
    you to fight the war?
I says, listen, baby, I got nothin'
    to fight for.

I ain' goin' down to no Red Cross
    Sto'.
I ain' playin in no rich man's show.

Tom Mooney Is Free

I wasn't much interested in high powered politics. Never aim to get a overdose of it if I can help it. But right is right and wrong is wrong. Shooting square is shooting square and framing and cheating is framing and cheating. Railroading a man to jail for 22 years with a crooked court set up and a bunch of lying witnesses is rape of the lowest kind. That's what they done to Mr. Tom Mooney. That's why I was glad the day he got out. I run home and hoed out this little song about him and about the Union and sung it a lot of times and lots of people liked it.

Mis - ter Tom Moon - ey is free!

Mis - ter Tom Moon - ey is free! Done got a par - don from that

old jail-house war-den, Mis-ter Cul-bert L. Ol-sen's de - cree.

Mr. Tom Mooney is Free!
Mr. Tom Mooney is Free!
Done got a pardon from that old
    jail house warden,
Mr. Culbert L. Olsen's decree.

How does it feel to be free?
How does it feel to be free?
How does it feel just to be out of
    jail,
Since the gov'ner has got your
    liberty?

It was way up in old Frisco town,
It was way up in old Frisco town,
Mr. Mooney and Billings was
    accused of a killing
And railroaded jail house bound.

Twenty two years have gone by,
Twenty two years have gone by,
And he spent the twenty two fer a
    crime he didn't do,
My! My! My! My!

Well the Truth caint be tied with a
    chain.
Well the Truth caint be tied with a
    chain.
From the cold clammy halls of the
    San Quentin walls,
Mister Tom Mooney is Free.

It was Culbert L. Olsen's decree!
It was Culbert L. Olsen's decree!
When he took that gov'nors chair,
    he said, I declare,
I got to set this state of California
    free.

Pity the Shape I'm In

I'm the poor wife of a company scab,
pit-y the shape I'm in, I wish I had mar-ried a
un-ion man, pit-y the shape I'm in.

I'm the poor wife of a company
  scab,
Pity the shape I'm in.
I wish I had married a Union man,
Pity the shape I'm in.

I'm the poor daughter of a company
  scab,
Pity the shape I'm in.
I wish I had me a Union dad,
Pity the shape I'm in.

I'm the son of a company scab,
Pity the shape I'm in.
Why don't you go in with the Union,
  dad?
Pity the shape I'm in.

I'm the poor dad of a company scab,
Pity the shape I'm in.
I wish that my boy was a Union lad,
Pity the shape I'm in.

I'm the poor mother of a company
  scab,
Pity the shape I'm in.
They say he's a coward, it makes
  me sad,
Pity the shape I'm in.

I'm the neighbor of a company scab,
Pity the shape I'm in.
To live next door to a scab is bad,
Pity the shape I'm in.

I am just a company scab,
Pity the shape I'm in.
Lost all of the friends I ever had,
Pity the shape I'm in.

Capitol City Cyclone

There has been a lot of cy-clones in my day, That come a-long and blow the town a - way, Swept up the farm and blow down the barn, and car- ry my chick-ens all a - way. But the big- gest blow I ev- er saw It blowed in from the Cap-i - tol. It was a wind - y sun of a gun, And here is what it done.

There has been a lot of cyclones in
  my day,
That come along and blow the town
  away,
Swept up the farm and blow down
  the barn,
And carry my chickens all away.

But the biggest blow I ever saw
It blowed in from the Capit-ol
It was a windy son of a gun,
And here is what it done.

It blowed down the wages and the
  pay,
It stretched out the hours of the day,
It blowed in the night, it was an
  awful sight,
It blowed down the W. P. A.

It cut down the flour and the meal,
It cut down the cotton in the field,
It cut down the hogs and cut down
  the lard,
You know just exactly how I feel.

O', it chopped down the folks on
  relief,
It left them with a lot of grief.
It took away the silk, it got the
  baby's milk,
It sheared all the wool off of the
  sheep.

It sucked all of the oil out of the
    ground,
It left it in a tank up here in town,
But the big oil company had it's
    name on the tank,
And the state man could never track
    it down.

It pulled all of the oranges from the
    trees,
It piled them in a dump to rot and
    freeze,
It poured on a coat of black creosote,
And called it a new orange squeeze.

It dug all the 'taters from the
    ground,
It made a dump a jillion miles
    around,
While the groceries was a soaking
    in black creosote
The children was hungry up in town.

O, I wonder how long it's gonna
    blow,
I wonder how long it's gonna blow,
That Capital City Cyclone's the
    worst I ever saw,
I wonder how long it's gonna blow.

Mister Congressman

Words by Agnes Cunningham. Tune of "Little Brown Jug." Last three verses added after World War II.
© 1965 by Agnes Cunningham.

Congressman, Mister Congressman,
Sittin' up there in Washington,
You'd better listen to our song,
Or you aint gonna be in Congress
  long.

Chorus:
No, no, no, no siree,
In Washington you will not be,
If you don't listen to our song,
You aint gonna be in Congress
  long.
(Repeat after each verse.)

Are you gonna listen to what we say,
Or let the big boys have their way?
Better get the people's point of view,
Or we're sure not a-gonna vote for
  you.

The vets want work at decent pay,
And we don't mean three bucks a
  day;
So, see that there are jobs for all,
Or you'll be looking for a job next
  fall.

Well, you know where the veteran
  lives,
Here and there with relatives.
If you think movin' around is fun,
We'll move you out of Washington.

A Fool There Was

Joseph Brandon

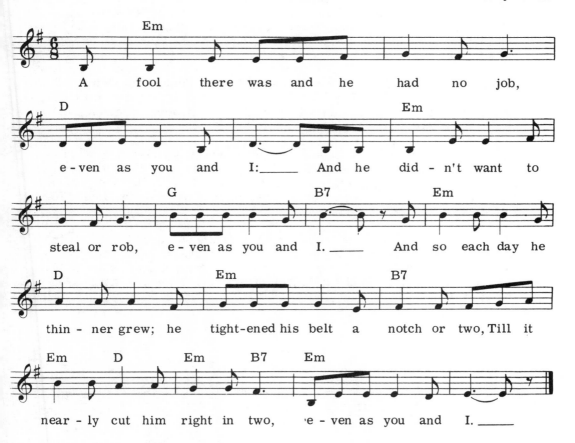

A fool there was and he had no
  job,
Even as you and I:
And he didn't want to steal or rob,
Even as you and I.
And so each day he thinner grew,
He tightened his belt a notch or
  two,
Til it nearly cut him right in two,
Even as you and I.

He voted for beer to ease his lot,
Even as you and I.
And they pledged him a chicken
  for his pot,
Even as you and I.
But after election all was grief,
He got no chicken, he got no beef,
And all that he got was home relief,
Even as you and I.

He watched depression growing
  worse,
Even as you and I,
But he heard Roosevelt on the
  radio,
Even as you and I.
They told him this was a country
  grand,
With plenty of everything in the
  land,
So he starved to death with a flag
  in his hand,
Even as you and I.

361

Why Do You Stand There In The Rain?

A few days before the 6,000 members of the American Youth Congress took their trip to Washington to ask the President for jobs and peace, I hoboed in from Galveston, Texas, up to the Missouri line, rode to Pittsburgh, then hit the road a walking again from Pittsburgh to New York in the snow.

It was snowing all of the way from Texas. Mississippi River was froze up worse than a Montana Well Digger; the Susquehannah River was 6 foot of solid ice, wind a blowin' like a Republican promise, and coldern'n a Wall Street kiss. But I got to town.

I hadn't been here but a couple or three days til I picked up a noise-paper and it said there that the 6,000 had been over to call on Roosevelt at his Whitehouse - and he called their trip and their stuff that they stood for "twaddle." It come up a big soaking rain and he made the kids a 30 minute speech in it.

Wrote up this little song about it. Ain't nothing fancy about it. Lots of better ones in this book made up by folks that was a fightin' and dyin' on Picket Lines, but -- anyhow, would like to dedicate this song to them 6,000 kids, and about 130 million others in this country that soaked the same day.

It was rain - ing might - y hard on the old cap-i-tol yard And the young folks gath-ered at the White House gate. The Pres - i - dent raised his head and to the young folks said, Tell me why have you come here in the

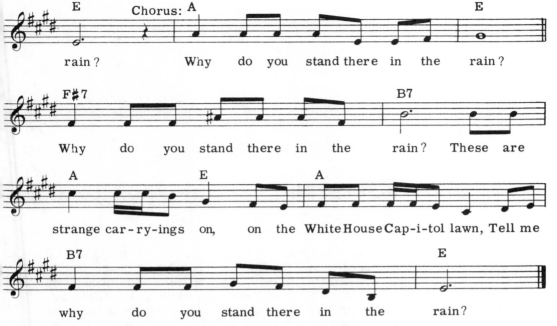

rain? Why do you stand there in the rain? Why do you stand there in the rain? These are strange car-ry-ings on, on the White House Cap-i-tol lawn, Tell me why do you stand there in the rain?

It was raining mighty hard on the
old Capitol yard,
And the young folks gathered at the
White House gate,
The President raised his head and
to the young folks said:
Tell me why do you come here in
the rain?

Chorus:
Why do you stand there in the
rain?
Why do you stand there in the
rain?
These are strange carryings on
On the White House Capitol lawn,
Tell me, why do you stand there
in the rain?
(Repeat after each verse)

My dear children, don't you know,
that unless by law you go,
That your journey here must all be
walked in vain.
You gotta make your resolution by
the U. S. Constitution,
Then you won't get left a standing
in the rain.

Well they tell me they got lands
where they will not let you stand
In the rain and ask for jobs upon
the lawn,
Thank God, in the U. S. A. you can
stand there every day,
But I wouldn't guarantee they'd take
you on.

Now before this storm could break,
Mr. John L. Lewis spake,
And he said you asked for jobs
what did you get?
A kid of seventeen, he was pretty
smart, it seemed,
Said we went there for a job - but
we got wet.

Now the guns in Europe roar as
they have so oft before,
And the war lords play the same
old game again,
They butcher and they kill, Uncle
Sammy foots the bill,
With his own dear children
standing in the rain.

Then the President's voice did
ring; "Why, this is the silliest
thing,
I have heard in all my fifty eight
years of life. "
But it all just stands to reason as
he passes another season,
He'll be smarter by the time he's
fifty nine.

COMPILER'S POSTSCRIPT   by Alan Lomax

Songs of a serious mould generally reflect the most important needs, anxieties and conflicts of a people. This is true even of "pop" songs, whose main theme is usually, "If only I had (or were with) you, I'd be happy," or in the cut-down, rock and roll variant, simply, "Hold me, baby". Worries about job security, though certainly present in the lives of the "pop" audience, are not considered suitable subjects for hit songs, probably because having a good job and being a desirable male are more or less equivalent in our middle class society. No middle class male in his right mind would approach his girl friend with a line such as, "I'm worried to death about my job and my future prospects: I don't know whether or not I can actually support a home and a family: and, for that reason, especially, please hold me close, be with me, love me."

Among the working class, however, where unemployment and money worries always have been a normal part of life, masculinity has never been equated with monetary success. If it had, there would be no population explosion. A large number of the British ballads of the Eighteenth and Nineteenth Century tell the stories of sailors, soldiers, farmers, craftsmen and house-servants caught not only in the net of love, but in struggles against economic and class difficulties. The songs and ballads of the American frontier - of the lumberjack, cowboy, farmer, sailor, and housewife go into detail about the wages, hours, living conditions, hardships and dangers of people on the job. One of the best lyric songs of the South is a frank statement of a young girl's worry about the future her swain may offer her...

> Come all Virginia girls and listen to my noise
> Don't go with those West Virginia boys,
> If you do, your fortune will be,
> Cornbread and hominey and sassafras tea...."

The simple theme of the loneliness that goes with poverty runs through many of our finest folk songs...

> I am a poor wayfaring stranger....

> I am a poor girl, my fortune's been bad....

I'm a poor boy and a long ways from home....

I'm a poor lonesome cowboy....

One dime was all I had....

In a broad but very genuine sense most of our traditional American songs can be considered songs of complaint or protest about the main economic and social problems that have always faced the mass of the American people as they struggled for a living, whether the scene of this struggle was on the bountiful but still harsh frontier, on a small farm, in a mine or a bunkhouse or - if the singer was a woman - in the kitchen of a little cabin or wooden shack somewhere. One of the problems everywhere was the rigid Nineteenth Century sexual code, which brought a feeling of keen deprivation into the lives of all Americans. The constant harping on the risks of falling in love and marrying, which is perhaps the central theme of Southern folk songs, can certainly be viewed as a complaint about the emotional hardship that sexual Puritanism imposed on our ancestors.

The literary scholars, who seldom went into the field and collected their song in the homes of the singers, have failed generally to perceive the undercurrent of tragedy and of protest that underlay the songs they footnoted and published. Since they had not been in the dismal prisons of the South; since they had not sat in the bare and flimsy shacks of sharecroppers and factory hands; since they had not seen the lines of sadness on the faces of the singers; or, even if they had seen such things; since they preferred not to see their singers as they were - people with a very low standard of living, - scholars usually have not regarded folk songs as relevant to the real problems of everyday life.

Since for most scholars folk song study has provided an escape from hum-drum scholarship, they have too often presented their findings as simply entertaining and amusing (which, of course, they are), as a quaint-ly phrased view of a bygone time or as a fantasy escape from life. This is the reason, it seems to me, that academic critics have generally refused to accept the validity of the more pointed songs of protest that Woody and I put together in this volume. At that time Bert Lloyd and Ewan MacColl had not presented their collections from the mines, factories and city streets of Great Britain. A look at these British collections shows that sharp, angry and self-conscious songs of protest have always formed a small but important part of the folk-song tradition of Great Britain. The early strikes and people's movements of England, Scotland and Ireland all had their topical folk songs set to traditional airs and couched in the idioms of popular poetry. Our own tradition contains many great folk songs with a powerful statement of social protest - The Factory Girl, Go Down Moses, Ain't No More Cane on the Brazos, The Buffalo Skinners, Single Girl, Going Down This Road Feeling Bad, Blow Boys Blow, to name only a few.

When the carriers and composers of this tradition were hit by the great depression in the '30s, when they joined in the union-organizing drive that gripped the whole country in the same period, when they voted for their New Deal and supported its programs, they naturally made new songs about all these crucial matters. As always before in their history, they took their favorite old tunes and set them to new texts - but these texts were in the vernacular of everyday speech and their style was "folk", rather than literary.

Most of these songs would, probably, have disappeared if they had not been collected or recorded at the time. They were evanescent pieces, pertinent only to the vents and times that produced them. In the Washington of the New Deal, however, there were many people, including the Roosevelts themselves, who wanted to know how the underprivileged people, how the people on the picket lines of America, felt about their times. In a sense we treasured these songs, because to us they were symbols of the fighting, democratic spirit of a whole sector of the population that is too often viewed as faceless, voiceless, supine and afraid. Aunt Molly Jackson, Ella Mae Wiggins, Woody Guthrie, John Handcox and the people they inspired were none of these things. They were courageous and genuine folk poets, who were as deeply involved in political and social change as any politician, union organizer or social critic. Since it was my responsibility, as the person in charge of the Folk Song Archive in Washington, to study the whole field of folk poetry, I was delighted to find that our tradition was still alive and concerned with contemporary problems. When, in the Spring of 1937, I ransacked the files of Columbia, Victor and Decca record companies for anything that had a folk flavor, I found not only the early Blue Grass, not only urban blues tradition, I found scores of songs of protest and social comment by urban and country folk singers. Some of these recorded topical songs praised the New Deal, some damned it; some recited the woes of the poor, some bitterly protested, - but, considered as a whole, they proved again that the American topical folk song tradition was live and productive.

When Woody Guthrie came along, the whole picture came together. Woody wrote and spoke the folk idiom of the Southwest with natural perfection. He had devoted years to singing for and about the Okies, and their migration out of the Dust Bowl. On top of that, he was a person of genius, as productive and unpredictable in his own idiom as Picasso is in his. Here was the heritor of the unknown folk poets, who had made the best of our ballads - Sam Bass, Jesse James, The State of Arkansas, John Hardy. Not only could Woody make songs with the electric impact of our best ballads, but he cared for nothing else. When he came across the Carter family recording of John Hardy in my house, he literally wore the record out. Presently he wrote Tom Joad to the tune of John Hardy.

Woody, then, was the logical person to write the commentary for my collection of topical folk songs. We were both pretty young at the time. We were both angry about the social injustice rampant in our world. In different ways we were both children of the Depression and we wanted to tell the story of what it had done to the people we knew. Woody, as a composer, believed that songs could change the world for the better. As a song editor, I believed that this collection was a testament to an unknown America, the folk poets who had become politically active and still kept their gift for song-making. Together we put together this angry book. No publisher would take it then, because post-war America was afraid to look reality in the eye. But the songs seeped out, one by one. Even more importantly, the range and validity of the American topical folk song was established in the mind of Woody Guthrie and of

Peter Seeger and many other singers of that day.

Now a new generation of topical singers is striking out against new brands of evil and injustice. I hope that these great young singers will enjoy meeting their grand-parents. They will, I am sure, get a charge out of an uninhibited, book-length monologue by Woody Guthrie, the most talented song-maker who ever thumbed a ride or picked on a Martin.

New York City
November 6, 1966

AFTERWORD 1999

by Pete Seeger

The University of Nebraska Press has asked 79-year-old me to add an "afterword" to this book, which 21-year-old me helped to put together in 1940. It was not published then. Irwin Silber and Alan Lomax tell in the publisher's foreword and the compiler's postscript how the book was finally published in 1967. My words are an oldster's view looking backward, and looking forward as well.

In 1937 Woody Guthrie's wife, Mary, was hanging laundry in her Pampa, Texas, backyard. She came inside, found a note on the icebox: "Gone to California. Will send for you. Woody." They'd discussed it; now he'd done it. A year later Woody had a job in Los Angeles for a dollar a day putting on a daily fifteen-minute program of songs and anecdotes for a little independent radio station. He made a few extra dollars selling a twenty-five-cent, self-mimeographed booklet of songs and jokes called "On A Slow Train Through California." As I remember, the second page had a notice like: "This book got an ironclad copyright No. 58643391072 and anyone caught singing one of these songs will be . . . a good friend of mine, 'cause that's why I wrote it."

Right after Woody's daily program was a fifteen-minute newscast by Ed Robbins, a reporter on the *People's World*, the West Coast Communist weekly paper.

One day in 1939 Woody said, "Ed, I listen to your program. Do you ever listen to mine?"

"I'm sorry, Woody. I guess I don't listen much to country music."

"Well, you listen tomorrow. I think you'll be interested."

The next day Woody sang "Mister Tom Mooney Is Free" (p. 356). Ed said, "Woody! That's a great song. Tonight there's a big rally for Tom Mooney. Could you come and sing it?" But then Ed had second thoughts, "Woody, it's a kind of a left wing gathering."

"Left wing, chicken wing. Don't matter to me. I been in the red all my life." That evening there was speech after speech. Woody fell asleep. Ed went over and shook him. "Woody, you're on!" Woody shook himself awake, walked to the mike, sang his song, and got an ovation from several thousand people. He had to sing the two-minute song twice. Hollywood actor Will Geer was in the audience and introduced himself. "Woody, I'm going north tomorrow to put on some entertainment for the striking workers in the lettuce fields. They're mostly Okies like you. Your songs would hit the spot."

Soon Will and Woody were a team at numerous fundraising gatherings in Southern California. In New York City I got a letter from Will, whom I had met there the year before when he taught at an off-Broadway theatre school. "Pete, I've met a great ballad maker named Woody. I hope he can get to New York and you can meet him."

Eight months later Will had the lead role in a Broadway play, *Tobacco Road*. He persuaded the producers to let the theatre be used for a midnight benefit concert for California agricultural workers. Alan Lomax and I drove up from Washington. On stage were Burl Ives, Josh White, Leadbelly, The Golden Gate Quartet, Margo Mayo's American Square Dance Group, and briefly me.

Woody was the hit of the evening. He stood very relaxed, spinning out jokes like Will Rogers, with his cowboy hat shoved back on his head, singing a few dust bowl songs like "Do Re Mi" (p. 230). The date was mid-March 1940.

Woody had hitchhiked from Los Angeles to New York the month before. Imagine him standing on the roadside in the February wind with his thumb stuck out and the cars passing—zooommm zooommm zooommm. In the diners where he went to warm up and get a cup of coffee the jukeboxes were playing that year's hit song. It was Kate Smith singing "Gob Bless America." This is where he started making up verses for his now most famous song, probably jotting down words with his coffee cup next to him. On the next page you can see it as he put it on paper when he got to New York. But none of us ever heard him sing it until 1949 when he changed the last line to what we now know. He then recorded it for Moses Asch and the tiny Folkways Recording Company. It got in the school songbooks. The rest is history.

At that 1940 midnight concert Alan Lomax immediately invited Woody to the Library of Congress in Washington. In two lengthy recording sessions Alan interviewed Woody and got his stories, songs, and life history. "Woody," said Alan seriously. "You are a great ballad maker. Don't let anything stop you from ballad making. This is your life's work."

I was working for Alan at the time. Fifteen dollars a week and overpaid at that, helping him go through stacks of old country music 78 rpm records. Woody must have liked my banjo picking, everything else about me must have seemed kind of strange. I didn't drink or smoke or chase girls. But I could back him up on any song he sang at first hearing. I had a good ear.

Now, how did this book get put together? It starts with young Alan Lomax. More than any single person he is responsible for starting off what has since been called "the American folksong revival." In 1933, his father, folksong collector John A. Lomax, had been made Honorary Curator (no pay) of the folksong archives at the Library of Congress. Alan, born in 1915, had for years been helping his father on collecting trips, and in July '36 was made the first paid staff-person at the archives. In '37 he started going through thousands of scratchy 78 rpm commercial recordings of country music and blues. They had been recorded in the 1920s and 1930s, not in Nashville or Detroit, but often in small southern towns by recording engineers looking for anything that might sell in their "Hillbilly" and "Race" catalogues. Some of them, Alan saw, reflected the realities of working people's lives and should be written down, words and music. In addition, through his contacts with union labor schools in Tennessee and Georgia, he had old mimeographed song sheets. He didn't have time to work on it all, and in April 1940, he presented that huge pile of mimeo'd song sheets and old 78 rpm discs to us and said, "Why don't the two of you work all of this into a book?"

We worked night and day on it in the spring of 1940, but then we had to put the book aside for awhile. Woody was traveling. Me too. Fortunately, friend Elizabeth Ambellan kept carbon copies of all Woody's pages.

In early 1941 Woody temporarily reunited with Mary and their three kids. I was in New York and started singing for left-wing fundraising parties with Arkansas songster Lee Hays and his roommate, New Jersey writer Millard Lampell. We needed a name for our group. I was reading to Lee one day from this songbook and came to the word 'almanac.' "Hold on," says Lee. "Back where I come from a family had two books in the house. A Bible to help 'em to the next world; and an almanac to help 'em get through this one. We have an almanac. 'Course, most congressmen can't read it."

God Blessed America
This Land Was made for You + me

This land is your land, this land is my land
From California to the New York Island,
From the Redwood Forest, to the Gulf stream waters,
God blessed America for me.

As I went walking that ribbon of highway
And saw above me that endless skyway,
And saw below me the golden valley, I said:
God blessed America for me.

I roamed and rambled, and followed my footsteps
To the sparkling sands of her diamond deserts,
And all around me, a voice was sounding:
God blessed America for me.

there
was a big high wall that tried to stop me
A sign was painted said: Private Property.
But on the back side it didn't say nothing —
God blessed America for me.

When the sun come shining, then I was strolling
In wheat fields waving, and dust clouds rolling;
The voice was chanting as the fog was lifting:
God blessed America for me.

One bright sunny morning in the shadow of the steeple
By the Relief office I saw my people —
As they stood hungry, I stood there wondering if
God blessed America for me.

*all you can write is
what you see.

Woody G.
N.Y., N.Y., N.Y.
Feb. 23, 1940
43rd St & 6th Ave.,
Hanover House

original copy
of this song

370

We became the Almanac Singers. I wrote Woody letters about what we were doing: making up peace songs, union songs, singing on picket lines. In May, Woody was in Oregon, writing songs like "Roll On Columbia," about the Grand Coulee Dam, and "Elekatricity And All," about cheap government electric power. In June of '41 he left his wife and children one more time and hitchhiked east to join us. He knocked on the door only a day or two after Hitler's June 22nd invasion of the Soviet Union. Almost his first words (with a wry grin) were:

"Well, I guess we won't be singing any more peace songs."

"You mean we have to support Churchill?"

"Yep. Churchill says 'All aid to the gallant Soviet allies.'"

"Is this the same Churchill who, in 1919, said, 'We must strangle the Bolshevik infant in its cradle?'"

"Yep. Churchill's flip-flopped. We got to flip-flop too."

Woody was right. We stopped singing peace songs, and with him making a four-some, we drove west in a huge old Buick, singing union songs for steel workers in Pittsburgh, and for a National Maritime Union convention in Ohio. In Chicago we arrived exhausted and slept on the living room floor of a young actor and his wife, Studs and Ida Terkel.

Next we hit union folks in Milwaukee, Denver, Salt Lake, and over the mountains into Californ-eye-ay. Got an ovation when we sang for longshoremen in Harry Bridges Union. In Los Angeles we met Theodore Dreiser and told him about our proposed book. We had in hand "Hard Hitting Songs For Hard-hit People" with a beautiful foreword by John Steinbeck. We asked Dreiser to look it over and give us some advice. Next day he returned it saying, "I'm afraid you've got a lot of work to do on this before it can be published." How right he was.

We weren't quite sure what to do with our manuscript. I had persuaded Woody to include "Why Do You Stand There In The Rain?" (p. 362). I tried unsuccessfully to locate John Handcox of the Southern Tenant Farmer's Union. A full thirty-five years later we connected. He and his family had gone to San Diego in WWII and never returned to Arkansas.

Back in New York in October the Almanacs were augmented by Sis Cunningham and Bess Lomax, Alan's younger sister. The Almanacs got three floors and basement of an old house in Greenwich Village for $100 a month. Woody and I kept tinkering with the book, added early IWW songs and an Earl Robinson song. Millard Lampell borrowed the manuscript to show some people in New Jersey and lost it in a bus station. Poor Mill had to endure Woody's wrath until it was found a few days later. In those days there were no such things as copy machines. Photostats were expensive. We had only one copy.

Came December 7th, Pearl Harbor. Now the Almanacs were making up songs about winning the war against Hitler, Tojo, and Mussolini. We quit singing songs about strikes; Communists helped push the labor movement to a no-strike pledge for the duration of the war.

July of '42, I was drafted into the U.S. Army. Soon after, Woody joined the merchant marine (he got torpedoed twice). The manuscript probably sat with a box of papers in my father's house near Washington, D.C., for the duration of the war. In December of '45 I was mustered out. Lee Hays and I started, in NYC, the songletter and organization *People's Songs* with the assistance of Alan Lomax, Herbert Haufrecht, Burl Ives, Oscar Brand, Early Robinson, Bob Russell, Robert Claiborn, Baldwin Hawes and Bess Lomax Hawes, Woody, John Hammond, and a few dozen others. The manuscript went into the "library" of *People's Songs* as Irwin Silber has already told you. Over the next twenty years it was split up before being reunited and published in '67.

As I leaf through the 197 songs and Woody's never-rewritten introductions and comments, I shake my head at the mistakes. Songs of textile workers should have had their own chapter like the songs of auto workers did. A number of songs were out of place, such as "Beans Bacon and Gravy" which should have been in chapter II not chapter V.

In 1940 it was a mistake not to point out that the book omitted songs of many important sectors of the American people, such as Latinos and Asians of the West Coast, Native Americans of the Southwest, Italian Americans and Jewish Americans of the eastern cities, and others.

The book had photos of songwriters Joe Hill, Leadbelly, Sis Cunningham, and Aunt Molly Jackson. But unfortunately none of John Handcox, who, it is now known, wrote "Roll the Union On" (in this edition, his photo is on p. 201).Well, rather than lament what's not in the book, let's point out that some of these songs, unknown then, have since become famous in the English speaking world: "Union Maid," "Which Side Are You On?," "Worried Man Blues," "Midnight Special," "Tom Joad," and others.

And while Woody and I didn't always put songs in the right order, we got 'em in.

Now, at the turn of the century, the millennium, what's the future of these songs? I want them looked over by young folks just learning the true history of this extraordinary mixed-up part of the world called the USA. They are growing up in it. There are probably several thousand songwriters in the USA who could be called "Woody's Children." I urge them to read this book but also to be aware that Woody also read a wide range of books and papers. I remember the week he read Rabelais. And he related his songs to events of the day. "Deportees" came out of a 3-inch story in the *New York Times*. Songwriters today should read the 1998 book *Hell, Healing, and Resistance* by Daniel William Hallock (Plough Publishers). In it you will discover that as many Vietnam veterans have committed suicide as were killed in Vietnam. "My husband's name is not on that wall," said the widow of one of them, "but he was also killed by the war."

There are ballads to be written here. Woody would have written some. He went into a hospital in '52 with Huntington's, a genetic disease he had inherited, which slowly destroyed his brain, until he died in '67. Now, songwriters: do you want to carry on his work? Try to read Hallock's book for a start.

Right now, I hope you will be looking over this book. I predict that many of these songs will be "rediscovered" perhaps by some adventurous young person now in diapers, who will put on a show for his or her school, church, or union, to let others know what their great-grandparents lived through. Who knows? A talented musician may find a new way of performing an old song, and with the help of recordings and airwaves it will reach millions who will hum it, memorize it, perhaps change it to fit new situations. It might be translated into another language, as has been done with similar songs. Ed McCurdy's peace song, "Last Night I Had The Strangest Dream" is so well known in Germany that it is thought to be a German Song. "We Shall Overcome" is sung in schools throughout India, in dozens of local languages. Students in other countries will discover that while they may hate the CIA or the Pentagon, they will love the American people whose lives are reflected here.

Historians studying the Great Depression will find themselves quoting verses that illuminate some particular point.

Hard Hitting Songs with all its flaws is a sixty-year-old document that deserves circulating. If there is a human race still here in two hundred years, music is one of the things that will save us. Future songwriters can learn from the honesty, the courage, the simplicity, the frankness of these hard hitting songs.

Not just songwriters. We can all learn.

Beacon, New York
January 1999

INDEX of SONGS